# THE WOMEN'S MOVEMENT AND WOMEN'S EMPLOYMENT IN NINETEENTH CENTURY BRITAIN

In the first half of the nineteenth century the main employment open to young women in Britain was in teaching, dressmaking, textile manufacture and domestic service. After 1850, however, young women began to enter previously all-male areas like medicine, pharmacy, librarianship, the civil service, clerical work and hairdressing, or areas previously restricted to older women like nursing, retail work and primary school teaching. This book examines the reasons for this change.

The author argues that the way femininity was defined in the first half of the century blinded employers in the new industries to the suitability of young female labour. This definition of femininity was, however, contested by certain women who argued that it not only denied women the full use of their talents but placed many of them in situations of economic insecurity. This was a particular concern of the Women's Movement in its early decades and their first response was a redefinition of femininity and the promotion of academic education for girls. The author demonstrates that as a result of these efforts, employers in the areas targeted began to see the advantages of employing young women, and young women were persuaded that working outside the home would not endanger their femininity.

Ellen Jordan's treatment of the expansion of middle class women's work is perhaps the most comprehensive available and is a valuable complement to existing works on the social and economic history of women. She also offers new perspectives on the Women's Movement, women's education, labour history and the history of feminism.

**Ellen Jordan** is based at the University of Newcastle, Australia. Her research is centred upon the history of women's work and gender in early childhood. She has published widely in these areas and edits the *Journal of Interdisciplinary Gender Studies*.

# ROUTLEDGE RESEARCH IN GENDER AND HISTORY

## 1 THE WOMEN'S MOVEMENT AND WOMEN'S EMPLOYMENT IN NINETEENTH CENTURY BRITAIN
*Ellen Jordan*

# THE WOMEN'S MOVEMENT AND WOMEN'S EMPLOYMENT IN NINETEENTH CENTURY BRITAIN

*Ellen Jordan*

London and New York

First published 1999
by Routledge
11 New Fetter Lane, London EC4P 4EE

Simultaneously published in the USA and Canada
by Routledge
29 West 35th Street, New York, NY 10001

*Routledge is an imprint of the Taylor & Francis Group*

Typeset in Garamond by Curran Publishing Services
Printed and bound in Great Britain by
TJ International Ltd, Padstow, Cornwall

*British Library Cataloguing in Publication Data*
A catalogue record for this book is available from the
British Library

*Library of Congress Cataloguing in Publication Data*
Jordan, Ellen, 1938—
The women's movement and women's employment in nineteenth
century Britain / Ellen Jordan.
280 pp. 15.6 x 23.4 cm.
Includes bibliographical references and index.
1. Women–employment–Great Britain–History–19th century.
2. Feminism–Great Britain–History–19th century. 3.
Women–Great Britain–Social conditions .I. Title.
HD6135.J667 1999
331.4'0941 09034–dc21                          98-51633
CIP

ISBN 0–415–18951–9

# CONTENTS

# FIGURES

All graphs, unless otherwise stated, are based on the census figures published in the following:
Parliamentary Papers 1844 vol. 27: 31–44, 48–51, 85–269; 1852–3 vol. 88: ccxxii–ccxxvii; 1863 vol. 53: xlii–lxv; 1873 vol. 71: xxxvii–xlviii, 65–607; 1883 vol. 80: x–xvii; 1893–4 vol. 106: x–xxv; 1903 vol. 84: 186–201; 1913 vol. 78: 6–11, 12–24, 75–88.

# TABLES

All tables, unless otherwise stated, are based on the census figures published in the following:
Parliamentary Papers 1844 vol. 27: 31–44, 48–51, 85–269; 1852–3 vol. 88: ccxxii–ccxxvii; 1863 vol. 53: xlii–lxv; 1873 vol. 71: xxxvii–xlviii, 65–607; 1883 vol. 80: x–xvii; 1893–4 vol. 106: x–xxv; 1903 vol. 84: 186–201; 1913 vol. 78: 6–11, 12–24, 75–88.

# PREFACE

When I was a pupil at a girls' secondary school in the mid-1950s, I and my fellow students had it very firmly impressed on us by our parents, and particularly our fathers, that we were not simply being educated to be suitable wives for men like our brothers. When our schooldays were over we were to go on to train for an independent career in one of the occupations regarded as suitable for women. Several of my schoolmates, in fact, married and had children without finishing their degrees. Although this was a time when very few women re-entered the workforce after marriage, the fathers of these women exerted considerable pressure on them to gain a qualification, their standard argument being, 'How else will you support yourself and your children if you are widowed?'

Many years later, when second-wave feminism focused attention on women and careers, I began to wonder where this set of beliefs had come from. In particular, I wondered whether convincing middle-class parents that their daughters should be trained for a career might not be one of the unrecorded achievements of the nineteenth-century Women's Movement. Further reading soon revealed that many of the occupations I grew up assuming to be immemorially feminine only became so during the second part of the nineteenth century, which raised the possibility that this, too, might be something my generation owed to the Women's Movement. These questions prompted the research and the answers recorded in this book.

No one researching in this area can fail to be grateful for the path-breaking efforts of three pioneering historians of women's work, Alice Clarke , Ivy Pinchbeck and Lee Holcombe. This book builds on their work and on the work of the many other historians of women's lives in the nineteenth century who have written in the last twenty-five years. I have tried to give credit to all insights and explanations taken from such books by naming the authors in the text and listing them in the index. I would also like to record my debt to the London librarians and archivists at the Fawcett Library, the Wellcome Insitute, the London Metropolitan Archives, the Guildhall Library, the Royal Pharmaceutical Society, the Prudential Insurance Corporation, the Public Records Office and the Family Records Centre, with particular thanks to

David Doughan, Lesley Hall, Shirley Dixon, Jonathan Draper, Lorraine Jones, Caroline Reed and Peter Traynor. Thanks also to contributors to the Victoria e-mail discussion list for suggestions of novels dealing with particular issues and other help relating to the period, in particular Sheldon Goldfarb, Patrick Leary, Beth Sutton-Ramspeck, and Helen Schinske. I am especially grateful to Sally Mitchell, also a generous member of the list, for sharing her profound knowledge of the period both in her writings and privately, and to Marion Diamond, whose work on Maria Rye has led to our fruitful discussions of the Women's Movement.

Friends and colleagues at the University of Newcastle to whom thanks are due for support and intellectual stimulation during the period when this book was in preparation are Inta Allegritti, Ari Brand, Lois Bryson, Linda Connor, Bethne Hart, Rob Irvine, Peter Khoury, Ken Lee, Helen Macallan, Dale Miller, Ross Morrow, Santi Rozario, Geoffrey Samuel, Ann Saul, Glenda Strachan, Maureen Strazzari, Stephen Tomsen, Judy Wells and Hilary Winchester, with particular thanks for their warm and supportive friendship to Hilary Carey, Chris Everingham, Deborah Stevenson, and Penny Warner-Smith.

# ABBREVIATIONS

| | |
|---|---|
| C&D | *Chemist and Druggist* |
| *Contemporary* | *Contemporary Review* |
| EWJ | *English Woman's Journal* |
| EWR | *Englishwoman's Review* |
| *Fraser's* | *Fraser's Magazine* |
| GW | *Good Words* |
| HW | *Household Words* |
| PJ&P | *Pharmaceutical Journal and Transactions* |
| PP | *Parliamentary Papers* |
| *James's* | *St James's Magazine* |
| TNAPSS | *Transactions of the National Association for the Promotion of Social Science* |
| WG | *Woman's Gazette* |

# Part I

# INTRODUCTION

# 1

# THE QUESTION OF
# MIDDLE CLASS
# WOMEN'S WORK

In the Britain of the 1840s the conditions in the two main occupations entered by middle-class women, those of governess and dressmaker, roused considerable public attention. In 1843 the Report to Parliament of the Commissioners on the Employment of Children was published. Among the revelations of this report were the very poor conditions offered to young women apprenticed to dressmakers. The sub-commissioner reported:

> The evidence of all parties establishes the fact that there is no class of persons in this country, living by their labour, whose happiness, health, and lives, are so unscrupulously sacrificed as those of the young dress-makers. They are, in a peculiar degree, unprotected and helpless; and I should fail in my duty if I did not distinctly state that, as a body, their employers have hitherto taken no steps to remedy the evils and misery which result from the existing system. . . . It may without exaggeration be stated that, in proportion to the numbers employed, there are no occupations, with one or two questionable exceptions such as needle-grinding, in which so much disease is produced as in dress-making, or which present so fearful a catalogue of distressing and frequently fatal maladies.
>
> (PP 1843, vol. 13: 122)

This concern was echoed by a number of journalists over the next few decades. An account of apprentice dressmakers' conditions published in *Fraser's Magazine* in 1846 expressed similar concern for their health:

> It is lamentable to see the change that sometimes comes over the country girl shortly after her admission as an apprentice. Arriving, perhaps, from her happy village home, where she has been the pride of honest and industrious parents, her cheeks redolent of rosy health, her step elastic, her spirits light and

buoyant . . . by degrees her pallid cheek and attenuated form shew that the loss of fresh air, and the absence of accustomed exercise are eating into the bud of youth.

(*Fraser's* 1846: 309)

The same story was still being repeated twenty years later when *Punch* published its famous picture *The Ghost in the Looking-Glass*, showing a fashionable woman admiring herself in a new ball gown, with Madame La Modiste, also fashionably dressed, saying, 'We would not have disappointed your ladyship at any sacrifice, and the robe is finished *à merveille*', while the plainly-dressed girl who has made it can be seen faintly in the mirror in a state of collapse (*Punch* 1863, vol. 45: 5).

Concern for governesses began with the focus on quite a different problem: the fate of the elderly. In 1841 a society called the Governesses' Benevolent Institution was founded to help those in distress. Brief accounts of the situations of the women who applied to it were published in the Annual Reports and included such cases as:

Miss E. A., aged fifty-eight. 1851. Her father died when she was very young; and her mother's second husband ruined the family. Greatly assisted her mother and sister. Being long crippled from a fall, and having some years since lost the use of her right arm and foot, is not only incapable of self-support, but entirely helpless.

Miss S. M .A., aged fifty-nine. 1856. Father a colonel in active service until Waterloo. Governess upon his death, and that of only brother. Assisted relations to the utmost of her power. Frequent illnesses have consumed her savings; is now in very delicate health. Earned only £10 in the past year.

Miss S. A., aged sixty-eight. 1857. Father a large calico printer; her mother having impoverished herself to assist her son's speculations, she gave up the whole of her property to her and became a governess; and to the same purpose devoted all her earnings. Is now entirely dependent upon the kindness of friends.

Mrs. O. S. G. B., aged fifty-seven. 1858. Father a captain in the army. Her husband, a surgeon, died suddenly, having made no provision for her and two children. Assisted her mother for some years. She suffering from chronic bronchitis and sciatica, and a daughter, also in very ill health, are without certain income, being dependent on the letting of her apartments.

(Parkes 1859a: 148, quoted)

Contemporaries argued that both these occupations were 'overstocked'. Too many women were pursuing too few positions and employers could exploit this oversupply by driving down wages and conditions (Crosswaithe 1863: 688; Jameson 1846: 235). As a writer in *Fraser's Magazine* put it: 'The market is glutted. If the supply were lessened, the demand would be greater' (*Fraser's* 1844: 580).

Yet by the beginning of the next century the situation had changed beyond recognition (Mitchell 1995: 23–32). Instead of being faced with the most obviously restricted and crowded labour market in the country, young middle-class women had a range of occupations they might enter, and a far higher percentage than in the past entered employment before marriage. The census of 1851 had recorded occupations for 56.5 per cent of young women aged from fifteen to twenty-four, and only 8.9 per cent of this age group were in occupations which could be called middle class: 7 per cent were milliners (which included dressmakers), 1 per cent were teachers, with the rest in various retail areas or engaged in literature and the arts.

By the end of the century a quite dramatic change had taken place. Middle-class women were now working as doctors, nurses, pharmacists and hospital dispensers, as teachers in publicly funded primary and secondary schools, as librarians, civil servants, clerks and shorthand typists, and as hairdressers and shop assistants (Bird 1911: 63–79, 90–1, 126–197, 233–4). The 1911 census showed that the number of young women listing an occupation had risen to 65.3 per cent of the age group (a rise of 8.8 per cent), and that most of this increase (7.85 per cent) was accounted for by the rise in the number of young women in middle-class occupations to 16.75 per cent of those in the age group (See Tables 4.3 and 4.5 in Chapter 4). Although the number of occupations available to women had been declining since the beginning of the eighteenth century (Hill 1989: 47–68), the period 1851 to 1911 saw a reversal of the trend, but a reversal that applied primarily to occupations for young middle-class women.

This change raises three sets of questions which this book attempts to answer.

First, why were dressmaking and teaching the only middle-class occupations employing young women in the 1840s, and why were conditions in them so bad?

Second, why, in the period after 1850, did young middle-class women begin to enter previously all-male areas like clerical work, hairdressing, dispensing, and librarianship, and others like nursing, retail work, and elementary school teaching previously restricted to older women, and why was almost all the recorded increase in the proportion of young working women the result of an increase in numbers in such middle-class occupations?

Third, why by the end of the century had it become customary for middle-class women to work before marriage when fifty years earlier this would have led them to 'lose caste'?

The answer suggested is that the understanding of the nature of masculinity and femininity, and of the work appropriate to each sex, had a determining effect on the kind of labour force that evolved during the industrial changes of the eighteenth and nineteenth centuries and this resulted in a contraction of the work opportunities available to women of all classes. More and more work was being done outside the households where women had previously worked with their fathers and husbands, and yet in only a very few industrial sectors did employers consider women an appropriate workforce. Thus female unemployment was high and some areas were grossly oversupplied.

As the century progressed the employment open to married women and young working-class women increased and decreased at the discretion of employers. It was their needs and, even more, their blindness to the cheapness and flexibility of female labour, which kept working-class women's industrial position stagnant.

With middle-class women, however, other factors intervened. The plight of governesses and dressmakers was written up in the serious press of the day and created a public awareness of their problems which ultimately reversed the trend where young middle-class women were concerned. Furthermore, some upper middle-class women were dissatisfied with the restricted field of activity allowed them, and began to demand the right to an occupation outside the home. In consequence, groups of philanthropists and intellectuals emerged who made it their business to alter the existing employment structure of their society to make a place for both the dissatisfied and the unemployed. They lighted on certain areas of work which they considered suitable for women, and then in campaigns with twofold purposes persuaded employers that young middle-class women were an ideal labour source and persuaded such women that the work they were suggesting was of a kind which would not compromise either their gentility or their femininity.

## Alternative explanations

This argument is at odds with the explanation currently accepted for the expansion of middle-class women's work, and reverts in part to a theory which that explanation was propounded to supersede. In the earlier decades of this century, particularly in accounting for the change in the middle-class attitude to young women working before marriage, it was assumed that the Women's Movement of the 1860s played a crucial role. Ray Strachey wrote in 1928:

> This large extension of wage-earners was, to some extent, accounted
> for by the rapid increase in the population, and in part by the general
> rise in the prosperity and business of the country; it was, however,
> also closely connected with the new stirrings of ambition and
> independence which education and the Women's Movement

'redundant women' who failed to find husbands to support them. A far higher proportion of women, it was believed, remained unmarried than in the past, and it was assumed that these elderly spinsters were not only the ones most obviously in poverty, but also swelled the numbers in these occupations so greatly that wages were driven down (Craik 1858: 2; HW 1852: 84; Smith 1857: 10). Various figures were bandied about, but the ones which had the widest currency were those which claimed that something like 30 per cent of women were unlikely to marry.

This was the figure proposed by W.R. Greg in 1862 in an article called 'Why are women redundant?' (Greg 1868: 346–8), based on the fact that in the 1851 census 43 per cent of women aged between twenty and forty were unmarried, and his estimate of the number likely to marry in the future. A closer look at the figures reveals that this was an over-gloomy projection even on the data available. The percentage of those still unmarried in the over-forty-five age groups was much lower, roughly 13 per cent (Anderson 1984: 379), while the 1871 census was to reveal that only 12 per cent of the women in Greg's 1851 cohort were still single twenty years later. Although the percentage of women remaining unmarried had risen from the low point reached in the late eighteenth centurey, it had not returned to the 15 per cent average of the late seventeeth century, and did not represent a drastic change from previous decades (Wrigley 1989: 112).

Moreover, the elderly composed only a small part of the numbers in dressmaking and teaching. Figure 1.1 is a graph showing the age distribution in 1851 of governesses, dressmakers, and domestic servants (excluding housekeepers) .

Although the proportion of older women remaining in the occupation was greater among governesses and milliners than among domestic servants, the general pattern was the same: most of the women in these occupations were concentrated in the under-thirty-five age group, a concentration presumably produced because most of them married before the age of thirty-five and left their occupation on marriage. It would seem, therefore, that the problem of overstocking in teaching and dressmaking was not caused by a large number of older women remaining in these occupations: almost 80 per cent of dressmakers and 70 per cent of governesses were under thirty-five years of age. The disproportion of men and women in the population was at most a minor factor; the real problem was the oversupply of young women looking for work *before* marriage.

Far closer to the truth were those who argued, as did a few scattered writers before 1857 (Adams 1849: 1370; *Fraser's* 1844: 580; HW 1853: 576) and the Women's Movement most vociferously after that date, that the cause of the overstocking was the very limited range of occupations open to women, and that the number of women seeking work was larger than the amount of work available in the occupations open to them.

I have argued elsewhere that unemployment was a problem which faced

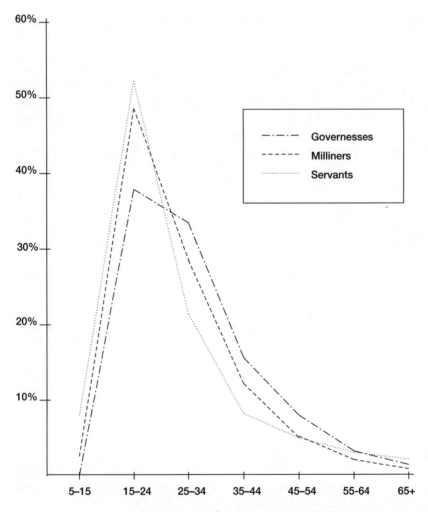

*Figure 1.1* Percentage of governesses, female milliners and domestic servants in various age groups as shown in the census of 1851

working-class women as well as the middle class, and that the regional variation in unemployment indicates that the cause lay in the limited range of occupations available.

In 1851, although the census returned only 10 per cent of males aged fifteen to nineteen (an age group chosen because it avoids the complications of having to allow for married women) as unoccupied, 37 per cent of females in the same age group were returned as having no occupation. Yet the regional variation was substantial. Unemployment figures for women aged fifteen to nineteen ranged from 15 per cent in Bedfordshire, where cottage industries like straw-plait and lace-making still survived, and 18 per cent in

Lancashire where cotton manufacture absorbed large numbers, to a massive 44 per cent in Durham and 41 per cent in Kent, with the other purely agricultural counties not far behind. Even by 1891 there was little improvement, with 10 per cent of males but 34 per cent of females in this age group returned as unoccupied. Once again, the rate of unemployment varied with locality. In the cotton towns of Blackburn and Burnley only 5 per cent and 6 per cent of women aged fifteen to nineteen were returned as unoccupied, whereas in the mining and iron and steel towns of West Bromwich and Gateshead 48 per cent and 46 per cent were recorded as unemployed, and in the ports of Middlesbrough and Sunderland 51 per cent and 50 per cent (Jordan 1988: 182–5).

Paid work for women, this regional variation makes clear, was available in only a few sectors of the workforce, and most new occupations created by expanding industrialism were closed to them. Though 89 per cent of domestic servants, 52 per cent of those employed in dressmaking, and 49 per cent of those in textiles were women, in metal manufacture only 7 per cent of the workforce was female, in transport and mining 3 per cent each, and in building and railway construction a negligible 0.2 per cent (Jordan 1989: 277–80). This difference was even more marked in middle-class occupations. The 'redundant' women crowding into dressmaking and teaching were redundant, not because there were no husbands for them, but because there was no other work on offer. In 1911, when the range of occupations for women had expanded, the conditions of governesses and dressmakers were no longer a matter for social concern, even though the percentage in each age group who had never married was measurably higher than in 1851 (Anderson 1984: 392).

## Economic determinates

The second question, why, with so many young women apparently available, in the 1840s they were being exploited only by employers of governesses and dressmakers, whereas by 1911 they were employed in considerable numbers in a range of previously all male occupations, was seriously addressed by Lee Holcombe in 1973, in her pioneering book *Victorian Ladies at Work*. In this she looked at the movement of 'ladies' into elementary school-teaching, nursing, office work and work as shop assistants. The oversupply of female labour, she argued, encountered an expanding economy which 'created a large and increasing demand for labour, a demand which better educated women could supply as well as men – and at lower cost' (Holcombe 1973: 18). Taking the increase in the numbers of shop assistants and office workers as the key areas to be explained, she suggested that employers turned to women when enterprises grew so large that low paid workers could be hired to do the unskilled parts of the work.

Shopkeeping in the early part of the century was, she argued, skilled work, and shop assistants were usually apprentices learning the trade to practise it themselves later. 'But the later nineteenth century saw a revolution in the distributive trades which parallelled the contemporary trend in industry toward large-scale organization, specialization and division of labour.' Goods were standardized and the manufacturers organized their distribution, and this in turn 'revolutionized the character of retailing by helping to destroy its craft tradition'. Both the number and size of shops increased, while 'at the same time, the decline of the craft tradition tended to transform shop assistants from skilled into unskilled workers' (Holcombe 1973: 104–5).

A similar change, she argued, lay behind the entry of women into clerical work. 'The expanding scope of industrial and commercial enterprises . . . led naturally to a growth in the size of business offices', to 'a tremendous increase in the amount of clerical work to be done', to 'rationalization and mechanization of office work', and to 'considerable specialization and division of labour within offices' (Holcombe 1973: 142, 144). The outcome in both areas was the creation of what later theorists were to call a dual labour market, with highly trained, trusted and well rewarded employees undertaking the demanding and responsible work, while the routine work was performed by a shifting group of low-paid, easily replaced workers who could be hired and fired as pressure of work demanded (Dex 1985: 131–4; Hakim 1979).

There can be little doubt that the kind of young women competing for work as dressmakers and governesses had much to offer an employer faced with the need to establish a dual labour market. In a much quoted passage, one of the early employers of female clerical labour has left on record his appreciation of their benefits. Frank Scudamore, the man who organised the transfer of the telegraph service, with its staff of young female operators, to the Post Office, wrote in a report to Parliament in 1871:

> In the first place, they have in an eminent degree the quickness of eye and ear, and the delicacy of touch, which are essential qualifications of a good operator.
>
> In the second place, they take more kindly than men or boys do to sedentary employment, and are more patient during long confinement to one place.
>
> In the third place, the wages, which will draw male operators from but an inferior class of the community, will draw female operators from a superior class.
>
> Female operators thus drawn from a superior class will, as a rule, write better than the male clerks, and spell more correctly; and, where the staff is mixed, the female clerks will raise the tone of the whole staff.
>
> They are also less disposed than men to combine for the purpose of extorting higher wages, and this is by no means an unimportant matter. . . .
>
> Permanently established civil servants invariably expect their

remuneration to increase with their years of service, and they look for this increased remuneration even in the cases, necessarily very numerous, in which from the very nature of their employment, they can be of no more use or value in the twentieth than in the fifth year of their service. . . .

Nor would it be possible for long to maintain a rule under which persons employed on certain classes of duties should perforce retire after a short term, say five or seven years of service.

Women, however, will solve these difficulties for the Department by retiring for the purpose of getting married as soon as they get the chance.

(Scudamore 1871: 78–9)

A hundred years later, Samuel Cohn put the last of these benefits in more academic language, concluding that women were sought after for areas of routine work where promotion opportunities were few, because their propensity to marry after only a few years in the workforce, combined with the ideological arguments for imposing marriage bars, got rid of the need to create a 'synthetic turnover' of staff to contain incremental wage increases. Rosemary Crompton and Gareth Jones have further pointed out that male career ladders in office work are dependent on the existence of 'unpromotable' categories – women, ethnic minorities, retired people – to do the bulk of the routine work (Cohn 1985: 93–7; Crompton and Jones 1984: 243). Other researchers have argued that similar qualities constituted the appeal of the young women increasingly employed in elementary school-teaching and nursing (Maggs 1983: 10–11, 138–43; Tropp 1957: 22, 117–8).

This straightforward economic determinist explanation has maintained a broad credibility for many historians, being repeated almost without qualification in work published in the 1980s by Gregory Anderson (1988), Margery Davies (1974), Graham S. Lowe (1987) and Carole Elizabeth Adams (1988) as the context for women's employment in offices not just in Britain but in the United States, Canada and Germany as well. Nevertheless, as more empirical work has been done in specific areas, it has begun to appear that only one of each of these pairs of occupations really conforms to the pattern described by Lee Holcombe. While women's presence in retail work coincides with the appearance of the large department store, the feminization of office work cannot be seen as a direct response to changed economic conditions.

Samuel Cohn's study comparing the entry of women clerks into the Post Office and the Great Western Railway shows that, in spite of similar problems and an almost identical external labour market, the timing of the introduction of female clerks differed markedly (Cohn 1985: 33). Furthermore, as Jane Lewis has pointed out, women did not in fact go first or in the largest numbers into the bureaucratized offices of banks, insurance companies and railways. Until 1914, she points out, 90 per cent of female office workers were classified by the census as 'commercial clerks', the term used to describe workers in the offices of factories and warehouses where numbers in each organization were low. Lewis concludes that the evidence does not support the view 'that changes in the economy are sufficient to explain the changes in women's work' (Lewis 1988: 34–6, 44–5).

There is a similar split in the pair of occupations, elementary school-teaching and nursing, in which young middle-class women replaced, not men, but older women. Whereas the growth in the number of young female teachers coincided with government regulation and subsidising of elementary school systems, the advent of the young middle-class hospital nurse in the 1860s occurred, as Monica Baly and Christopher Maggs have pointed out, between the two great expansions of hospitals, the first of which took place at the beginning of the century and the second during the 1880s (Baly 1980: 61; Maggs 1983: 7).

It is not possible, it would seem, to relate women's entry into new occupations directly to either a 'pull' from employers or a 'push' from changes in the social demography. Primarily structural explanations are not sufficient to explain the developments which occurred. It will be suggested in what follows that it would have been to the benefit of employers to engage young middle-class women decades before the step was actually taken, that they were blinded to the possibility by contemporary conceptions of gentility and femininity, and that similar conceptions inhibited the young women from undertaking work in any but traditionally feminine occupations. The considerable expansion after mid-century cannot, therefore, be explained without reference to the arguments and activities of the Women's Movement which opened the eyes of employers to the benefits and viability of employing young women, and convinced young women that it was in their interest to train for an occupation and practice it before marriage.

Such an approach, however, makes it necessary to move beyond the economic determinism that has since the 1950s been taken as the axiomatic basis for explaining the expansion of middle-class women's work, and look at the changes in terms of the poststructuralism, with its emphasis on discourse and understanding, which is found increasingly helpful both in social history in general and in labour history in particular.

## The 'linguistic turn'

In the 1970s and 1980s most labour history research was conducted within an economic determinist framework and was directed towards establishing that class, gender and ethnic inequalities were not the outcome of the characteristics of individuals, but created by and perpetuated through the social structure. There was not, of course, unanimity in this project, which was marked by heated disagreement over 'agency' between structural and humanist Marxists, disagreement, that is, about whether people should be seen primarily as 'bearers of the structures', or whether importance should be given to their resistance to oppression, but the emphasis on the broad economic and institutional determinates was shared (Barrett 1992a: 85–96; Connell and Irving 1992: 4–6). However, once the fact that inequality was structural was established, new questions arose. How was it established, how was it reproduced and perpetuated? What were the dynamics of the process? The time had come for poststructuralist analyses and explanations.

Much of the really exciting and innovative work now being done in labour history is conceptualized within the framework of poststructuralism, and more specifically discourse theory as it derives from Foucault, Derrida and Lacan. What is called the 'linguistic turn' has occurred, and it is being argued that language constructs social reality rather than simply reflecting it. Whereas historians like E. P. Thompson focused on people's experiences in examining class, more recent historians argue that these experiences are mediated through language, that people can only understand them in terms of the discourses currently available to them (Joyce 1993; Steinberg 1996: 193–5). Derrida's technique of deconstruction (in particular his focus on the idea of binary oppositions) is also much in vogue as a method the historian can use for demystifying the social reality (Scott 1988: 37–8).

Feminist poststructuralist historians now argue that the discourses which constrained people's ways of thinking about gender have been as significant in determining the sexual division of labour as the needs of capitalism. The gendered world of the workplace must be seen as influenced by the way gender is experienced in other sites (Baron 1991; Davidoff 1990: 234–40; Kessler-Harris 1993; Poovey 1988: 160–2). Alice Kessler-Harris writes:

> In our zeal to understand how pervasive these forces [the changes caused by industrialism] were, we have interpreted identity, social relations, customs, and culture as greater or lesser reflections of this process and of the narrowly-defined class struggle. We have blurred aspects of a continuity located in households and communities. But fundamental forms of identity, derived from the household (created and shaped by women and men), survived even the depredations of capital.
>
> (Kessler-Harris 1993: 197)

The way gender is understood and lived in household and community, she argues, should be seen not simply as responding to but as shaping capitalist labour relations (Kessler-Harris 1993: 197–201).

I have argued in an earlier publication (Jordan 1989) that, because of the way femininity was defined within their own middle-class world, employers of working-class labour were blind to the existence of women as a potential labour source except in cases where they had been part of the preindustrial workforce in the same industry. This androcentrism, I suggested, was responsible for the very limited number of occupations which employed working-class women. Women were likely to be found in an industry only if it had developed gradually out of an eighteenth century system of 'putting out' manufacture. In such cases women, already given a role in the family division of labour, moved with the process into the workshops and factories, and once there were likely to be used even when the process changed, employers being already aware of the cheapness and docility of female labour. Thus in 1851 52 per cent of those employed in textiles were women, 49 per cent of those in paper manufacture, and 31 per cent in earthenware manufacture.

On the other hand, when an industry was organised anew, employers' androcentric view of the new industrial world prevented them from visualizing women in the new situation, though they easily saw men in it. Thus huge sectors of the new industrial economy – railways, metal production, mining for example – virtually ignored women. Only 7 per cent of those employed in metals and machines, 3 per cent in conveyance, and 0.2 per cent in building were female (Jordan 1989: 277–85). A similar 'androcentric blindness' seems a plausible explanation for the similar failure to employ middle-class women throughout the first three quarters of the century.

The questions to be pursued in this book, however, are: what were the characteristics of contemporary thought that created this blindness to economic benefits, and what happened to change the views of the employers who turned to middle-class women after 1860? The first of these questions can be answered within the explanatory framework outlined above. The second question, however, raises the question of agency. Is the Women's Movement to be given some credit for this change, or should determinism through 'structure' be extended to include determinism through discourse? Though the debate still continues, the emphasis on resistance and agency stressed by cultural Marxist critics of determinism like E. P. Thompson and Eugene Genovese has been found congruent with a poststructuralist approach (Steinberg 1996: 193–5), and feminist theorists argue that acceptance of the poststructuralist emphasis on discourse does not necessarily mean conceiving of individuals as no more than the intersections of discourses (Baron 1991: 31; Levine 1990: 7–8). Individuals can choose from among existing discourses those which will constitute them as powerful and which will, if used strategically, achieve political ends (Walkerdine 1990: 14; Weedon 1987: 108–9).

The activities of agents making expedient use of the discourses available to them can thus be investigated as a contribution to the dynamics of two features seen in current poststructuralist thought as characteristic of social change: contingency and historical specificity (Barrett 1992b: 202–4; Fraser and Nicholson 1988: 91–2). Social change is, it is argued, unpredictable and historically specific because it is the outcome of the actions and interactions of individuals contending in multiple microsites of power, and so explanation must focus on agency and discourse.

Such an explanatory framework does not deny the significance of structural factors in determining the context for, and setting constraints on the outcome of, the actions of these agents. Nevertheless it draws attention to the fact that the particular form taken by the change was contingent on the form their action took. Thus though it cannot be claimed that women would never have entered the new occupations created by industrialism without the intervention of the Women's Movement, that some other agents might not have pushed change in the same direction, it can be shown that the intervention of the Women's Movement determined the time when the change actually occurred, the kind of young women who undertook this work, and thus the conditions under which women entered these new areas. It further raises the question of what motives drove these agents to act as they did, and what understandings of their society determined and constrained their tactics.

## Agents of change

The members of the Women's Movement who concerned themselves with women's work were part of the much larger group of British intellectuals and philanthropists, named 'social cranks' by Harold Perkin, who were committed to changing their society (Perkin 1969: 220–1, 256–7). According to Karl Mannheim, changes and syntheses of political ideas are typically brought about by 'socially unattached intellectuals', and occur because there exists in a society this 'relatively classless stratum which is not too firmly situated in the social order' and whose members participate less than most people 'directly in the economic process'. Although they tend to preserve some class interests and affiliations, they can see the point of view of other groups and so produce social theory that seems to have a true and universal character, thus transforming 'the conflict of interest into a conflict of ideas' (Mannheim 1936: 137–42). The members of the Women's Movement who devoted themselves to persuading employers to offer work to women, and women that they should train for work, belonged to such a group. Most of them were possessed of private means and very few took advantage of the changes initiated, yet as Philippa Levine has demonstrated, their whole lives, including family and friendship networks, were structured around their commitment to their causes (Levine 1990).

Given this stress on discourse and agency, it might seem that the most suitable theoretical framework to use in examining what the Women's Movement attempted and achieved would be Michel Foucault's analysis of the power struggles involved in defining 'truth' (Foucault 1980). The kind of struggles that Foucault investigated are not, however, strictly analogous to the changes to be considered here. The Women's Movement was confronting in the area of women's work, not a 'truth' used to defend a self-interested position, but an understanding of the way society functioned, coming from what Schutz has named the 'intersubjective stock of knowledge' (Schutz 1967: 81–4, 118–26), which had created the employers' androcentric blindness described above.

The work of Pierre Bourdieu has provided a more flexible framework (and a particularly useful vocabulary) with which to analyse both the way in which employers' 'knowledge' created this blindness and the tactics used by the Women's Movement to change it. Bourdieu's concept of 'habitus' ('a system of acquired dispositions functioning on the practical level as categories of perception and assessment') offers a way of understanding how this knowledge is acquired and used. A person's habitus is his or her knowledge of the way things are and can be done in the 'historically constituted areas of activity with their specific institutions and their own laws of functioning' which he calls 'fields' (Bourdieu 1990a: 87). This knowledge is 'embodied', and therefore determines people's actions (including speech) in an unreflective instantaneous manner.

Each individual's habitus is historically constructed, from 'knowledge' that has been acquired from family and class. Some of it is discursive, in the form of proverbs, sayings, jokes and anecdotes, but a lot is simply undiscussed practice, gained by watching and copying (Bourdieu 1977: 78, 85; Bourdieu 1990a: 13–14). 'For as long as habitus and field are in agreement,' he writes, 'the habitus "comes at just the right moment" and, without the need for any calculation, its anticipations forestall the logic of the objective world' (Bourdieu 1990a: 91). Thus Bourdieu does not conceptualize such actors as self-consciously rational or calculative, but as devising, with greater or lesser skill, 'strategies' which allow them to gain the ends they seek while acting in a manner defined as appropriate by the various social fields between which their activities are divided (Bourdieu 1990a: 62–6; Bourdieu 1990b: 7–14). Bourdieu lays stress on the fact that there are a number of these fields in which individuals must learn to operate, and that everyone's habitus comprises knowledge of their difference and of the different discourses and practices appropriate to each (Bourdieu 1990a: 87–91).

This conceptualization, he argues, provides a way of understanding how both agency and constraint are present in social life (Bourdieu 1990a: 46). Every social field is continually in flux, full of people acting as agents, all pursuing strategies to serve their own interests, and yet constrained by the historically entrenched discourses and practices of the field. These fields are also full of people successfully and unsuccessfully trying to apply the practices of one field in another, of those with what he calls 'symbolic capital' modifying the practices of their own fields in the ways that suit them, of parvenus and upstarts coming in and debasing the current practices by following them in inappropriate ways. No social field stays the same and its nature at any one time is the outcome of its own specialized history created through the agency of those who inhabit it.

The socially unattached intellectuals of the Women's Movement were possessed of the symbolic capital that allowed them to bend and stretch the rules of the fields in which they moved, but their attack on the sexual division of labour was discursive as well. The tactic they used has been pinpointed by

Mary Poovey and Philippa Levine: discovering contradictions between the way women were treated and the broad principles it was believed informed their society, and then 'rewriting the political script' by capitalizing 'on inconsistencies and confusions in their society' (Levine 1990: 178; Poovey 1988: 127, 166, 179). Bourdieu once again provides a framework in which to theorize this achievement. The habitus, he suggests, is composed of a 'universe of the undiscussed (undisputed)' which he calls 'doxa', and a 'universe of discourse (or argument)'. When a set of ideas which has previously been part of the undisputed doxa of a field is challenged, it moves into the universe of discourse. The ideas proposed by the challengers then become a heterodoxy, and the previously undisputed ideas become the orthodoxy within that field (Bourdieu 1977: 168–70).

Two different sets of female unattached intellectuals, it will be argued in what follows, used the logical and rational incompatibility of the current definition of women's work with certain widely accepted discourses in other fields to convert it from doxa to an orthodoxy, proposing their own heterodoxies as alternatives. In the first part of the century, female writers, philanthropists and educational reformers argued for its incompatibility with their religious principles, and in the second half the Women's Movement members opposed it in terms provided by political and economic liberalism.

The evidence which this theoretical framework is used to interpret comes from a variety of sources. The discussion of the general attitudes to women and women's work comes from a detailed examination of the periodical literature of the period 1800–80, supplemented by novels, letters (published and unpublished), and polemical and proto-sociological texts on women.

The argument for the involvement of the Women's Movement in the expansion of occupations is developed by identifying the changes in the patterns in women's occupations revealed by the census figures and noting the congruence with the occupations recommended by the Women's Movement and the dates when this occurred. Where archival material is available, for example in the records of the early nursing institutions, the Post Office and the Prudential Assurance Company, this is used to give a more detailed picture of the process in particular sites. Use is also made of the substantial historiography on nursing, teaching and women's education produced during the last thirty years.

## Argument of the book

It will be argued that the problems facing young women in the 1840s, though indubitably a product of increasing industrialism, were a contingent and not an inevitable outcome of these changes. While the reorganization of industry stemmed from economic and technological changes, the factors which determined employers' choice of a labour force had a different provenance. They came from the 'knowledge' of the differences between men and women embedded in the practices of the pre-industrial workplace and in the new discourses that were emerging to understand the changes taking place.

These new discourses, it will be argued in Chapters 2 and 3, grew out of earlier conceptions of masculinity and femininity, and were developed as a means of understanding and mediating the social impact of the technological and organizational changes in manufacturing and commerce in the early years of the nineteenth century. They placed discursive constraints on the manner in which young women participated in the new industrial world, constraints now usually known as the 'domestic ideology'.[1] The interaction of this belief system with wider economic and social changes, it will be suggested, created most of the tangle of problems known to contemporaries as the 'woman question' (Helsinger, Sheets, and Veeder 1983, vol. 2: xi–xv). It caused grave personal dissatisfaction to the many women it confined to the home sphere, it imposed conditions which denied individual liberty to those who entered the workforce, and, by restricting women to a small range of badly paid occupations, ensured that only in the homes of fathers or husbands could they find economic security.

The next section looks at the first group of women to challenge the domestic ideology: the 'strong-minded women' who found that it placed intolerable limitations on the use of their talents and energies. These women, it is suggested in Chapter 5, challenged these restraints by creating what I have called the 'religious heterodoxy', arguing that religion placed men and women in the same relation to God, and that therefore the same imperatives to succour the needy and develop their talents to the full applied to both sexes. By the 1850s they had introduced intellectual and artistic components into the standard 'English education' offered to middle-class girls, and made it acceptable for adult women to practise as writers and artists and to play a major part in the burgeoning organised philanthropy that was a feature of the period. Chapters 6 and 7 look at how the religious heterodoxy was used during the 1850s to legitimate the foundation of public schools for middle-class girls and to claim hospital nursing as suitable work for unmarried middle-class women.

The final section deals with the manner in which the Women's Movement built on the foundations laid by the religious heterodoxy. Chapter 8 describes the foundation of the movement and the creation of what I have called the liberal heterodoxy to challenge the domestic ideology even further. Chapter 9 gives an account of the efforts of one branch of the Movement, the Society for Promoting the Employment of Women, to open a range of previously male-dominated lower middle-class occupations to women. Chapter 10 looks at how the education branch opened universities and the medical profession to women, and argues that, by establishing public schools for middle-class girls and staffing them with its university-educated supporters, the Movement was able to spread the message to students and their parents that working in any of the new occupations before marriage would jeopardize neither a young woman's femininity nor the gentility of her family.

# Part II

# THE CONSTRAINTS ON WOMEN'S WORK

# 2

# THE CONSTRAINTS OF GENTILITY

## The separation of work and home and the emergence of the male breadwinner norm

In 1859 Bessie Rayner Parkes, one of the founders of the Women's Movement in England, addressed a Social Science Congress on the problems facing 'educated women':

> Everybody here present will at once admit that the theory of civilised life in this and all other countries, not excluding the democratic States of America, is that women of the upper and middle classes are supported by their male relatives: daughters by their fathers, wives by their husbands. If a lady has to work for her livelihood, it is universally considered to be a misfortune, an exception to the ordinary rule. All good fathers wish to provide for their daughters; all good husbands think it their bounden duty to keep their wives. All our laws are framed strictly in accordance with this hypothesis; and all our social customs adhere to it more strictly still. We make no room in our social framework for any other idea, and in no moral or practical sphere do the exceptions more lamentably and thoroughly prove the rule. Women of the lower class may work, *must* work, in the house if not out of it – too often out of it! But among us, it is judged best to carefully train the woman as the moraliser, the refiner, the spiritual element.
>
> (Parkes 1859a: 145–6)

Yet many middle-class women, too, were forced into work. 'Probably every person present,' she continued, 'has a female relative or intimate friend whom trade-failures, the exigencies of a numerous household, or the early death of husband or father has compelled to this course; it is the experience of every family.' (Parkes 1859a: 146).

Such women had not been trained for any profession or trade and so the only work they could find was passing on the kind of education they had received to others. The presence of these 'ladies' had, she argued, encouraged 'ideas of the superior gentility of governesship' and consequently 'trades-people, housekeepers and widows of all ranks' were making governesses of their daughters and creating 'a frightful competition and depression of salaries' (ibid.: 150).

Yet, as the two pioneer historians of women in Britain, Alice Clark and Ivy Pinchbeck demonstrated many years ago (Clark 1919; Pinchbeck 1930), and as Women's Movement members themselves realized (Davies 1866: 97), 'the theory of civilised life' outlined by Bessie Rayner Parkes was of quite recent origin. Even fifty years earlier most women were part of what Louise Tilly and Joan Scott (Tilly and Scott 1979) refer to as a 'family economy', and were expected to make a contribution to the family's income. The fundamental cause of this change, these historians argue, was the separation of home and work that accompanied industrialism as it emerged in Britain in the early years of the nineteenth century. New kinds of household economy were developed to cope with this change, and the family economy began to be replaced by two rather different forms which coexisted (and still coexist) with it and which I shall refer to as the multi-wage family and the male breadwinner family.[1]

However these new household forms, I shall be arguing in this chapter and the next, were not an inevitable outcome of the technological and organizational changes in manufacturing and commerce which created the separation of work and home. The particular form they took was decided by the new discourses that were developed as a means of understanding and mediating the social impact of these changes. These discourses placed discursive constraints on the manner in which young women participated in the new industrial world, constraints that were identified by Maria Grey, a leading educational reformer of the second half of the century, in the title of a pamphlet as the *Idols of Society, or Gentility and Femininity* (reviewed in EWR, 1875: 21–2).

Three broad problems emerged, which were identified by contemporaries as part of the 'woman question' (Helsinger 1983, Vol 2: xi-xv; Jordan 1994). First there was the problem of 'nothing to do', the fact that many women, expected to live as ladies in a domestic environment, found their lives intolerably constraining and dull with no chance to develop their talents or make use of their practical energies. Second, middle-class women's economic situation was precarious, since most were totally dependent on the earnings of their husbands and fathers, and could be left in distressed circumstances if these failed through illness or death. Finally, the only occupations open to those who needed to earn their livings, teaching and dressmaking, were badly paid and alienating, and yet demand for the work exceeded the supply.

## The family economy

At the end of the eighteenth century, the economic base of most households in Britain was some form of family economy, in that there was economic interdependence between family members, and women were customarily contributors to the family income in the way considered appropriate to their class or their family situation (Hill 1989: 24). At this date, it is generally agreed, British society consisted of three broad social groups: the gentry, the middle ranks and the lower orders or labouring poor (Marshall 1973: 89–91; Perkin 1969: 22–3). The impact of industrialism on each group was different, but except in the wealthiest groups the outcome for women in almost all cases was an increased dependence, and an economic vulnerability of which the difficulties faced by governesses and dressmakers were symptomatic.

At the top of the social pyramid, among the nobility and gentry, it was expected that both husband and wife would contribute to the family income, and that the woman would therefore bring with her a dowry commensurate with her husband's income. The aristocracy and gentry in Britain were from the first heavily involved in the financial changes that preceded industrialism and the richest among them were already relying on investments as much as on rents from land (McCord 1991: 92–3; Perkin 1969: 75–8). Thus the woman's fortune was normally in the form of capital.

Readers of Jane Austen will remember the easy way in which a woman's fortune could be described, as with Mary Crawford's thirty thousand pounds, or the expectation in *Pride and Prejudice* that the younger son of a peer 'unless the elder brother is sickly . . . would not ask above fifty thousand pounds' (Austen 1813: 195). In spite of the common law expectation that a woman's property became her husband's on marriage, such fortunes were usually well protected by preceding marriage settlements. Thus a woman's fortune could be held in trust for her to pass to her children on her death, or if it went into her husband's hands, there was a provision made for the amount of pin money she would receive during the marriage and the jointure to be paid to her by the estate if widowed (Stone 1977: 242–4).

At the other end of the social scale the cottagers, the closest England came to a peasant class, were equally embedded in and dependent on a family economy. They were people who could never expect to own much or make much money. They did not live on wages, but rather on the food they produced themselves and what they could sell. They lived in cottages, often on waste or common land. They rented and farmed one or two strips of land in the open fields, ran a few animals on the common, went out sometimes as day labourers to the big farmers and engaged in certain cottage industries which were gradually becoming capitalized on the 'putting-out' system, such as spinning, weaving, lace-making and straw-plaiting. Both husbands and wives were engaged in the work which produced an income. Their children, male and female, went off at the age of twelve or thirteen to work as farm servants for the big tenant farmers. Again they did not get weekly wages, only their bed and board and a small annual sum which they tried to save for setting up as cottagers themselves when they married (Hill 1989: 69–84; Pinchbeck 1930: 19–26).

Between these two was the group known as the middle ranks. These were the people who in the seventeenth and eighteenth century undertook most of the commercial provision of food, consumer goods and services: the larger tenant farmers who produced for a local market; the merchants who imported spices, currants, silks, muslins, furs etc. from overseas and sold them from warehouses in the big ports; the craftsmen belonging to the town guilds, the potters, shoe-makers, blacksmiths, carpenters, glovers (like Shakespeare's father), hairdressers, tailors, hatmakers; those who provided prepared food, butchers, bakers, brewers, inn-keepers; and the group who ultimately became the major professionals, the attorneys, surgeons and apothecaries, and estate managers (who became accountants). Sons and daughters of this group were usually apprenticed at about fourteen or fifteen and went off to live in another household. They married one another and when married set up in business together (Clark 1919: 167–89; Hill 1989: 25–33, 85–7).

The wives and daughters within the middle ranks were, Clark and Pinchbeck argued, an absolutely vital part of the money-making enterprise. Farmers' wives had responsibility for the dairy and the poultry and for selling their goods at the local markets, and this, unlike the selling of wheat or wool which was an annual one-off, brought in an income to cover incidental expenses. Among the merchants, the craftsmen, the shopkeepers and the proto-professionals, the women handled the commercial side, ordering materials, taking orders from customers, selling in the shop. Ivy Pinchbeck noted:

> Where the workshop was attached to the home it was customary for the whole family to work together in the craft. Goldsmiths' daughters, for example, were frequently skilled in designing and chasing, and furniture makers, stone masons and engravers brought up their daughters to assist them in carving, sculpture, drawing and graving. The craftsman's wife was usually so well acquainted with her husband's business as to be 'mistress of the managing part of it,' and she could therefore carry on in his absence or after his death, although she herself might lack technical skill. Marriage was, in fact, as much a business partnership as it was among the small clothiers and the farming classes. Servants were kept for domestic work so that the mistress could give her attention to more important business affairs.
>
> (Pinchbeck 1930: 282)

These households were seen by Clark and Pinchbeck as largely benign and based on an economic partnership between husband and wife, but this view has been challenged by later historians (Davidoff and Hall 1987:25, 30; Middleton 1985). The male heads of these households, they contend, exercised autocratic power, and the households conformed to Max Weber's definition of 'patriarchalism': 'the authority of the father, the husband, the senior of the house, the sib elder, over the members of the household and sib; the rule of the master and patron over bondsmen, serfs, freed men; of the lord over the domestic servants and household officials' (Weber 1948: 296). In such households the head – father, husband, master (or, more rarely, mother or mistress) – had control over the life choices and daily routine of all those economically dependent on him (or her) and made decisions in terms of the needs of the family enterprise rather than the individuals who composed it.

This kind of control was exerted even over those who were paid a wage. Servants, apprentices, and journeymen usually lived in the household, received much of the reward for their work in the form of board and lodging, and were consequently subject to the same kind of domination by the head of the family as his wife and children. It was commonplace for families with too many young people to place them in other households, but they were in no sense independent. The control of the father was replaced by that of the master, while it was expected that most of their cash earnings would be handed over to their parents, and in some cases even paid directly by the master to them (Davidoff 1974; Tilly and Scott 1979:37, 109–10)

During the early nineteenth century, however, increasing industrialism was causing a change in the manner in which income-producing work was carried out, a change which transformed the three ranks of the preindustrial period into four classes, upper, upper-middle, lower-middle and working classes, and caused new household structures to emerge in place of the once nearly universal family economy. These transitions took place at different times and different rates in different parts of the country, but the trend was consistently in the same direction.

## The separation of work and home

By the mid-seventeenth century Britain was a most successful capitalist country (Crafts 1989: 65–71) with its trade and supporting financial institutions the equal of any in Europe, but this period also saw the beginnings of a new kind of capitalism, called by Karl Marx capitalist production (Marx 1867) and now more usually described by historians as industrial capitalism. Capitalist producers began by taking advantage of households based on the family economy, with merchants moving from buying up the products of patriarchal households to 'putting out' the work to such households, that is, supplying the households with the raw materials, indicating the kind of product required and then paying for the work done. The earliest industrial machines such as spinning jennies, flying shuttles and knitting frames were designed to be used in such household contexts. In some manufactures, handloom weaving, frame-knitting, earthenware, and small metal goods, for example, the whole household was engaged in the work. In other cases, spinning, lace-making, straw-plait, slop clothing, the work was done primarily by women and young children (Jordan 1989 : 291–2).

In the first half of the nineteenth century, much of this work began to be concentrated into small workshops and factories where a single master could oversee the quality of the work. These masters did not, however, create patriarchal households for this purpose. Instead, they imported into manufacturing the conditions of employment which had previously applied to the intermittent use of day labour in agriculture: workers lived in their own homes and received all the reward for their labour in cash, but could only expect to earn when the employer had a direct need for their work.

Thus, although in the early stages of industrialism whole families were still occupied in industries such as textiles, earthenware and mining, the situation had been transformed, as Marx pointed out (Marx 1867: 279–80), into one where an individual sold his or her labour power during a set period of time to the employer for cash, rather than one where a whole family lived by consuming or selling the product of a household's labour (Jordan 1989: 291–2; Seccombe 1993: 22–8).

A similar process was occurring in farming where the enclosure of the open fields and the common land was transforming cottagers into agricultural labourers (Humphries 1990).

With work no longer done primarily in the household, and businesses gradually approaching a scale and a relationship with employees that could not be contained within a home, economic, as well as political, activity began to be considered as belonging to the public rather than the private sphere. The relationship between employer and employed was conceived of as a civil contract rather than a patriarchal commitment, and when work moved out of the home it also moved out of the private sphere (Pateman 1988: 55–60). Now when a merchant or manufacturer left his parlour or kitchen and went to his warehouse or factory he left the private sphere and entered the public, and those he employed also left their homes to work in the public sphere.

This separation of work and home meant for the labouring poor a transition from households based on a family economy to ones that relied on the wages of the individual members, and the emergence of a group with the characteristics of the modern industrial working class. It also meant, to a very considerable degree, a decline in the patriarchal control that could be exercised over young men and women. If they earned wages that were expected to cover their whole subsistence, they were no longer dependent on fathers or masters for their board and lodging, and it was possible for them to break away from all patriarchal control outside the hours of work.

In practice, as multiple studies have shown, the interdependence of the family economy was replaced, not by an atomistic existence, but by an interdependent multi-waged family unit. Nevertheless, the possibility for independence was there and, indeed, throughout the century, caused widespread concern among those who felt it their duty to supervise the morals of the nation (Seccombe 1993: 54–60).

These changes had an equally profound effect on the old middle ranks, and here too the family economy ceased to be the dominant form of household. This group produced the individuals most instrumental in the industrial transformation of the nineteenth century: the big farmers who pressed for and benefited from the enclosures of the open fields and commons, and the merchants, tradesmen and shopkeepers who transformed themselves into factory owners. Industrialism polarized this group into an upper and a lower middle class, into capitalist employers and skilled waged employees like clerks and artisans, with a group of professionals, tradesmen and shopkeepers who continued to live by selling goods and services, distributed in status terms (size of income, where they lived, whom they married) between the two. In the upper middle class the male-breadwinner family emerged as the dominant household form, whereas in the lower middle class both male-breadwinner and multi-waged forms could be found, together with many households where the family economy persisted. These were the groups from which the women came who overstocked the occupations of dressmaker and governess.

The major catalyst, once again, seems to have been the movement of manufacture from the household to the factory and workshop. At first, as Leonore Davidoff and Catherine Hall have discovered in their study of Birmingham, the tendency was to build a separate dwelling place close to the place of work. However, as the manufacturingprocesses became increasingly dirty and noisy and the streets surrounding the place of work become filled with the houses of the growing workforce, they were tempted to move away and travel to work daily (Davidoff and Hall 1987:359–69). The same situation became inevitable for their middle-class employees. Increasingly, as enterprises grew larger, they needed the work of skilled clerks and artisans. Many of these people were given considerable responsibility, and needed commensurate wages to secure their trustworthiness and loyalty, wages which would allow them to marry and establish their own households (Hobsbawm 1963: 273–5; Lockwood 1989: 19–20). Since they, like the factory workers, were selling their time to the employers, they too expected to spend their leisure time away from the plae of work, and they followed the example of their employers in looking for residences away from the noise and grime of the workplace and its workforce.

This demand provided a lucrative market niche for property developers and builders, and suburbs and residential squares designed for the middle class were built in all the major centres of population (Davidoff and Hall 1987: 360–4). Soon they were being occupied by almost the full range of those who could be defined by occupation as middle class. Each development inevitably contained households with roughly equivalent incomes, yet the sources of those incomes were far from being the same.

A check on those living in two London squares at the time of the 1851 census reveals that businessmen, civil servants, professional men, and those with unearned incomes were living side by side.[2] It also reveals that not one of the women living in them claimed to have any occupation beyond being a relation or servant of the head of the household, or having independent means. A thirty-seven-year-old unmarried woman visiting in one of the houses identified herself as 'clergyman's daughter'. Yet in most cases these were not places of business and there is ample evidence that when men left the house to go to work their wives and daughters did not accompany them (Cobbe 1862: 230; Craik 1858: 227–8; Davidoff and Hall 1987: 364–75; Milne 1857: 23).

As Ivy Pinchbeck pointed out, there was no longer any opportunity for the wives and daughters to play an active part in most of these occupations. Wives and daughters of merchants and manufacturers were no longer at hand to observe and import into their habitus the way the business was run. When household heads in this class were salary earners there was even less chance. While it was becoming possible for men to earn an upper-middle-class income in the increasingly bureaucratised areas of business and government, there was no possibility of their wives participating. Civil servants and the officers in the large banks and insurance companies worked for salaries and their assistants were appointed and paid by the organizations they served. Even in situations, such as in professional households, where home and work had not yet been separated, there was a similar exclusion of wives and daughters. Professional practice was increasingly regulated by examinations rather than apprenticeships, and overseen by chartered societies, so that even if a professional man still worked from home, there was strong pressure against his wife or daughter acquiring his skills by acting as his assistant. (Holloway 1991: 261–3; Reader 1966: 68–9).

It would seem that in the upper middle class, to a very considerable extent the family economy had been replaced by a male breadwinner economy. But it was apparently not because they were wives but because they were female that women remained in the home. Daughters too were now usually cut off from connection with the family business. It had become customary for sons from such families to choose, and for their parents to afford them the choice, either of entering the business as a working partner, going into business on their own, becoming professional men, or even, if the concern had been particularly prosperous, becoming leisured gentlemen living on rents or dividends (Tosh 1996: 54). With daughters, however, there was no such choice. It was assumed, all the evidence from the period suggests, that they would remain with their mothers in the family home, helping with whatever tasks she undertook, until they married and took on these tasks as principals.

Historians of women's work have long been faced with the question of why the separation of work and home was accompanied by the segregation of women within the home, why at the turn of the eighteenth century the women of the middle ranks ceased to be economically active while men from the same segment of society increasingly took part in the much more varied economic activities now available. The answers, over the century and a half

30

during which the matter has been known, have become increasingly complex and sophisticated. From the first, however, there have been suggestions that discursive as well as economic pressures played a part.

Gentility, as Bessie Rayner Parkes's remarks quoted at the beginning of this chapter show, was the earliest of these pressures to be identified. When she and other members of the Women's Movement began in the 1860s to suggest that young middle-class women should train for occupations, they encountered strong resistance, the most obvious basis for which was a belief that their families would 'lose caste' if the women were seen to be earning money. After fifteen years of such work the Society for Promoting the Employment of Women noted in its annual report:

> There are ladies who are so afraid of being known to do anything towards their own maintenance that they beg to be allowed to work under an assumed name; these poor ladies will submit to any privation, undergo any hardship, to keep up appearances, and it is impossible for any-one who is not intimately connected with the working of the Society to estimate how difficult it is to help them.
>
> (EWR 1875: 172)

This explanation was taken up by the early historians of women's work like Ivy Pinchbeck (1930: 315). The status of a family was judged by the amount of leisure available to the women, and thus the emergence of what Wally Seccombe (1993: 111–24) has called the 'male-breadwinner norm' in the earlier part of the century was not simply a consequence of the separation of work and home. It was, as well, the basis on which a new way of demonstrating social status was built, with the amount and kind of work the women of the family did being strongly related to the status pretensions of the family.

## The aspiration to gentility

The most widely recognized status division in England, or at least the one which figures most prominently in the written record, was the line separating ladies and gentlemen from the rest of the population. In the eighteenth century this line separated the top group, the nobility and gentry from both the middle ranks and the labouring poor (Marshall 1973: 89–91; Perkin 1969: 18–23), but as the class structure changed from three groups to four, this defining line also changed its position.

Landed society in Britain had always been relatively open. Rich merchants who bought country estates usually found themselves accepted by the longer established families (McKendrick 1974: 191–5; Mingay 1963: 26; Reader 1966: 3). Readers of Jane Austen's will recall how in *Pride and Prejudice*, though the Bennets' neighbours the Lucases had made their money in the

City, they mixed with the landed families among whom they had settled and one daughter married a clergyman, the heir to the Bennets' estate, and how in *Emma* the Coles, 'of low origin, in trade, and only moderately genteel' saw in their increasing wealth almost an obligation to move a rung up the social ladder and invite the older established families to dine with them (Austen 1816: 204, 205).

This tendency, Janet Roebuck has argued, continued throughout the nineteenth century, extended right down the social scale, and 'promoted a curious cohesiveness in this basically divided and sub-divided society':

> Because the pace-setters of each class aped the class above, eventually all socially ambitious segments of society came to share certain similar standards, aspirations and behaviour patterns, with the result that they had more in common than might have been expected.
> (Roebuck 1973: 20)

For example, the suburban villas and city squares and terraces into which the new middle class of manufacturers and professional men moved were modelled on the country estates and the town houses of the landed gentry, while the cottages and terraces built for their lower-middle-class employees, the waged clerks and artisans, were even more modest versions of the same models.

It was not just the material aspects of the lives of the gentry that were being copied: their 'gentility', the morals and manners that were assumed to justify their right to enjoy political and economic superiority (Mingay 1963: 139), was being appropriated, and to a considerable extent redefined, by the new upper middle class.

By the 1840s the dividing line that separated ladies and gentlemen from the rest had slipped. Instead of lying below the landed classes and their offspring, it formed a barrier separating the wealthier section of the old middle ranks from those below (Clark 1962: 252–74; Davidoff and Hall 1987: 24–5). Above the line were now included merchants, manufacturers, and a group of occupations – attorney, surgeon, apothecary, engineer – which had previously been seen as roughly on a level with carpenter, barber, watchmaker, tailor and the like, but whose members had, in the early nineteenth century, begun to form themselves into chartered professional bodies (Reader 1966: 68–9).[3]

The clearest listing I have come across of which occupations placed a family above the line is one made by the Prudential Insurance Company in the 1870s when it was decided to employ 'ladies' as clerks. The company would employ only women whose nearest male relatives were officers of the army and navy, clergymen, bankers, merchants, wholesale dealers, members of the stock exchange, 'professional men (viz medical men)', lawyers, artists and 'purely literary men', managers, secretaries and chief officials of companies, clerks in the Houses of Parliament, and 'any exceptional cases in harmony with the above principle to be considered by the Board' (Jordan 1996: 66 quoted).[4] Such men were increasingly being educated in the public schools which expanded in number with the demand, and by mid-century the typical definition of a gentleman was one who had received a gentlemen's education (Clark 1962: 255, 267–70; Perkin 1989: 83–5, Tosh 1997: 47).

Moreover with this change in personnel, the moral qualities believed to define a gentleman also changed. The aristocratic code of honour was replaced by the conception of the Christian gentleman as preached in the reformed public schools (Clark 1962: 253; Houghton 1957: 282–4; Perkin 1969: 273–8). Ladies too had a very similar code, one summed up by George Eliot as comprising 'high veracity, delicate honour in her dealings, deference to others, and refined personal habits' (Eliot 1861: 97).

Though the title of gentleman was employed to cover wholesale traders, manufacturers and professional men, there was no assumption that they had moved out of the middle ranks. Dinah Mulock Craik wrote of 'we "ladies" of the middle and upper ranks', and Bessie Rayner Parkes spoke of ladies as coming from the 'upper and middle classes' (Craik 1858: 66; Parkes 1865: 74) while George du Maurier wrote of his hero in Trilby in 1894:

He had a well-brought-up, middle-class young Englishman's belief in the infallible efficacy of gentle birth – for gentle he considered his own . . . and that of most of the good people he lived among in England – all people, in short, whose two parents and four grandparents had received a liberal education and belonged to the professional class.

(Du Maurier 1894: 38)

## The upper middle class

Harold Perkin has demonstrated that during the nineteenth century a split developed in the gentry and that those landed families who invested in new commercial enterprises became observably richer than those who relied primarily on land for their income. Between 1850 and 1870 they were joined in a new upper class by the richest of the businessmen from the old middle ranks who, because of the ease of transport provided by the railways, could purchase and occupy landed estates while continuing to control their business (Perkin 1969: 428–436). Thus that section of the community known as 'high society', 'the best circles' or the 'upper ten thousand', which had once been confined to the landed nobility and gentry and had revolved around the court, became, during the second half of the nineteenth century, increasingly a mixture of landed and business interests, where anyone rich enough to play a part, South Africans and Americans included, was acceptable. Style, elegance, and above all money, rather than birth and education separated this group from the group below (Davidoff 1973: 59).

Though the section of the older landed gentry that was not incorporated into the new upper class still regarded itself as superior to the merchants and professional men who were obliged to earn rather than manage money (Perkin 1969: 23), they increasingly found themselves incorporated into the new upper middle class by relationship and marriage. Traditionally the strict observance of primogeniture by landowners had meant that not all their sons could become landowners too, but if these sons entered one of the acceptable occupations – law (as a barrister), medicine (as a physician), the church, the army, the navy, the civil service – they did not lose their right to be considered gentlemen or to marry ladies. They were thus little different in their way of earning a living from the rising members of the old middle ranks where the richer merchants and manufacturers were sending their sons to the schools and universities patronised by the upper class and placing them in the established professions.

This mixing of the sons in educational establishments and professionally made it possible for those from diverse backgrounds to meld into a single status group. Although as Harold Perkin has noted 'from top to bottom the middle class was riddled with . . . divisions and petty snobberies, not only of income and geography but also of religion' (Perkin 1989: 78–101), nevertheless the similarities in education, type of residence, and lifestyle generally, made it acceptable for all members of the group to eat at the same table and find marriage partners within the whole broad group, thus fulfilling the conditions of 'commensality' and 'connubium' that Max Weber identified as defining the boundaries of a status group (Weber 1968: 306). The upper middle class was not large, probably not more than 2.5 per cent of the total population at any time between 1840 and 1910 (Banks 1978: 197; Perkin 1969: 420), but it still emerged as the group which defined not just manners and customs, but the morality which was intricately related to conceptions of gentility.

The aspiration to be regarded as gentlemen had little impact on the working lives of upper-middle-class men, but the impact on their wives and daughters was very different. Though men left the villas and squares where they spent their evenings to go to their places of business each morning, their wives and daughters did not accompany them into this now public arena. As with housing, the practices of the lesser gentry provided the model on which their lives were based. The wives and daughters of the lesser gentry usually brought to the marriage an income of their own, and they expected that their married lives should offer them that leisure that was one of the defining characteristics, the status conventions, of the upper class, leisure not necessarily to be idle, but to follow up their personal interests, social, political, artistic, or charitable (Perkin 1969: 55–6). Even those whose husbands had to earn their livings as soldiers, sailors, civil servants, clergymen, barristers or physicians, expected not to be involved in this process, though they undertook the supervision of the servants, and continued to pursue the 'leisured' life of women in the landed gentry (Purvis 1991: 5–7).

This, then, offered a model to the rising professional and commercial families. Even when the place of business was still attached to the dwelling, as with a doctor's surgery or a lawyer's office, for those who wished to claim 'gentle' status, the public and private areas of the house had to be distinctly defined. No longer did the merchant's wife keep accounts and check bills of lading, the apothecary's wife help by measuring out the drugs, or the attorney's daughter copy out the long, involved wills and settlements in which her father dealt. What Carroll Smith-Rosenberg (1979) has called the female world of love and ritual became their sole source of occupation. They were also, their critics noted, committed to 'aping the life of the aristocracy' (Parkes 1865: 156), paying morning calls, giving dinner parties, and joining with the wives of squires and clergymen in visiting the poor, running clothing clubs for them, and teaching in the Sunday School (Craik 1858 : 227–8; Milne 1857: 23).

J. A. Banks has shown that it was customary for those with above £400 a year to employ at least three servants, and with this staff the mistress's duties were purely supervisory; few of them had to do any physical housework beyond arranging the flowers and dusting the most precious ornaments, though they seem to have done a great deal of sewing. (Banks 1954: 77; Banks and Banks 1965: 65). As Bessie Rayner Parkes wrote in 1865: 'Deep into the heart of English society eats this cankering notion that women of the middle class lose caste by household activity' (Parkes 1865: 82). Furthermore, perhaps because they had less to occupy them than their husbands, it was apparently the women of these families who worked hardest at raising the social level of the family. Frances Power Cobbe wrote in 1862:

> It is nearly always the *wives* of shopkeepers, merchants, professional men and smaller gentry who are found pushing their families into the grade a step higher and urging the often-recalcitrant husband to the needful toadyism and expenditure.
>
> (Cobbe 1862a: 230)

Consequently the prohibition against women entering the public sphere was extended within the upper middle class, to a prohibition against their using any of their ample leisure time to add to the family's income even by doing work which did not involve leaving the privacy of the home.[5]

Contemporary commentators agreed that paid work for ladies was considered quite out of the question (Banks and Banks 1965: 30; Milne 1857: 8; Pinchbeck 1930: 315). When Sophia Jex-Blake, a rebel from early childhood and one of the first Englishwomen to qualify in medicine took a position as tutor at Queen's College in 1859 her father wrote to her:

35

I have only this moment heard that you contemplate being *paid* for the tutorship. It would be quite beneath you, darling, and I *cannot consent* to it. Take the post as one of honour and usefulness, and I shall be glad, and *you will be no loser*, be quite sure. But to be *paid* for the work would be to alter the thing *completely*, and would lower you sadly in the eyes of almost everybody. Do not think about it, dearest, and you will rejoice greatly by and bye with all who love you best.

(Todd 1918: 67, quoted)

Yet her brother earned his living as a schoolmaster. When Charlotte M. Yonge's first novel was ready for publication a family council was held to decide whether this was permissible. 'In consenting,' wrote her biographer, 'there was an understanding that she would not take the money herself for it, but that it would be used for some good work.' (Coleridge 1903: 153.)

## The lower middle class

Establishing status through the lifestyle of the women was not a practice confined to upper-middle-class families, but extended to many of those on the other side of the line dividing ladies and gentlemen from the rest of the population. The status customs of this group, for which the most convenient title seems to be lower middle class, were even more varied than in the class above, while estimates of its size depend on which groups are seen as composing it. Some investigators tend to accept Rowntree's definition of the middle class as the servant keeping class (McBride 1976: 18; Roebuck 1973: 23–4) and there is plenty of contemporary evidence that many below the line of gentility kept servants. 'The vast tradesman class, and the small manufacturers, and the superior artisans', the 'richer mechanics', 'small shopkeepers', and farmers were described as the main employers of maids-of-all-work, or, as the census called them, general servants (Martineau 1859: 308; Phillips 1861: 87).[6]

Modern historians seem to be agreed that the 'labour aristocracy' to which these 'richer mechanics' and 'superior artisans' belonged had a great deal in common, both in income and in life style, with the clerks, shopkeepers and self-employed tradesmen who were defined by contemporary observers like Booth as middle class (Armstrong 1972: 209; Booth 1902: 52–3; Hobsbawm 1963: 273–4; Perkin 1969: 144). Estimates of the size of the group vary, but the proportion was possibly as high as 37 per cent (Perkin 1969: 144, 420). Within this wide group, each of the family forms seems to have had a substantial presence.

Most of the families where the family economy continued to determine lifestyle belonged to this new lower middle class. In the 1851 census, farmers' wives and daughters were given their own categories and included in the farming rather than the domestic class. The wives of shopkeepers, innkeepers, shoemakers and so on, were similarly placed in the same occupational category as their husbands, and the enumerators' books seem to suggest that in some cases at least, the daughters, though not given a separate category like farmer's daughters, were returned as pursuing their fathers' occupations. Other contemporary accounts suggest that many daughters helped shopkeeper fathers and there is evidence that as late as the 1890s daughters in tailors' families acted as assistants (Collet 1902: 150–1; Martineau 1859: 311).

More generally, however, the practice of helping craftsman fathers seems to have died out. There were scattered references in the 1870s in the Women's Movement journal, the *Englishwoman's Review,* to girls trained by their fathers to be printers, goldsmiths, dentists, and so on, but the eagerness with which these cases were pounced on suggests that such practices were not customary.

However, if there were two or three grown daughters, too many for the needs of farm, shop, or household, the traditional custom of the family economy, that of sending them out to work elsewhere, seems to have continued, and this was equally the case with families where the father earned a wage. There were three occupations – teacher, dressmaker, and shop assistant – where employers expected a woman to have training, manners, and personal presentation which could only be acquired by women from middle-class backgrounds, and middle-class women were in demand for the more confidential posts in domestic service such as children's nurse and lady's maid (Boucherett 1863: 23–6; Butler 1868: 5; Milne 1857: 130, 180; Yonge 1877: 192, 201). Three of these – sewing, teaching and domestic service – were all long-established as suitable work for women, with only retail work relatively new and giving a hint of where future opportunities were to lie.

Many lower-middle-class wives also contributed to the family's cash income. This was not by any means a new development. Families at the lower end of the middle ranks had always employed multiple strategies for gaining an income. In the seventeenth and eighteenth centuries, wives in some households ran their own independent enterprises to add to the family income, ranging from manufacturing (with the primary focus on the luxury end of the dress trade), through various forms of shopkeeping to taking in lodgers (Hill 1989: 92–3; Pinchbeck 1930: 287–303). This tradition seems to have continued, and to have been practised by the wives of employed men. However once again, as with the daughters, there was little adaptation to a world in which wage-labour was increasing. Unlike their husbands and sons, they did not work for wages, but, like women in earlier generations engaged in small, home-based entrepreneurial ventures, running girls' schools, dressmaking establishments, shops of various kinds, and of course taking in lodgers (Anderson 1984: 384–5; Davidoff 1979).

Some of these households, however, may have retained the family economy from necessity rather than choice. Those at the bottom of the group were anxious to distance themselves from the unskilled labouring poor, while many of those at the top seem to have modelled themselves as far as possible on the upper middle class with a similar aspiration to gentility (McKendrick 1974 : 191–2; Roebuck 1973: 20). In an interesting study based on the attitudes revealed in two widely read penny weeklies, the *London Journal* and the *Family Herald*, Sally Mitchell notes:

> The readers . . . actively sought information about the values, standards, and mechanical details of living in a milieu which was new to them. Their letters to the correspondence column reveal their conscious mobility. They want to eradicate the traces of their origin that linger in their grammar and pronunciation. They ask the kind of questions about etiquette and general knowledge that would be impossible for anyone with a polite background and more than a rudimentary education.
>
> (Mitchell 1977: 34)

In the fiction in these papers, it seems, there was a tendency to claim for the lower middle class the moral right to gentility. The stories demonstrated 'to the woman of narrow means that ladyhood is not dependent on income nor destroyed by the necessity of working, but lies in manners and bearing' (ibid.: 40).

Nevertheless, many of the more prosperous members of the lower middle class, particularly the large farmers and shopkeepers, followed the upper-middle-class pattern, and began to rely on the single male breadwinner for income, while the women of the family demonstrated their gentility by distancing themselves from earning money. Like merchants and professionals, farmers and shopkeepers began to make a strong distinction between their workplace and their living quarters, the space allotted to the servants and to the family. This is particularly well documented with farmhouses. Whereas it had been customary for farm servants to eat with the farmer and his wife and to share the sleeping accommodation of his family, increasingly throughout the first part of the century, they created separate dining rooms for themselves, built cottages to house their skilled workers and used day labourers rather than live-in servants for the farm work (Mingay 1963: 240; Pinchbeck 1930: 35–7).

The education of the daughters of the family played a similar role in establishing gentility and status. Evidence from the first part of the century suggests that a sizable minority of lower-middle-class families were paying for some sort of education for their daughters well into their teens. It may be remembered that in Jane Austen's *Emma* the teenaged sisters of a farmer were attending Mrs Goddard's school, and such schools were still being described at mid-century (*Athenaeum*, 1848: 461; *Fraser's*, 1860: 360).

The census figures for students aged fifteen to nineteen give some idea of the proportions for the latter part of the century. In 1851, 4 per cent of girls aged fifteen to nineteen were returned as 'scholars', in 1871, 6.9 per cent as 'students and others' and in 1891, 4.5 per cent as 'students', whereas the equivalent figures for boys were 3.4 per cent, 4.8 per cent and 4 per cent. Since there was little educational provision for those over seventeen, these figures would suggest that double these percentages of girls aged fifteen to seventeen were being supported by their fathers throughout their teens, and presumably from then until they married. Since the upper and upper middle class together accounted for less than 3 per cent of the population, the rest must necessarily have been lower middle class, and it would therefore seem that a sizable minority of lower-middle-class households (ranging between 5 per cent and 11 per cent of the total population) had adopted the same economic pattern as the upper middle class.

Furthermore, in the schools where they were educated the curriculum was based on that of the schools for the class above. There was plenty of upper-middle- class scorn for this practice. Criticism of farmers for their aspirations for their daughters began in the late eighteenth century and continued well into the next century (*Athenaeum* 1848: 461; Pinchbeck 1930: 35–7). *Fraser's Magazine* reported in 1860:

> Female education in the upper classes of society has been frequently denounced as frivolous and low-toned, but in the classes below these it is far worse. We find there a bad imitation of a bad thing. The same frivolity without the refinement; the flashiness without the elegance; the same absence of all that is practically or intellectually useful with the additional disadvantage of a position in which the useful qualities of head and hand are most likely to be needed; in which habits of idleness are not merely a folly, a mental suicide as among the rich, but a sin against the dearest interests of home, a barrier that may make it forever impossible to maintain independence or respectability.
>
> (*Fraser's*, 1860: 360)

Low grade or not, this education seems to have been eagerly sought for their daughters by those sections of the lower middle class which could afford it, and served, along with wives who occupied their time with household supervision and sociability, and daughters who lived as ladies at home until marriage, to establish the status credentials of the family. Indeed, the lower-middle-class claim to the name 'lady' was so determined that upper-middle-class women even began to suggest that the term 'gentlewomen' should be used to distinguish their true refinement from the pseudo-refinement of farmers' and shopkeepers' daughters (Hubbard 1875: 45; Phillips 1861: 1–2).

The male-breadwinner norm was becoming firmly established even among employed clerks and the 'aristocracy of labour', the skilled artisans.

These families, having abandoned the older forms of patriarchal family labour and gaining their money in the same way as the new working class of free wage labourers, had a strong incentive to distinguish themselves socially from this group. Like the upper middle class, they too were being forced to adapt to the separation of work and home, and they seem to have used the fact of having wives and daughters who did not contribute to the family income as a way of distinguishing themselves from the class below.

Furthermore, as a number of historians have convincingly argued, clerks and artisans in industry felt very deeply their displacement from the position of power enjoyed by their fathers as heads of patriarchal manufacturing or retailing households. Their pride and their definition of their own masculinity thus became deeply implicated with their notion of themselves as breadwinners for their families and controllers of their wives' and children's destinies, and throughout the nineteenth century, the male-breadwinner norm was made the basis for demands for a 'family wage' (Alexander 1984: 133–7; Benenson 1984: 7–8; Seccombe 1993: 112–3).

When, however, the question of resisting the introduction of female employees into previously all-male occupations arose, the unionists did not refer directly to their status needs for such a wage. Instead they turned to a different set of beliefs which they shared with their employers, the belief that women did not belong in the public sphere of work. In 1811 the journeymen tailors were complaining that women had been 'unfairly driven from their proper sphere in the social scale, unfeelingly torn from the maternal duties of a parent and unjustly encouraged to compete with men in ruining the money-value of labour' (Drake 1920: 4), in the 1840s wood-engravers protested that the opening of the Female School of Design would 'tempt the women to forgo those household employments more befitting their sex' (Jameson 1846: 245), and in 1877 the union leader Henry Broadhurst told TUC members that:

> It was their duty as men and husbands to use their utmost efforts to bring about a condition of things where their wives should be in their proper sphere at home, instead of being dragged into competition for livelihood against the great and strong men of the world.
>
> (Drake 1920: 16)

The unionists' rhetoric here implied that they were basing their objections on a set of beliefs about the relations of the sexes that was an unchallengeable 'truth' for both parties to the negotiations. They were making a moral appeal to values which they believed were accepted as what Bourdieu has called 'doxa' by their upper-middle-class employers, and which were part of the habitus of many members of the employed lower middle class, and played a significant part in establishing their self-esteem and social status. This raises the question of whether the 'aspiration to gentility' credited by the Women's

Movement workers and the early historians of women's work as the primary cause of the relegation of women to the home can be seen as a sufficient explanation, or whether it was, rather, the most obvious, the one must capable of being described and disputed. I would suggest that this aspiration was in fact supported by the undiscussed and undisputed set of beliefs about the relations of the sexes to which the male unionists referred.

Maria Grey, in adding femininity to gentility as the 'idols of society' which were at the root of the 'woman question', had identified a far greater barrier to change than the more obvious concern with gentility. Whereas the concern with 'losing caste' could be rejected by Women's Movement members on moral and religious grounds as part of the 'pomps and vanities of this wicked world', definitions of femininity and 'woman's mission' were more resilient. This conception of femininity was, I shall argue in the next chapter, far more deeply integrated into the habitus of the men and women of the day than conceptions of gentility, and indeed the constraints of gentility were so powerful only because they were built on this doxic base.

'Victorian' ideas about gender and femininity have, over the last fifteen years, been seen as part of a broad discourse usually referred to as the domestic ideology. June Purvis has suggested that the domestic ideology embodied three major assumptions: first that the biological differences between men and women made it natural that they should occupy 'separate spheres', second that women were what Sarah Stickney Ellis described as 'relative creatures', defined by their relation to the men of their families, and thirdly that they were inferior to men (Purvis 1991: 2–5). The next chapter will look at the contribution of these three assumptions to determining that the separation of work and home in the nineteenth century left women positioned in the home.

# 3

# THE CONSTRAINTS
# OF FEMININITY

## The domestic ideology

The assumption that men's and women's lives were to be lived in different spheres, which surfaced in the speeches of trade unionists, can be found in even richer detail in the journalism addressed to an upper-middle-class audience. The novelist Margaret Oliphant wrote: 'Man goes out to his work and labour till the evening. Woman prepares for him, waits for him, serves him at home' (Oliphant 1869: 585). A writer in *Blackwoods' Magazine* asserted that 'while man's business was in the bustle of the world, in the hot contest of life, with its disappointments no less than its rewards and distinctions, woman's sphere was within the shelter and retreat of a tranquil home' (Atkinson 1861: 470). It was widely believed that this separation of spheres had existed from time immemorial. *Punch* argued that 'in parcelling out life into two great fields, the one inside, the other outside the house doors, and in creating two beings so distinct in mind, body, and affections, as men and women, the Framer of the Universe must have meant the two for different functions', while a writer in the *Westminster Review* believed that 'God made man *and* woman, is guiding their destiny on earth, and that the result can be no world-wide mistake' (Adams 1849: 352).

It was claimed that the basis of this doctrine of separate spheres was the biblical description of the creation where God said, 'It is not good that man should be alone: I will make him an help meet for him.' (Gen. 2:18), and the term was widely used in the period: 'To be man's help-meet is woman's true vocation: for this, in the happy garden, she was given to the first Adam; and to be this, no longer Man's drudge or his plaything, the coming of the second Adam has restored her' (Greenwell 1862: 64). God, it was thus demonstrated, had created separate spheres for men and women, and it was only in these divinely ordained spheres that they could fulfil the destiny for which they were created. Man was independent, woman dependent on man. Man's sphere was the world, woman's the home. Man's duty was to provide materially for the woman, the woman's to comfort and succour the man.

Such language is redolent with what recent poststructuralist theory refers to as binary oppositions (Scott 1988: 37), in this case the opposition between home and work, between (to use the Marxist terminology) production and consumption, between the man's and the woman's sphere. Linked distinctions such as mind/body, public/private, reason/desire had long been part of western thinking, and in the transition to industrialism work/home was added to them. However with the doctrine of separate spheres a new feature appears to be added: the oppositions are gendered. The first term in each opposition is seen as masculine and the second as feminine. Wives might always have been regarded as helpmeets, but before the nineteenth century, the help was, as was argued in the last chapter, specifically directed to raising the income of the family, and there was little distinction between home and workplace. The relationship of husband and wife had been seen as hierarchical; now it was increasingly regarded as one of opposition, of mutual exclusion. What the man was, the woman was not, and vice versa. This is not to claim that there were no gendered oppositions before the nineteenth century. At the level of discourse many such can be found, for example the classic statement of male and female virtues: 'All the brothers were valiant and all the sisters were virtuous', while at the practical level most work within family economy households was gendered. Nevertheless, as a number of historians have pointed out, there was an increasing tendency to move from a hierarchic view of gender to a dichotomous one (Laqueur 1990: 5–6; Poovey 1988: 6–9).

## 'Relative creatures'

The research of feminist political philosophers like Jean Bethke Elshtain, Linda Nicholson and Carol Pateman has focussed attention on the relationship between this trend and the spread of democratic ideas. They have noted the exclusion of women from the right to participate as citizens in the public sphere during the time when it was being claimed for all men. The emergence of social contract theory during the seventeenth and eighteenth centuries saw the gradual replacement of a patriarchal conception of society with all men and women owing loyalty and obedience to a god-appointed king just as they did to a father, with a belief in a social contract between subjects and their rulers where men stood in the relation of brothers to one another (Elshtain 1981; Nicholson 1986: 105–30). This transition, as Pateman points out, has been built into a heroic narrative by the historians of political thought: the oppressive paternal rule of the monarch was overthrown in the late eighteenth century by a group of men claiming liberty, equality and fraternity. But this, Pateman stresses, is a narrative that sees as 'natural' the exclusion of women (Pateman 1988 Chap. 4).

In the early stages of this transition, the right to participate in the public sphere where the social contract was negotiated was not claimed for all men, only for those who were property owners. Thus the public sphere was not gendered during the first phases of the transition. These property owners acted on behalf of all the members of their households and the communities in which they were the leaders. The economic changes in the way work was organized, its movement out of the household and the increasing number of men who earned substantial incomes without owning property, gradually changed this. The bulk of men who worked for others, even the poorest farm labourers and factory hands, were no longer in a patriarchal relationship with their employers, expecting to be housed and fed and accepting that their relationship to the state and the public sphere generally was mediated by their master. They were employed as individuals, and as free labourers, entering into a contract to sell a certain amount of time or labour in return for an agreed cash payment and buying their food and negotiating the rent for their housing in an open market. This, after a good deal of political struggle, was recognized as establishing them as individual parties to the social contract, and thus as entitled to the political rights and duties of citizens.

As the feminist historians of political thought have pointed out, there was strong resistance to extending these political rights to women. Although Robert Filmer posited the 'natural' liberty of women as a *reductio ad absurdum* of the contract argument in his *Patriarchia* (1680) (Pateman 1988: 183), and the early 'women's rights' theorists like Mary Wollstonecraft (1792) put the same case quite seriously, only some of the most extreme political radicals accepted that the universalist form in which contract theory was stated meant that, logically, women too should be admitted to citizenship (Taylor 1983: 15–18).[1] For most people it seemed quite out of the question that women should ever act in independence as citizens in their own right. They were 'relative creatures' defined by their relationship with men and created to serve their interests. Poets ranging in period and stature from John Milton to the anonymous author of a poem celebrating the 'lofty pine' and 'clinging vine' copied into a woman's commonplace book in the 1820s (Davidoff and Hall 1987: 397) stressed this. Milton has Eve tell Adam:

> God is thy law, thou mine: to know no more
> Is woman's happiest knowledge and her praise
> (Milton, *Paradise Lost* IV: 637)

The dominance of men over women, the belief that women were the property of their male relatives, was seen as so 'natural' that it scarcely needed defending. Although, as Pateman has shown (1988: 83–8), Locke made efforts to deal with Filmer's argument, and those who looked to the Bible to establish truth could find verses from Genesis to St Paul to justify the position (Davidoff and Hall 1987: 132–3), it was a truth so widely accepted that it seems to have been, in most circles, what Bourdieu has called 'doxa', 'undiscussed and undisputed', part of everyone's 'knowledge' of how the world operated. Indeed it was and is a belief so deeply held by people who otherwise differ very widely in their world views, and so little defended despite almost two centuries of challenges by feminists, that it is still very difficult to identify its basis.[2] Its consequences can, however, be explored. The focus in what follows will be on its importance in the emergence of the doctrine of separate spheres and the impact of this new mode of interpreting the world on the working lives of women, and the extent to which this was responsible for restricting the range of occupations open to them.

## Separate spheres

The most significant consequence for women's future employment of the gendering of the public/private division was a similar gendering of the notion of patriarchal control. Whereas it was increasingly assumed that adult men were independent citizens, free from dominance by fathers or masters, it was believed that women were defined by their relation to their male relatives, and must therefore be under some form of patriarchal control, and that such control should be exercised in the private sphere of the household. Just as it was felt inappropriate for women to become citizens, there was a similar strong feeling in many quarters that they did not belong in the public sphere of work as free wage labourers. Thus, the separation of work and home and the consequent establishment of free labour conditions in most industrial sectors had a very different impact on men and women. Work, as well as politics, was now part of the public sphere where free individuals made contracts with one another, but whereas this set the scene for men of all ranks to become citizens, women were not and could not be free individuals.[3]

Here, once again, the newly gendered binary opposition of public and private was interpreted in terms of older conceptions of modesty, chastity and family honour which applied to women and not to men (Hill 1989: 184; Rogers 1982: 9–11).[4] Women known to be sexually active outside marriage brought dishonour on a family, and their male relations felt impelled to fight (with swords and pistols at the top end of the society, with whips and fists below) both their 'betrayers' and any other men who alluded to the circumstance. Women who worked outside the home were therefore believed to be running the risk of 'unsexing' themselves and bringing shame on their families.

This belief was not a direct product of the increase in wage labour for men, but it was highlighted by the consequent diminution of work for women within the home. In 1787 the writer of children's educational texts, Sarah Trimmer (1741–1810), expressed deep concern at the lack of work which women could do in their own homes:

> It is a most lamentable sight to enter a cottage, and behold a poor woman sitting in rags surrounded by a set of dirty children: we are shocked, and turn away with disgust, condemning her in our hearts for sloth and untidiness; but let us stop an instant, and hear her apology.
>
> (Trimmer 1787: 62)

45

Yet she did not believe the answer lay in joining men in the fields.

> Instead of sitting down in peace and quietness in her own little neat apartment, surrounded by playful innocents, she finds in the fields or gardens a set of reprobates who shock her ears with oaths, blasphemies, and indecency. Her mind is filled with anxiety for her children's safety; she is not at liberty to return home to prepare a comfortable supper for her husband. He may be enticed for the sake of a good fire, and other refreshments, which if she had spinning or knitting she could provide, to go to the alehouse; she may herself be prevailed on, when overcome with fatigue or faintness, to drink destructive spirits, and by degrees become a dram-drinker. She must become a Sabbath breaker, by either continuing her occupation, or washing, ironing, or cleaning house. In short, innumerable evils may be the consequence of her removal to a place where she is excluded from the employments of her early days. . . . I have great reason to believe, from observation, that many men, who when they first marry are soberly inclined, gradually become sots, from their wives working out of doors.
>
> (ibid.: 66–7)

She believed that the answer was for women to be provided with work they could do in their own homes:

> I cannot help thinking that there are enow of the other sex to perform the usual business of agriculture, and that it is invading their province for women to forsake their spinning, needle-work, and knitting, to work the whole summer long, and in winter also, in the fields and gardens; yet what can they do if there is no suitable employment to be had.
>
> (ibid.: 68)

The same views were still being expressed almost a hundred years later. The topic came up over and over again at the Social Science Congresses held to discuss public affairs in the late 1850s and 1860s. Work within a family economy was still felt to be the ideal for women. One speaker talked glowingly of 'the unbroken family circle, united in all its interests, and happy in the constant alternation of hearty work with social inter-course' (TNAPSS 1863: 705). Most were adamant that work should not take a married woman out of her home and away from her family. Bessie Rayner Parkes wrote:

> In the working class where the mother is also nurse and home-servant, where all the cleanliness, economy, and comfort of home

46

depend on her actual and constant superintendence, her absence at any trade is as bad in a money as in a moral point of view.

(Parkes 1865: 151)

Like Mrs Trimmer, many speakers blamed men's drinking on this neglect of home comforts, while the practice of women working in factories was also seen as contributing to infant mortality (TNAPSS 1857: 543, 546, 547; 1859: 725; 1861: 686; 1868: 606, 607).[5]

For women in the middle class the older prescriptions designed to preserve female modesty and chastity now had tied to them the new prescriptions of gentility, about behaving as a 'lady', both lumped together under the general heading of 'propriety'. Without even the freedoms made necessary by their contribution to the family income, women found themselves hedged about by numerous prohibitions restricting what they could do, say or even think. Spontaneous speaking and acting and expressions of personal idiosyncrasy were inhibited by a constant fear of what the neighbours, often personified as 'Mrs Grundy', would think (Craik 1858: 227–33; Houghton 1957: 394–9).

These constraints were not accepted without some murmuring and objections. Though for some what Carroll Smith-Rosenberg (1979) has called 'the female world of love and ritual' was enough, particularly among the relatively wealthy who could afford the interests of visits and clothes, there were others who found the round of social activities and the 'proper' behaviour necessary to maintain the family's status stifling. A major grievance was that all individuality was suppressed by the imposed social role, by the need to move in society and to be available on call, for all members of the family. The most famous expression of this view is that in Charlotte Bronte's *Shirley* (Bronte 1849: 203-4), but there were many others. In 1844 Charlotte M. Yonge had her very first heroine say of her social duties:

> Here am I in Abbeychurch, and must make the best of it. I must be as polite and hypocritical as I can make myself. I must waste my time and endure dulness.
>
> (Yonge 1844: 106)

Margaretta Grey wrote in her diary in 1851:

> What I remonstrate against is the negative forms of employment; the wasting of energy; the crippling of talent under false ideas of station, propriety and refinement that seem to shut off a large portion of women of our generation from proper spheres of work and adequate exercise of powers. For, now, regular arrangement of hours and systematic occupation give place to all manner of casualties – visiting, note writing, dressing for morning and evening

engagements, or making or receiving calls. The wise and unwise, the gifted and the imbecile yield to the inheritance of custom and limit themselves to what has been fashionable in their circle and station.

(Butler 1954: 402, quoted)

Florence Nightingale poured out bitter complaints about the sacrifice of female talents and energy to the demands of family life:

Women never have an half-hour in all their lives (excepting before or after anybody is up in the house) that they can call their own, without fear of offending or hurting someone. . . . Everybody reads aloud out of their own book or newspaper – or every five minutes, something is said. And what is it to be 'read aloud to'? The most miserable exercise of the human intellect. Or rather, is it any exercise at all? It is like lying on one's back, with one's hands tied and having liquid poured down one's throat.

(Strachey 1978: 402, quoted)

And again:

O weary days – oh evenings that seem never to end – for how many years have I watched that drawing-room clock and thought it would never reach ten! and for twenty, thirty years more to do this!

(Woodham-Smith 1950: 92–3, quoted)

Yet though the complaints were made, throughout the first half of the century the moral pressure on women to accept the restrictions of propriety increased.

## The Angel in the House

By the 1850s a new discourse had appeared which reconciled some women, at least, to their 'relative' status, but which in consequence set up a barrier to future attempts to challenge the doctrine of separate spheres. A moral imperative had been added to the status demands that women stay at home and devote themselves to their male relatives. Though as June Purvis (1991: 2–5) has suggested there is substantial evidence that it was widely assumed that women were inferior to men, this assumption was losing the almost doxic status it had held in the eighteenth century.

A new interpretation of the significance of the separate spheres which saw women not as men's inferiors but as spiritually their superiors had emerged, and though it was not accepted as universally as the notion of separate spheres and women's subordinate place, it played a major role in reinforcing the dictates of 'propriety'. I have chosen to call it, following Virginia Woolf's use of the title of Patmore's poem, the Angel in the House myth.

Though the doctrine of separate spheres was usually legitimated by reference to the biblical story of the creation, the interpretations of this story which had obtained in the seventeenth and eighteenth centuries where not ones that brought much joy to women. It was argued in many a misogynistic sermon that, because Eve had tempted Adam, women were infinitely inferior to men and deserving scorn and castigation (Nussbaum 1984; Stenton 1977: 204–6). This explanation of their situation had little appeal for middle-class women with time to spare and the status of their family to maintain through their social efforts. From the end of the eighteenth century there is evidence that women were looking for some form of heroic justification for the pattern of their lives.

Davidoff and Hall (1987: 157–67) have pointed out that in the decades spanning the turn of the century a number of writers who celebrated the moral superiority of the retired domestic life enjoyed considerable popularity. One of the writers they discuss, the evangelical propagandist Hannah More (1745–1833), though never failing to assert that women must accept that God had designed for them a subordinate position in a patriarchal household, also argued that this position offered them great opportunities for exercising a Christian influence over their husbands and children and through them influencing the life of the nation. In her novel, *Coelebs in Search of a Wife* (1808), she drew a picture of the ideal wife as a woman as well educated as her husband and with an even more refined morality who was, nevertheless, prepared to live a quiet restrained life, influencing her husband for good, but not seeking any activity beyond the household.

More's earlier works also carried the message to women that they had an obligation to use the power of their influence for the good of the nation. The first chapter of her two volume *Strictures on the Modern System of Female Education* (1799) was called 'Address to women of rank and fortune, on the effects of their influence on society. – Suggestions for the exertion of it in various instances', and in it she wrote wistfully of the pure and holy influence women had wielded in the days of chivalry:

> I do not wish to bring back the frantic reign of chivalry, nor to reinstate women in that fantastic empire in which they sat enthroned in the hearts, or rather in the imaginations of men. . . . But let us not forget, in the insolence of acknowledged superiority, that it was *religion* and *chastity*, operating on the romantic spirit of those times, which established the despotic sway of woman: and though, in this altered scene of things, she now no longer looks down on her adoring votaries from the pedestal to which an absurd idolatry had lifted her; yet let her remember that it is the same religion and the same chastity which once raised her to such an

elevation, that must still furnish the noblest energies of her character; must still attract the admiration, still retain the respect of the other sex.

(More 1799 vol. I: 19–20)

By the 1830s there were, however, women who were intent on reclaiming that pedestal, and they were encouraged in that endeavour by works being published by major writers on the continent. The most famous statement of the idea that inspired them appeared in Goethe's *Faust* in 1832 when he wrote that 'the eternal in woman draws us on', but the discourse seems to have been prevalent in France at the same time and to have reached England by this route.[6] In 1834 Louis Aimé -Martin won a prize for a book called *The Education of Mothers of Families; or, the Civilisation of the Human Race by Women.* In this he stressed the power women exercised over men:

Thus, this young girl, who scarcely yet knows herself, who till this day has only known how to obey without reflecting; to whom nothing has been taught of what is going on in the world; this young girl, without knowledge, without experience, becomes all at once powerful and sovereign. She disposes of the life and the honour of a man, guided by his passion; she wishes, and her wishes are fulfilled; she wills, and is directly obeyed. Her childish will may give an hero to his country, or an assassin to the family, according to the loftiness of her soul, or the blindness of her passion. O, woman, you reign, and man is subject to your dominion! you reign over your sons, your lovers, your husbands! In vain do they call themselves your masters, they become men only when you have rendered their existence complete: in vain do they boast of their superiority; their glory, and their shame, are alike derived from you.

(Aimé-Martin 1834: 20–1)

He went on to ask why this had not been incorporated into the writings of moralists and the work of legislators.

For it cannot be too often remarked, that all the evil that women have done us is derived from us, and all the good which they do us comes from themselves. It is in spite of our stupid education that they have thoughts, an intellect and a soul; it is in spite of our barbarous prejudices that they are at the present day the glory of Europe, and the companions of our lives.

(ibid.: 21)

Significant nineteenth-century French publicists soon made their own contributions to the new discourse. The historian Jules Michelet took up the theme in his *L'Amour* and the philosopher Auguste Comte devoted a chapter of his *General View of Positivism* to the role of women. Comte saw women as playing the same role in the private sphere as philosophers did in the public: they were not called on to act but to define and defend the moral principles on which action should be based (Comte 1865: Chap. 4).

It was, however, by way of Aimé-Martin's book that the discourse made its first appearance in England, and here it was women who were its first propagandists. In 1839 Sarah Lewis, a working governess, translated parts of his book, added some ideas of her own and published it as *Woman's Mission*, creating, as Judith Johnston (1997: 208) has pointed out, three phrases that passed into general currency by adding the word 'woman's' to 'sphere', 'influence' and 'mission'. The book had already run through six editions by 1841, and other female writers took up the theme, notably Sarah Stickney Ellis in her addresses throughout the 1840s to the *Women, Wives, Mothers* and *Daughters of England* (Davidoff and Hall 1987: 180–5). Anna Jameson summed up (and seems at that date to have endorsed) their message:

> Open one of these books – or indeed open any book whatever, of morals, physics, travels , history, – they tell us, one and all, that the chief distinction between savage and civilized life, between Heathendom and Christendom, lies in the condition and treatment of the women. . . They assume, as a principle, that in every class of Christian life there is what is called *domestic life*, and that this domestic life supposes as its primary element – the presence, the cares, the devotion of woman. Her sphere is home, her vocation the maternal (not meaning thereby the literal bringing forth of children, but the nourishing, cherishing, and teaching of the young). In all the relations between the sexes, she is the refiner and the comforter of man; it is hers to keep alive all those purer, gentler, and more genial sympathies, those refinements in morals, in sentiment, in manners, without which we men, in this rough working-day world, would degenerate (*do* degenerate, for the case is not hypothetical) into mere brutes.
>
> (Jameson 1843: 257)

Indeed by the 1850s the Angel in the House myth can be found embedded in almost all public representations of women and their position.

The doctrine of separate spheres saw women's main function as succouring men, but according to the Angel in the House myth it was not, in the upper middle class at least, the physical and practical providing of comforts but spiritual inspiration which was their main contribution. The women were shut up in the house not just to do the housework and bring up the children but to be a sort of externalised conscience for men. A clergyman wrote in the *Westminster Review* in 1849:

The true woman speaks to every true man who sees her, refining and exalting his intellect and feeling, making him indeed know his true manhood to consist in the noble action of his soul. She sends him from her with all the subtle threads of his being in firmer tension, and remembering only that he too 'is a little lower than the angels.' She can make him work, and dare even death for his work, and his heart ever beating with the love of the highest love. She can do this without knowing it, and because her *genius* is *influence*. Yes; to warm, to cherish into purer life the motive that shall lead to the heroic act – this is her genius, her madness, her song flowing out, she knows not how, going she knows not whither, but returning never again.

(Adams 1849: 354)

Women had been created noble and angelic for the purpose of serving husband and family:

Selfishness is a male vice, par excellence, and is in some remote degree *with* men excusable. They have to hew their way to every achievement by mowing down so many obstacles that they are obliged to think of themselves, or they would never get on. Women have, or should have, *no identity wholly their own*, no separate existence in themselves – this is treating of women in their natural state of alliance with men. If a woman (speaking generally) so allied has any thought at all, except for her husband and children, she is nothing.

(*All the Year Round* 1858: 370)

A widely accepted theory of the different but complementary natures of men and women was developed. Emily Davies (who did not accept it) summed it up thus in 1863:

The strength of the woman, we are told, is in the heart; the strength of the man, in the head. The woman can suffer patiently; the man can act bravely. The woman has a loving care for the individual; the man an unimpassioned reverence for the general and universal. These, and such as these, are represented as the outward tokens of essential differences, which cannot be mistaken, and ought never, in any system of education, or work of life, to be overlooked.

(Davies 1863: 264)

It was accepted that women could perform acts of outstanding courage and physical bravery, and they were celebrated for them, but only if they fitted within the framework of 'woman's mission', and could be seen to arise from this 'loving care for the individual'. Two paintings by Millais of courageous women, *The Order of Release, 1746* and *The Proscribed Royalist* demonstrate this theme. The first shows a wounded highlander emerging from prison to embrace his barefoot wife with a child in her shawl his release papers in her hand. In the second, a woman in puritan dress is bringing food to a hidden royalist. Biographies of such heroic women were offered to young girls as examples to emulate. Anne Mozley's *Tales of Female Heroism* (1846), for example, gave short accounts of twenty heroic women ranging from 'The Miller's Maid' and 'A Rustic Heroine' to the Countess of Nithsdale and Flora Macdonald. The author wrote in the preface:

> Love of adventure, constitutional indifference to danger, and a consciousness of superior powers, have led women to the successful performance of many high and daring exploits; but it has been wished to prove that such constitutional peculiarities are not required to make a heroine; while the natural emotions of timidity and fear need be no hindrance to the development of true heroism. It only needs that the mind, trained and disciplined to obey the will, shall have force to overcome the weakness of body; that, clear to see its duty, the heart shall be prompt, at any sacrifice, to perform it. Not that there shall be no natural fear or shrinking, but that the occasion shall be felt great enough to overcome them. Every one who accustoms herself, in small as well as great things, to do at once, and in a cheerful spirit what is to be done – who takes upon herself the duties that fall to her lot – who uses no vain delays – who does the thing she fears, and thus learns to know the joy and strength that every such effort brings with it – is educating herself to be a heroine.
>
> (Mozley 1846: v–vi)

Women, it would seem, could if required act heroically in the public sphere, their womanly sympathies could triumph over their equally feminine timidity, but only if they had prepared themselves for such a contingency through living the life of continual selflessness and self-abnegation dictated by the Angel in the House myth.

Although modesty, timidity and selflessness were claimed on the one hand to be essential parts of women's natures, and women who violated these claims were called unfeminine and unnatural, the logically incompatible view was also held that women had to be trained to be women by a careful sheltered upbringing. Though the potential to be an angel was theoretically born in women, appropriate social conditioning, it was felt, was necessary for its full flowering. The myth determined the kind of upbringing recommended by moralists for women, and indeed describing the kind of education that was needed was the main purpose of both Aimé-Martin and Sarah Lewis. A writer in *Fraser's Magazine* in 1845 felt that the 'single eye and a simple faith' which gave women 'the filtering power' to see only what was 'clear and fresh' in men's interests, were possible only because they did not mingle 'with the stained current of the world' (*Fraser's* 1845: 708). 'The duties of a wife and mother' said a speaker at a Social Science Congress, '. . . were the noblest ends of a woman's life, and everything that encroached on them . . . should be looked on as an evil disease, and utterly eradicated' (TNAPSS 1868: 606).

A girl's upbringing must be sheltered not just from all knowledge of sin and evil, but from situations where she might need to be dominating and aggressive. A writer in *Fraser's Magazine* in 1845 believed:

> Men, who are made for the world, must, sooner or later, exchange the innocence of ignorance for that victory over evil, only gained by fighting the enemy at every inch; but woman, in her lowest and most destitute estate, was made for home. *She*, at least, may be saved from even touching the edged tools which man must learn to wield.
>
> (*Fraser's* 1845: 708)

Once again the lower middle class, sharing as it did the separation of home and work and the economic dependence of women with the upper middle class, seems to have adopted the same discursive interpretation. Sally Mitchell, in her study of magazines read by the lower middle class, finds acceptance of the Angel in the House myth implicit in their stories:

> Aggression, competitiveness, and hard-heartedness were necessary for worldly success – and yet they, too, were qualities in conflict with religion and social conscience. And so the ideal was expressed in the person of the woman enclosed within the family. There, fulfilling her duty to her husband, she could be free of the taint of sexual desire; there, because she lacked selfishness, she could create the peace in which moral virtues could rule. But it was only possible within the security of the family. Woman could not possess the aggressive qualities needed to compete in the world and still retain moral superiority. Without male protection she must be helpless.
>
> (Mitchell 1977: 50–1)

The appeal of the Angel in the House myth to women is easy enough to explain. Forced into idleness and economic dependence by the demands of the status system, they were given a reason for their existence which allowed them to maintain their self-esteem in this situation. Though in every practical way inferior to men, they could feel morally superior. However there were men too who found in the myth a 'truth' that coincided with their experience (Tosh 1997: 43). According to Walter E. Houghton many men felt a considerable contradiction between evangelical religion and the business ethic, while others were disturbed by the question of preserving ethical standards when religious doubt had destroyed their theological base. Thus the home came to be seen as:

a source of virtues and emotions which were nowhere else to be found, least of all in business and society. . . . It was a place apart a walled garden, in which certain virtues too easily crushed by modern life could be preserved and certain desires of the heart too much thwarted be fulfilled.

(Houghton 1957: 343)

It is inconceivable that all middle-class men and women believed the myth to be a representation of reality. Indeed, if writers of children's fiction, from Charlotte M. Yonge in the 1850s to E. Nesbit in the early twentieth century are to be believed, many boys were strongly imbued with a sense of their own superiority, and were as scornful of girls as the most misogynistic eighteenth century parson. Yet, though it lingered on in popular comic literature, in pictures of domineering wives, in mother-in-law and old maid jokes, after the 1830s the sweeping disparagement of women seems to have vanished from the serious periodical press, and presumably from the pulpit as well. Certainly John Stuart Mill (1869: 258) believed it to be a thing of the past.[7]

This may have been because the many men and women for whom the Angel in the House myth filled profound psychological needs, and who had incorporated it into their world view, were deeply shocked, almost shattered, if it were questioned. Examples of this sort of response can be found in the reports of the Social Science Congresses in the 1860s. Whenever members of the Women's Movement made proposals which seemed contrary to the myth there were members of the audience (frequently clergymen) prepared to jump up and protest vociferously. Each move made by Emily Davies in her education campaign provoked this response (Stephen 1927: 85–97, 103–4, 177–8), and it can be seen in articles criticising the Women's Movement in the 1860s (Greenwell 1862; Oliphant 1869). Before the Women's Movement appeared it is likely that after producing this reaction once or twice, the unconvinced took the line of least resistance and paid lip service to the myth. It had become part of the weaponry of Mrs Grundy.

Thus even if the Angel in the House myth with its assertion of women's moral superiority was not universally accepted, its prescriptions for the socialisation and occupations of women were. Just as the public school Christianity became the moral code defining a gentleman, so the Angel in the House myth become the code by which a lady lived. The practices it prescribed became grafted on to the status definition of a lady, and had to be acceded to even by those who did not accept their underlying moral basis. It was not only the doctrine of separate spheres which was doxa for the middle class; the Angel in the House definition of women's mission was equally undisputed.

Middle-class women, then, though they did not necessarily find themselves revered as angels, had their way of life defined by the Angel in the

House myth. If they hoped to maintain an image of themselves as 'ladies', or even as 'true' women, they had to accept the sphere defined for them by the myth, and live within its prescriptive boundaries, no matter how high the price paid.

The separation of work and home, the combined result of the status aspirations of the upper middle class, and the changes in methods of production resulting from industrialism, had created what seemed an appropriate ideology to explain the changed conditions. Yet in the same decade that the Angel in the House myth was being confirmed came the revelations about governesses and dressmakers noted in Chapter 1. Anna Jameson, in a continuation of the passage quoted above wrote:

> Such is the beautiful theory of woman's existence, preached to her by moralists, sung to her by poets! Let man, the bread-winner, go abroad – let woman stay *at home*; let her not be seen in the haunts of rude labour any more than in those of vicious pleasure – for is she not *the mother?* – highest holiest, dearest title to the respect and the tenderness of her 'protector man!' We really beg pardon of our readers for repeating these truisms – we merely quote them here to show that, while they are admitted, promulgated, taught as indisputable, the real state of things is utterly at variance with them. Our social system abounds with strange contradictions in law, morals, government, religion. But the greatest, the most absurd, the most cruel of all is the anomalous condition of the women in this Christian land of ours. We call it anomalous because it inculcates one thing as the rule of right and decrees another as the rule of necessity. 'Woman's mission,' of which people can talk so well and write so prettily, is irreconcilable with woman's position of which no one dares to think, much less to speak.
>
> (Jameson 1843: 257)

By the mid-1850s, however, major social commentators were taking it as an accepted fact that middle-class women were economically vulnerable, that male protectors were not always there to support them, and that how this was to be dealt with became part of the 'woman question' which was such a topic of discussion in the 1840s and 1850s (Helsinger 1983: 11–12).

## Economic insecurity

Even though in the pre-industrial period 'the widow and the fatherless' were frequent objects of Christian charity, within each grade of society there had been accepted ways of providing for wives and daughters. Among the gentry the usual way was provision of a capital sum or an annuity to be paid by the estate left to the main male heir, and single women were seen as the financial responsibility of their male relatives. Where the family was rich enough this continued to be the means of support in the upper middle class, and, indeed, many of the single women active in the Woman's Movement acquired the time and resources for their work in this way. Louisa Hubbard, the daughter of a cotton merchant who had bought an estate outside London, was given a house on that estate by her brother when her father died (Pratt 1898: 5–6). Frances Power Cobbe's father left her £200 a year to be paid from the estate left to her brother and expected that she would continue to live in the family home, a provision which, given the family income and the fact that she had been her father's housekeeper for many years, she felt should have been more generous (Cobbe 1894 vol. 1: 214).

In the old middle ranks, security came not from being left an income but a business, and within the section of the lower middle class where the family economy persisted, these customs continued without a break (Pinchbeck 1930: 284–6). Women whose fathers or husbands had been shopkeepers, farmers or even tradesmen like blacksmiths whose work as master craftsmen involved sizable capital investment in equipment and materials, were able to continue the family business until they retired, married, or had a son old enough to take over and support them. This could be the case even if they had not helped in the business during the life of the husband or father. The woman blacksmith and postmistress for whom Flora Thompson worked in the 1890s had been able to continue her father's trade most prosperously with the help of a foreman and without ever touching a tool herself (Thompson 1931: 411–12).

Figure 3.1 is a graph showing the striking rise in the numbers of women in various occupations as the age of the group increased, presumably representing widows who had taken over the family business. It would seem that practices varied in the different trades. Butchers' widows seem to have abandoned their husbands' trade unless they inherited in their middle years; bakers' and innkeepers' widows seem to have persevered longer, while the widows of farmers seem to have domineered over their inheritance to the bitter end just as the 1920s novelists caricatured in *Cold Comfort Farm* suggested (Gibbons 1932). Nevertheless, the graph as a whole suggests that women in family businesses did not necessarily need to fear destitution when the male head of the family died.

In families where the male-breadwinner norm had been established, however, particularly if the husband was a professional man or worked for a salary or wages, things were different.[8] Women in the less prosperous section of the upper middle class were particularly vulnerable. The prosperity and way of life of the family now depended entirely on the earning powers of the male head. Most of the capital such a man had received from his family and through his wife was likely to be sunk in his house and his business, and it was his efforts which made it productive. If he died, the bulk of the income died with him. Yet it was this income that his wives and daughters depended on to keep a roof over their heads, and find them their dress allowances, and

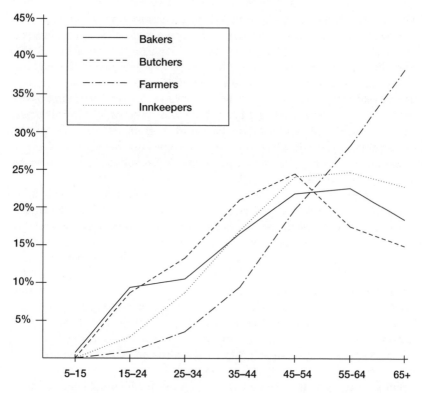

*Figure 3.1* Percentage of female bakers, butchers, farmers and innkeepers in various age groups as shown in the census of 1851

the savings from it were the main source for the dowry which men of this class still expected with their wives (Parkes 1865: 83; Yonge 1879: 6).

Moreover, this was a period when business was precarious and bankruptcies and bank failures frequent, and these too could cause an abrupt cessation of income. Some provision for wives and children could be made through insurance companies, and writers of the period stressed the wisdom of this course (Parkes 1865: 83; Warren 1865a: 12, 91; Yonge 1873: 36), but even so, on the early death of a breadwinner, the standard of living of his wife and daughters was likely to decline drastically. A writer in the *Athenaeum* in 1851 spoke of 'those women – and their name is Legion – of refined habits and elegant tastes whom the premature deaths of protectors or other misfortunes leave stranded on the bleak shores of existence' (p. 631). The novelist Dinah Mulock Craik wrote:

> Every one's experience may furnish dozens of cases of poor women suddenly thrown adrift – widows with families, orphan girls, reduced gentlewomen – clinging helplessly to every male relative or

friend they have, year after year, sinking deeper in poverty or debt, eating the bitter bread of charity, or compelled to bow an honest pride to the cruellest humiliations.

(Craik 1858: 27)

Many women thus thrown on the world had somehow to support themselves, and when in the 1860s societies were formed to promote the employment of women, they were besieged by such women desperately hoping for suitable work. Some of these women's accounts were preserved and later published by Emily Faithfull, one of the members of the Society for Promoting the Employment of Women:

I am the daughter of a Commander in the navy, and have now lost both my parents. I am totally unprovided for, and have been trying in vain for a situation as companion.

My father was a clergyman in a small parish in . . . , and I am now penniless and homeless, with my mother a confirmed invalid; and if you will only give me work to do by which I can support her, you will confer a blessing on me.

I am the youngest of three sisters, and we have lost everything we possessed by the failure of . . . Bank; I am thirty years of age, and will gladly take any work you can suggest.

(Faithfull 1884: 281)

Though a few women from upper-middle-class backgrounds thrown on the world became writers or practised the fine arts (the novelists Dinah Mulock Craik and Margaret Oliphant are examples (Todd 1991: 489–90, 510–1)), it was generally accepted by contemporaries that the obvious occupation for those fallen on hard times was some form of teaching. Elizabeth Eastlake wrote in 1848:

The real definition of a governess, in the English sense, is a being who is our equal in birth, manners, and education, but our inferior in worldly wealth. Take a lady in every meaning of the word, born and bred, and let her father pass through the gazette, [i.e. go bankrupt] and she wants nothing more to suit our highest *beau ideal* of a guide and instructress to our children . . . There is no other class which so cruelly requires its members to be, in birth, mind, and manners, above their station, in order to fit them for their station.

(Eastlake 1848: 176–7)

Although, as will be argued in the next chapter, the majority of governesses were not upper-middle-class women from families where the economic base had collapsed, many of those who turned to charities like the Governesses' Benevolent Institution seem to have had such backgrounds (Eastlake 1848: 183; Parkes 1859a: 147–8).

The situation of women in lower-middle-class families where the father earned a wage as a clerk, craftsman, or skilled artisan in industry was equally precarious. Only those women who made entrepreneurial use of the skills they had acquired through their education or their domestic experience and ran their own schools, dressmaking establishments, lodging-houses or shops could get an income comparable to the one which died with the male bread-winner (Davidoff and Hall 1987: 293–308). Those who looked for waged employment could seldom survive without support from relatives. Many were without skills or training, and even if they had been definitely trained at considerable expense to work as governesses or dressmakers, they, like the upper-middle-class women who entered teaching as a last resort, found that the wages were usually too low to provide more than a bare subsistence for a woman with no family in the background to tide her over periods of illness and unemployment. Unlike their brothers, they found few opportunities for supporting a middle-class way of life in the expanding world of paid employment.

Nevertheless, though working for a living could cause a decline in status, work did not, in itself, threaten her femininity if the conditions were appropriate. In all the discussions of the wrongs of governesses and dressmakers, the objection was to the conditions of work, not to the work itself. While it was accepted that for any 'lady' to work as a governess implied a loss of status, and that dressmakers and shop assistants could not claim gentility at all (Craik 1858 : 69), there was never any suggestion that the femininity of these women was being compromised, that they were in any way unfitting themselves for 'woman's mission'. Although, as Mary Poovey has suggested, the fascination with governesses may have been due to the fact that 'the governesses' "plight" articulated the contradiction between the moral role women had been assigned in capitalist society and the economic position into which they were being driven in increasing numbers' (Poovey 1988: 162), there was no suggestion that women caught in this trap should not be governesses. If women had to earn an income, teaching and dressmaking were the occupations where it could suitably be done.

The question then arises: what was it about these occupations that made them incontrovertibly 'feminine', and, further, what was it about the two new occupations for young women that began to open in the 1840s, retail work and elementary school teaching, that placed them in this category? The constraints of gentility explain why so few women were looking for paid work, and why the 'push' factor was relatively weak, but this makes it even more extraordinary that the occupations open to them were so crowded. Why was there no 'pull' from employers in an expanding economy where new types of work were constantly emerging? Why were so few of them considered feminine?

In the next chapter it will be argued that all these occupations seemed compatible with the middle class's 'knowledge' of what was 'women's work' because they preserved the patriarchal conditions of work within a family economy that had prevailed in the pre-industrial period. All involved work which might later be useful to a married woman, and all were carried on in a more or less domestic setting. Above all, in these occupations women were not paid a wage which covered their living expenses, instead they were provided with board and lodging and given only a few pounds a year pocket money. Hence the employer had the power, and was assumed to use it, to control the girls not just during working hours but during their leisure time as well. Thus patriarchal control was transferred from the father to the employer, and the girl could not escape it. She was, as Leonore Davidoff puts it, 'mastered for life' (Davidoff 1974). Employers offering these conditions, unlike those looking for free wage labour, had no difficulty in seeing women as appropriate employees, and parents had no qualms about the honour of their family being compromised if their daughters entered them.

# 4

# WHAT WAS 'WOMEN'S WORK'?

## The patriarchal household and employers' 'knowledge'

In his much discussed article called 'Why are women redundant?', published in the *National Review* in 1862, the literary journalist W .R. Greg argued that if woman had to work for their livings, domestic service was the most appropriate occupation. Female servants, he argued:

> are in no sense redundant; we have not to cudgel our brains to find a niche or an occupation for *them*; they are fully and usefully employed; they discharge a most important and indispensable function; they do not follow an obligatorily independent, and therefore for their sex an unnatural, career:— on the contrary, they are attached to others and are connected with other existences, which they embellish, facilitate, and serve. In a word, they fulfil both essentials of woman's being; *they are supported by, and they minister to, men.*
>
> (Greg 1868: 363–4)

Greg was basing his argument on the two assumptions that were doxa to believers in the domestic ideology: that women were 'relative creatures', intended by nature to devote themselves to serving the needs of their male relatives, and that their lives must therefore be lived within the private, domestic sphere. He, like others concerned about the situation of women, accepted that it might be necessary for some women to contribute to the family income. What he could not accept was that it might be done in the non-patriarchal conditions that were becoming typical of work in the new industrial sectors and which had, in consequence, moved such work from the private to the public sphere. Such work placed women in the unfeminine position of negotiating free labour contracts with employers; they were no longer 'mastered for life'.

The domestic ideology seems to have laid down some fairly stringent conditions which had to be fulfilled before the work could be considered 'feminine'. The nature of these essential requirements does not emerge very coherently from contemporary writings about the middle-class occupations, but a clearer picture can be gained from the reactions of middle-class philanthropists to the sort of work undertaken by working-class women. These requirements were presented as necessary to retain the purity and delicacy which the Angel in the House myth saw as natural to women, but the means to this was seen as preserving patriarchal control over the girl.

## Patriarchal conditions

For preserving the girl's delicacy, the criteria seem to have been that the work itself should not involve contact with industrial grime (household dirt was apparently unobjectionable), or baring the body or the wearing of trousers. It should not involve continuous muscular effort, and it must not be carried on in company with men. These criteria, as much as the threat to health, provided the emotive force behind the legislation forbidding the employment of women underground in the mines. One of the sub-commissioners on the Children's Employment Commission reported: 'One of the most disgusting sights I have ever seen was that of young females, dressed like boys in trousers, crawling on all fours with belts round their waists, and chains passing between their legs' (PP 1842 vol. 15: 76). Twenty years later Bessie Rayner Parkes wrote: 'In Staffordshire they make nails; and unless my readers have seen them, I cannot represent to the imagination the extraordinary figures they present – black with soot, muscular, brawny – undelightful to the last degree' (Parkes 1865: 22). Such work was regarded as 'unsexing'.

It was similarly 'unsexing' for women to work with men. J. S. Wright, a factory owner who in general did not feel that factory work harmed a girl's morals, told the Social Science Congress in 1857 that 'when women work promiscuously with men, we shall almost be sure to find low and depraved habits'. A later speaker added that 'the indiscriminate mixing of the sexes . . . too soon rubbed out all natural modesty, and the consequences to morality might be inferred' (TNAPSS 1857: 544, 545). In 1867 this belief was enshrined in the legislation covering agricultural gangs, (groups of labourers available for hire for short periods of intensive work), which forbad gang leaders to have men and women in the same gang. This view is reported as held by the women themselves. 'As a rule,' wrote M. Mostyn Bird of factory workers in 1911, 'the better class girls avoid all work that brings them into contact with men workers.' (Bird 1911: 21).

All work done outside a domestic setting was seen as open to objection. Factory work was usually criticised for two reasons. First, it gave a girl no training for her future domestic duties (TNAPSS 1857: 547; 1859: 724; Parkes 1861: 637, 639), and second, it gave girls an appalling freedom from patriarchal control. Girls who worked in factories, with their weekly wages in their pockets, could defy attempts by their parents to curb or coerce them. The 1857 Social Science Congress was told by one speaker:

At fourteen or fifteen years of age . . . if they had any cause to be dissatisfied with the conduct of their parents, they would leave them. He had known a young girl of fifteen, whose parents objected to her 'keeping company' with a navvy, leave home and take lodgings next door.

(TNAPSS 1857: 545)

This was in Coventry, another speaker the same year reported similar customs in Birmingham (TNAPSS 1857: 542), and in 1859 the girls of Yorkshire and Lancashire were said to behave in the same way. These reports horrified the novelist Margaret Oliphant. She wrote:

We ask nothing about the morality of these young feminine nomads. Perhaps their independence may help preserve a certain savage virtue in them. But let anybody imagine a little commonwealth pervaded by these free, flippant, uncontrolled, and uneducated creatures, a whole future generation coming from them.

(Oliphant 1860: 711)

For work to be suitable for a young woman, it seems, it had to preserve the conditions that had prevailed in the pre-industrial period.

## The established occupations

At the beginning of the nineteenth century three occupations had been considered suitable for girls in the middle ranks, with domestic service by far the most accessible. At this date, except in 'gentlemen's service', domestic service was not characterized by a difference in status between employer and employee, but by one of age. In a society where the family economy was predominant in the middle ranks, there was a sharing around among families of labour resources. Families with too many young women for the needs of the family industry sent them out to service in families where the girls had either not yet grown up or had married and left home (Tilly and Scott 1979: 33–5). Usually this was an exchange between social equals, farmers, craftsmen, tradesmen, etc. making it possible for the more routine domestic chores to be left to young women while the mistress of the family took on more specialised tasks – dairy work, selling in the market, keeping the accounts of the business – which fell to her share in the family division of labour (Hill 1989: 83; Pinchbeck 1930: 282). The basic assumption of status equality in these arrangements can be seen in the practice of all servants and apprentices eating with the family (Pinchbeck 1930: 35; Stone 1977: 255).

By the 1850s, however, the pattern of recruitment for servants had changed, and large numbers were now the daughters of agricultural labourers. The census enumerators' books show that in the 1850s London servants

64

were 'young, single and rural born', while Harriet Martineau noted in 1859 that most 'maids of all work', that is the typical servants in lower-middle-class families, came from labourers' cottages (Martineau 1859: 307; McBride 1976: 35–7). Charlotte M. Yonge wrote in 1877 that the best servants for the upper middle class 'used to be the daughters of small farmers, but this class is all but extinct; and the best we have now are the children of coachmen, gardeners, gamekeepers and village tradesmen', while what most mistresses had to cope with was 'the thorough cottage girl only civilised by school', that is the daughter of a farm labourer (Yonge 1877: 192, 193).

This influx of cottage girls into domestic service seems to have driven out girls from the lower middle class by causing the whole occupation to lose its status (Hubbard 1875: 144). Lower-middle-class girls who entered gentleman's service because of the cachet attached to entering into a personal relationship, even if one of subordination, with members of a higher class, must have been affronted when they found themselves expected to share a kitchen, and perhaps even a bed, with a girl from a labourer's cottage. Nor can it have been satisfactory socially for such young women to help out in other tradesmen's families when their neighbours were employing heavy-booted, broad-vowelled girls from the villages in similar positions. By 1863 Jessie Boucherett, who could claim to have had more dealings with this sort of girl than most women of her day, was writing, 'Tradesmen's daughters do not want to be taught to be servants' (Boucherett 1863: 26).

The predominant occupation for lower-middle-class girls in the middle of the century was thus dressmaking. Jessie Boucherett wrote that it was 'to persons in a certain position in life, what teaching is to those of the rank above them, viz. the most genteel occupation within reach', and that 'girls of the middle class beginning life seldom think of becoming anything else' (ibid.). The census figures for 1851 attest its popularity. In the fifteen to twenty-four age group, in which only 57 per cent of women were returned as occupied, 6.7 per cent (that is, almost 12 per cent of those returned as occupied) were returned as milliners, a category which seems in this census to have covered those employed as dressmakers as well, conditions and training in the two areas being nearly identical.

The Children's Employment Commission of 1843 reported:

> The age at which young women usually commence the millinery business is fourteen; they begin first as apprentices, the ordinary term of apprenticeship being two years at the expiration of which time it is customary to enter the large and fashionable houses as 'improvers'; great numbers of young women coming to London from the country, every year for this purpose, being generally between sixteen and seventeen years of age.
>
> (PP 1843 vol. 13: 114)

Girls beginning their apprenticeship paid a premium, lived in the house of the employer, and had all their food provided, though they expected no payment until their apprenticeship was finished. 'Improvers' sometimes paid an additional premium, but usually worked for six months for their board and lodging. The size of the premiums asked was between £20 and £60 and so girls entering the occupation by this route must not only have been lower middle class, but must have come from the more prosperous section of it (*Fraser's* 1846: 308; PP 1864 vol. 22: xlviii, 105).

Conditions of work in dressmaking were notoriously bad. The Children's Employment Commission of 1843 reported that the hours worked could rise to twenty a day at the height of the London season when orders had to be completed at short notice. Because of the high rents charged for shops in fashionable areas, employers skimped on the work rooms which were cramped and stuffy, and although women were ostensibly offered a family life, their sleeping places were worse than the work rooms, the food was of poor quality, and the girls were often expected to be off the premises all day on Sunday. It was generally agreed that their health suffered and they were prone to many chest diseases, especially consumption (Greg 1844: 146–7).

Though for the really skilful the reward was high, the general level of payment was not generous. Fully trained women employed as 'indoor hands' living on the premises under the same conditions as apprentices received between £8 and £16 a year, though those expert in cutting and fitting who rose to be 'first hands' in expensive houses could earn up to £70. For the ambitious, their training could lead to independence and prosperity. Experienced first hands sometimes set up in business for themselves (PP 1864 vol. 22: 103–4), and many others, after they married, supplemented the family income by making for their neighbours. However, for those whose abilities were only moderate, or lacked the drive and confidence to set up for themselves and did not marry, the expensive training and the long hours worked did not ensure an income which left much over to save for sickness and old age.

Becoming a dressmaker was not cheap, but there were girls from prosperous families in the lower middle class who set their sights higher, and given the cost of and conditions in dressmaking one can hardly wonder at them. They aimed at the one unequivocally genteel occupation: being a governess. Women with an education at a cheap girls' school behind them were becoming governesses 'just as men sometimes go into the Church or the army in order to become gentlemen by profession' (Boucherett 1863: 25). Indeed, although the fiction of the period gives a contrary impression, women from lower-middle-class backgrounds seem to have formed the bulk of governesses. It is unlikely that with only 90,000 families in the £300 to £1,000 income bracket in the 1860s there could have been enough with sinking fortunes to provide the 24,770 governesses returned in the 1861 census. Nor do the poorer clergy provide the answer. There were only 19,195 clergymen altogether returned in the 1861 census and by no means all of these would have had grown up daughters or been so badly off that their daughters needed to work.

Comments in the periodical press confirm this impression. According to the *Saturday Review*:

> The best governesses are not ladies who have had unexpectedly to earn their bread, but professional governesses, born and bred to the trade, regularly educated in the duties of this particular office, and anxious to succeed in it, as in a profession which it is their lot in life to follow.
>
> (*Saturday Review* 1858: 111)

Elizabeth Sewell wrote that the choice of a governess lay 'in great measure between well-born, well-bred ladies, driven by circumstances to a profession for which they are imperfectly qualified, and under-bred, but clever women, who really know what they profess to teach' (Davies 1866: 512–3 quoted ). Other commentators also remarked on this division in the profession (*Athenaeum* 1848: 462; Boucherett 1863: 25; Eastlake 1848: 180). There seems to have been a recognized form of training for governesses from the lower middle class. According to *Fraser's Magazine* in 1845, the under mistresses at fashionable girls' schools were 'very often articled pupils from second-rate boarding schools', 'undergoing a state of probation for more lucrative and independent posts hereafter' (*Fraser's* 1845: 708). (One thinks of Becky Sharp at the Misses Pinkerton's.)

As details from the reports of the Governesses' Benevolent Institution given in Chapter 1 show, governesses, though better paid than dressmakers (the average salary was about £35 though it could rise to over £100 for those who worked for the nobility), found it equally difficult to save for sickness, periods of unemployment, and old age.

## The new occupations

Though status considerations and the contemporary definition of femininity were constraints on the expansion of middle-class women's employment, they did not inhibit all change. Even before the middle of the century, increasing feminization was evident in both retail work and in elementary school-teaching. In these occupations change in scale and increase in female numbers went hand in hand, suggesting that Lee Holcombe's argument that this was a response to employers' needs has in these cases some validity. What will be argued here is that this was possible because the factors which inhibited the employment of women, the definition of femininity dictated by the doctrine of separate spheres and the consequent androcentric blindness of the employers of free wage labour, did not apply in these cases. Well before the expansion in the retail trade and elementary schools began, this work had been accepted as suitable for middle-class women.

The census figures suggest that from 1841 onwards women were increasingly employed in the retail trade and the age group was becoming progressively younger. Lee Holcombe has suggested that this can be put down to changes taking place in retail trading, changes leading to deskilling and the creation of a dual labour force. She argues that there was little place for women employees in small family businesses where the shopkeeper needed to develop his own sources of supply and be a good judge of quality, and where the usual assistant was an apprentice learning the trade so that he could later set up on his own. However, as the factories increasingly turned out standardised goods this changed. Manufacturers and wholesalers now performed many of the functions of the shopkeepers. Goods could be ordered and sold at standard prices. Thus one knowledgeable man could acquire a great mass of goods and needed as assistants only relatively unskilled people who would deal directly with the public. Thus the department store came into existence, staffed by a few knowledgeable, well-paid buyers and supervisors and a mass of low-paid, unskilled, easily replaced shop assistants, for whom the only requirements were basic knowledge of arithmetic, a respectable appearance, and polite manners (Holcombe 1973:104–6).

The creation of the new kind of shop began, as Alison Adburgham has shown, in the 1840s, when certain 'retail adventurers' began expanding their traditional drapers' shops, marking the price of each article clearly, encouraging the public to walk around without necessarily being expected to buy, and even holding reduction sales. By the 1870s this trend had produced the full-scale department stores, shops offering almost everything the householder might wish to buy (Adburgham 1964: 138; Jefferys 1954: 328). Thus the increase in the number of young women in the retail trade seems to coincide with organizational changes within that sector of the economy.

It is possible, however, that Lee Holcombe has overstressed the importance of deskilling for women's entry into retail work. It seems likely that the new department stores, though they increased the demand for young female shop assistants, were not crucial in establishing it as an occupation for young middle-class women. The retailing of food does not seem to have undergone the changes which took place in the selling of clothing and household goods. Butchers, bakers, greengrocers and grocers must still have had to deal directly with suppliers, using their own judgement as in the first part of the century, so deskilling could scarcely have been occurring here. Yet in these shops too there was a steady rise in the proportion of young female shop assistants. Table 4.1 shows that young women were already established in food shops in the 1850s, and that the proportion of them in this occupation increased steadily throughout the rest of the century.

No information on who these women were or why shopkeepers increasingly employed them is available in the periodical literature I have examined,

*Table 4.1* Number of women aged 15–24 in selected retail occupations and percentage in 1851, 1871, 1891 and 1911

| Occupation | 1851 | | | 1871 | | |
|---|---|---|---|---|---|---|
| | Number | % of occupation | % of age group | Number | % of occupation | % of age group |
| Draper | 2,750 | 6.80 | 0.16 | 10,458 | 14.10 | 0.49 |
| Hosier, haberdasher | 789 | 13.80 | 0.04 | 1,602 | 18.80 | 0.07 |
| Butcher | 140 | 0.23 | 0.01 | 685 | 0.90 | 0.03 |
| Fishmonger | 439 | 4.00 | 0.03 | 408 | 2.70 | 0.02 |
| Baker | 575 | 1.11 | 0.03 | 1,393 | 2.40 | 0.06 |
| Grocer | 1,464 | 1.30 | 0.05 | 3,244 | 2.90 | 0.15 |
| Greengrocer | 580 | 4.30 | 0.03 | 939 | 3.60 | 0.04 |

| Occupation | 1891 | | | 1911 | | |
|---|---|---|---|---|---|---|
| | Number | % of occupation | % of age group | Number | % of occupation | % of age group |
| Draper | 26,307 | 24.60 | 0.90 | 50,475 | 33.40 | 1.50 |
| Hosier, haberdasher | 3,221 | 25.80 | 0.10 | 782 | 8.03 | 0.02 |
| Butcher | 977 | 1.00 | 0.03 | 1,996 | 1.50 | 0.06 |
| Fishmonger | 963 | 3.20 | 0.03 | 1,683 | 3.80 | 0.05 |
| Baker | 3,263 | 3.90 | 0.11 | 20,860 | 19.00 | 0.62 |
| Grocer | 9,068 | 5.00 | 0.31 | 10,959 | 5.00 | 0.33 |
| Greengrocer | 2,614 | 6.40 | 0.09 | 5,566 | 7.70 | 0.17 |

and nothing seems, as yet, to have been turned up by historians of women's work. Nevertheless it can be tentatively suggested that an explanation may be found in the tendency of shopkeepers to make young ladies of their daughters. The figures for students quoted in Chapter 2 suggest that more and more families in the lower middle class were giving their daughters a young lady's education, and this must have cut down the numbers of daughters available to help their fathers in the shop. Therefore it seems likely that such men turned, as perhaps they had always done when their children were young, to the daughters of less prosperous neighbours to fill the gap. Possibly in the earlier part of the century such girls had been taken on as domestic servants, expected to give a hand in the shop when required, but by mid-century, with the lower middle class rejection of domestic service as a suitable employment, they had to be hired for work in the shop alone.

The fact that shop assistant was already a recognized, if sparsely practised, occupation may explain why the expanding drapers' shops and later the department stores retained so many of the trappings of the patriarchal household. Certainly the 'retail adventurers' do not seem to have treated their employees, male or female, as free wage labour. In the 1860s the big London shops like Swan and Edgar of Regent Street and Marshall and Snelgrove of Oxford Street housed and fed their shop assistants, and were presumed to be offering them the moral protection and supervision that this traditionally implied. Even some vestiges of the apprenticeship system were retained. New employees, male and female, were required to pay a small premium, though according to H.G. Wells, who worked for a time as a draper's assistant, this did not guarantee their being taught anything which would allow them to move to more responsible positions (PP 1864 vol. 22:109–14; Wells 1934 vol. 2: 116). Part of the reason for maintaining this system may have been the long trading hours. Shops were open six or seven days a week until almost midnight (TNAPSS 1857: 549), and as well as making it necessary for an employer to provide all meals for the employees, it may well have been hard for them to find lodgings close enough to suit these hours.

On the other hand, the appearance of a patriarchal household may have been necessary to attract the kind of neatly dressed, well-spoken young men and women the shopkeepers wanted. Conditions which conformed to those offered by a more genuine apprenticeship must have made the occupation seem more 'genteel' to girls who wished to maintain their lower-middle-class status but could not afford the high premiums demanded in dressmaking. The demand for a small premium may well have served to make the work look less like a working-class occupation. In the United States similar conditions of work had been provided by the Lowell family to entice the daughters of New England farmers into the cotton mills (Kessler-Harris 1976: 333).

These conditions had become a grievance by the end of the century (PP 1893–4 vol. 37: 3–4, 85; Bird 1911: 65; Bulley and Whitley 1894: 49–63), but in the early days they probably did something to establish the middle-class status of the work, and provided employers with a steady stream of respectable country girls who might not have risked coming to town if they had not been convinced that lodging was available. Though this work, unlike the occupations to be discussed later, never became recognized as appropriate to the upper middle class, it was, in spite of the appalling conditions, much sought after by those on the borderline between the lower middle class and the working class. By the end of the century shop assistants were described as being 'the daughters of artisans, of agricultural labourers, of skilled mechanics, of struggling and of prosperous shopkeepers, of clerks and of professional men' (Bird 1911: 65).

Though the initial employment of women in retail work cannot be explained by Lee Holcombe's deskilling thesis, deskilling would seem to have contributed to the increasing feminization of work in drapers' shops. However, even more significant may have been the need, identified by Rosemary Crompton, Gareth Jones and Samuel Cohn, for an 'unpromotable' category of workers most of whom will not remain in the position for more than a few years, a need which young women with low expectations and expecting to leave on marriage supplied (Cohn 1985: 93–7; Crompton and Jones 1984: 243). This can be seen if one compares the percentage of women working in draper's shops, with those selling food and drink. Whereas in 1851 15.3 per cent of those of all ages returned in the census as drapers were female and 15.3 per cent of those in food and drink, by 1911 the proportion had risen to 56 per cent in drapery but only 26.4 per cent in food and drink. It was in drapery that the scale of the enterprise increased and that the ratio of secondary to primary sector labour rose, whereas in food and drink, where the small family shop dominated, the ratio of shopkeepers to shop assistants must have stayed much as it was at mid-century.

For employers to turn to young women did not require any modification of their 'knowledge' of men's and women's work. Customers were used to being served by women – witness the number of wives of shopkeepers returned in the 1851 census as sharing their husbands' occupations – and for parents, the work as it was organized, violated none of the lower middle class's expectations for its daughters since many of the features of the apprenticeship system were retained and girls continued to live in what was ostensibly a patriarchal household. Thus though feminization of retail work can be explained by the changed needs of employers, it must also be taken into account that this feminization occurred in a manner completely compatible with the gender beliefs of the middle class.

A second area in which the numbers of women employed grew strikingly in the latter half of the nineteenth century was elementary school teaching. Here once again, though opportunities for work expanded dramatically and there was a strong tendency towards feminization, the employment of women did not require any change in employers' 'knowledge'. Women were firmly entrenched in the occupation before expansion began. The class and age of the group changed, but there was nothing new about the fact of employing women to teach the children of the poor.

Public elementary schooling, in the early part of the century was organized by two major voluntary charities, the Anglican National Society and the non-conformist British and Foreign Society. Both societies provided schooling for boys and girls, often, because of the lack of finance and small numbers, in mixed classes (Purvis 1991: 20–2). Moreover the sex of the teacher was by no means fixed. There was no accepted pattern of entry into the occupation, and teachers tended to be refugees from other occupations which required a knowledge of reading and writing: semi-skilled craftsmen, shopkeepers, clerks, and 'superior' domestic servants (Tropp 1957: 10–11). Sometimes these people were women, sometimes men. When Hannah More set up a system of schools in the Mendips in the 1790s, she chose a woman for her first teacher, but later employed men and married couples (Yonge 1888: 86, 93, 96). Thus when the government first began to take a hand in education, it was already accepted that women could be elementary schoolteachers.

71

In 1839 the government, which had been subsidising the two religious societies since 1833, set up a Committee of the Privy Council on Education to supervise these grants, and thereafter the development of elementary education was directed by a national policy. One of the first acts of this committee, under the guidance of its secretary Dr J.P. Kay (later Sir James Kay-Shuttleworth, 1804–1877) was to institute inspections of schools and make the subsidy dependent on their efficiency (Kamm 1965: 156). This led to a sudden burgeoning of teacher training colleges. In 1839 there were three. Then in 1840 Kay set the example by establishing, on his own initiative and independently of the government, a demonstration school (for boys only) at Battersea where teachers could be trained under guidance, and this example was followed in many provincial centres. By 1845 there were twenty-four training institutions in existence running courses ranging in length from three months to five years, with almost 400 men and 200 women enrolled (Rich 1933: 80–1).

In 1846 Kay persuaded the Privy Council Committee to undertake a further scheme, the pupil teacher system, with a five year apprenticeship and a competitive examination with the possibility of winning a 'Queen's Scholarship' to a training college. This scheme transformed elementary teaching from an occupation for old people to one for ambitious young men and women. In this scheme, too, there was no formal distinction made between males and females. Taking pupil teachers added to the income of the person to whom they were apprenticed, and both schoolmasters and schoolmistresses could take such pupils, while the pupil teachers themselves could be either boys or girls (Rich 1933, 119–23). There were, however, some differences. Girls had to be able to sew, their training college courses were less rigorous, and women were paid only two-thirds of the male wage augmentation by the government (Bergen 1982: 13–14). Furthermore, training college provision for women was not as great proportionally as for men. In 1899 2,556 men and 7,572 women passed the Queen's Scholarship examination. Of these 1,008 men (39 per cent) and 1,724 women (23 per cent) were admitted to training colleges (Tropp 1957: 118).

Patriarchal control was not as absolute, nor did it continue so long among elementary school teachers as among shop assistants. Nevertheless it was built into the conditions of their early years. Pupil teachers were expected to come from respectable local homes, and if these did not reach a high enough standard the boys and girls were boarded elsewhere. Government inspectors were instructed to make sure that they lived under 'the constant influence of a good example', and they were expressly forbidden to lodge in public houses (Tropp 1957: 21). They were even more strictly restrained at the training colleges. The female students slept in large barrack-like dormitories and were expected to do most of the domestic work (Widdowson 1980: 52–3). After they left, however, this sort of patriarchal control was lifted. No doubt they were subject to community scrutiny and criticism, but their daily comings and goings were not controlled. Nevertheless the conditions of entry, with their apprenticeships and residential training colleges, were not such as to raise fears in lower-middle-class parents that their daughters' femininity, and so the family honour, would be compromised. The occupation thus became one which young lower-middle-class women of the sort who might otherwise have become dressmakers or shop assistants were entering in increasing numbers.

Frances Widdowson has produced an interesting picture of this process in action by examining the admissions registers of Whitelands College, an Anglican training college for women teachers established in Chelsea in London in 1841, and comparing the family backgrounds of those entering in 1851 (the earliest for which information is available) and in 1857. The earlier entrants, she notes, seem to have been similar, at a lower level of society, to those whom family misfortune drove to becoming governesses. In the 1851 intake fourteen (45 per cent) of the thirty-one women admitted were orphans or the daughters of widows. The others were daughters of farmers, clerks, shopkeepers and artisans, with the working class represented only by two daughters of labourers. By 1857 the number of orphaned or part orphaned had fallen to six (10 per cent), the number of artisans' daughters (twenty-five) had risen to almost half of the fifty-five (out of fifty-eight) whose parents' occupations were known, while there were eight who, as daughters of labourers and domestic servants, could be considered working class (Widdowson 1980: 26–7).

In the 1850s the government began deliberately encouraging the entry of the lower-middle-class group. In 1855 the Queen's Scholarship examination was opened to those who had not been pupil teachers, and in 1858 it became possible to become a pupil teacher at the age of sixteen and work for only two years of the standard five year apprenticeship (Rich 1933: 133–4). Thus it became possible for girls and boys whose parents were able to send them to fee-paying schools to enter the occupation. The teachers themselves were convinced that they were an upwardly mobile group, that their education and the work they did gave them a claim, whatever their origins, to be considered middle class. Complaints are recorded as early as 1853 that teachers' 'social condition' was not high enough, and that they were not accorded the respect they deserved, and male teachers also complained that the occupation did not offer enough opportunities for advancement (Tropp 1957: 35–9).

It would appear that elementary school teaching was another occupation where employers could see advantages in an 'unpromotable' category of workers with a brisk turnover. Women cost less than men, and, since there were limited opportunities for rising, while a very large number of lower level employees was needed, the high turnover created by women leaving to be married tended to ease the situation.

Feminization duly occurred, (and, Barry H. Bergen (1982: 1–21) has suggested, created problems for those seeking to 'professionalize' the occupation). In 1849 32 per cent of pupil teachers were girls, but this figure rose to 41 per cent in 1854 and 46 per cent in 1859, and by 1899, 80 per cent were women. Moreover the supply of training college places had not kept up with the number of teachers needed. In 1879 the number of uncertificated teachers had been 25 per cent of the total number; by 1899 it was 44 per cent. In 1899 61 per cent of the 62,000 certificated teachers were female, and there were in addition 30,000 uncertificated or provisionally certificated teachers of whom 84 per cent were female, and a further 17,000 'additional women teachers' without any formal qualifications, making women 73 per cent of the total 109,000 employed elementary school teachers (Tropp 1957: 22, 117–8).

Dressmaking, the retail trade and teaching were the only areas in which lower-middle-class women aged fifteen to twenty-four numbered more than 2,000 in 1871. However as the tables to follow show, while a marginally lower percentage of the age group were engaged in dressmaking at that date than in 1851, in the other two occupations the numbers had increased not just numerically, but as a percentage of the age group, and in proportion to the number of men in the occupation. These were, then, the only two occupations where, in the middle decades of the century, large numbers of employers seem to have taken advantage of the existing reserve army of unemployed lower-middle-class girls which the census figures reveal, and which middle-class commentators put down to the overstocking in dressmaking.

The two occupations had, as has been suggested, common features which made them likely areas for feminization. Both were expanding rapidly to fulfil a demand in the society at large, both were labour intensive and in both there was little chance of promotion for the bulk of employees. However they had one more thing in common which is not usually included in theories of feminization: both had been recognized as 'women's work' before the period of expansion began. There was no need for employers in either to modify their 'knowledge' of the sexual division of labour before they could recognize the benefits of women as employees.

## Changes after 1860

In the period after 1860 middle-class women's employment no longer conformed to the pattern of declining opportunities that characterized working--class employment. The numbers in the occupations considered middle class continued to expand, whereas opportunities for working-class girls seem to have become stationary. Furthermore, unlike the decades at mid-century, this increase was not simply an expansion of the traditional areas. This would appear to suggest that the major constraints on middle-class women's work, employers' 'knowledge' of what was 'women's work', the belief, upheld by the Angel in the House myth, that women should be under patriarchal control for life, and even the status demand that middle-class women should demonstrate the family's gentility by not working at all, were being broken down.

In Figure 4.1 and Table 4.2 an attempt has been made to show the extent of these changes. The age group fifteen to twenty-four has been chosen as covering the bulk of unmarried women, and the occupations used in the census have been grouped into the broad categories of agriculture, manufacturing, and service, with manufacturing and service broken down again to show the difference between the expanding and stagnating areas of women's employment. As illustrated, a higher percentage of the age group was employed in 1911 than in 1851, the rises being by 5 per cent of the age group by 1871, by 2 per cent by 1891, and by a further 2 per cent by 1911.

Between 1851 and 1871 the main area of expansion seems to have been domestic service, though the increase in the number of teachers and shop assistants also contributed, as did the expansion in the 'other manufacturing' sector. Between 1871 and 1891 the movement into domestic service levelled off (from 30 per cent of the age group in 1871, to 29.5 per cent in 1881, 27 per cent in 1891, 22 per cent in 1911), but the other trends continued, with 'other manufacturing' absorbing 1.5 per cent more of the age group in 1891, and a further 3 per cent by 1911, and 'other service' rising by 2 per cent and 4 per cent of the age group in the same periods.

These two expanding sectors gave work to rather different segments of the population. The 'other service' sector gave middle-class status to the employee, while manufacturing work was considered suitable only for working-class girls. No doubt improved elementary education after 1870 made it possible for clever girls from working-class backgrounds to enter middle-class occupations, but the reverse was less likely to happen. Table 4.3 rearranges the figures in Table 4.2 to show the comparative employment opportunities in the occupations carrying middle-class status and those considered irredeemably working class.

It can be seen that though middle-class work offered positions to almost 8 per cent more of the age group in 1911 than in 1851, working-class occupations absorbed only 1 per cent more of the age group in the same period, and between 1871 and 1911 dropped by more than 2 per cent of the age group.[2] It would appear that though work for working-class girls was failing to keep up with the growth in population, and so presumably doing nothing to reduce endemic female unemployment, the position of middle-class girls was definitely improving.

For middle-class girls not only did the number of positions available increase, there was an increase in the variety of work as well. The period 1871 to 1891 saw the entry of young women into service areas quite new to them: nursing, librarianship, hairdressing, medicine, and, above all, clerical work in both the civil service and the private sector. Clerical work, in particular, was to be of immense importance to them, and was to be one of the major growth areas of women's employment in the next century. In 1881 women

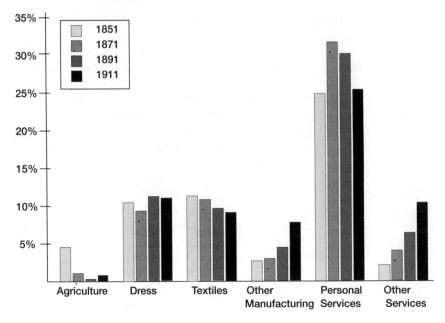

*Figure 4.1* Percentage of women aged 15–24 in industrial sectors in 1851, 1871, 1891 and 1911

were only 2.5 per cent of the total number in the commercial sector. By 1911, however, their share of the positions had risen to 16.1 per cent, in 1931 they occupied almost half (44.54 per cent) and by 1951 outnumbered the men, holding 59.6 per cent of the positions (Marsh 1977: 136).

Tables 4.4, 4.5, and 4.6 show the progress of those occupations usually considered middle class for which the census gives specific numbers, both the growing proportion of women in each of these occupations, and the particular share appropriated by the 15-24 age group. It can be seen that in all these occupations except dressmaking the percentage of women employed increased over the sixty year period, though in the case of teaching the peak was reached in 1901 rather than 1911. There also seems to have been a tendency for the 15-24 age group to gain a greater share of the positions, the anomalies here being teaching, medicine, and the civil and telegraph services. It would seem that in many areas young middle-class women were increasing their share of the workforce at the expense of both men and older women.

This picture of a much wider range of available occupations presented by the censuses is confirmed by the books written about work for women. Whereas books and articles of the 1850s and early 1860s had seen middle-class women as restricted to dressmaking and teaching (Boucherett 1863: 23–8; Butler 1868: 5; Craik 1858: 69; Milne 1857: 130, 180), books written

Table 4.2  Percentage of women aged 15–24 in occupational categories based on the censuses of 1851, 1871, 1891 and 1911

| Census year | 1851 | | 1871 | | 1891 | | 1911 | |
|---|---|---|---|---|---|---|---|---|
| Total number of women | 1,755,105 | | 2,148,542 | | 2,884,756 | | 3,354,792 | |
| **Agriculture** | | | | | | | | |
| Farmers | 0.01 | | 0.01 | | 0.01 | | | |
| Farm servants | 3.86 | | 0.41 | | | | | |
| Labourers and others | 0.72 | 4.59 | 0.71 | 1.13 | 0.36 | 0.37 | | 1.11 |
| **Manufacture** | | | | | | | | |
| Dressmakers, milliners, staymakers | 6.70 | | 5.79 | | 7.32 | | 6.37 | |
| Other dress | 3.94 | 10.64 | 3.57 | 9.36 | 3.98 | 11.30 | 4.73 | 11.10 |
| Textiles | 11.36 | | 10.88 | | 9.69 | | 9.14 | |
| Other | 2.73 | 24.73 | 3.04 | 23.28 | 4.53 | 25.52 | 7.83 | 28.07 |
| **Service** | | | | | | | | |
| Household and inn | 23.58 | | 29.70 | | 28.34 | | | |
| Other personal | 1.30 | 24.88 | 2.02 | 31.72 | 1.86 | 30.20 | | 25.43 |
| Government | 0.01 | | 0.07 | | 0.15 | | 0.51 | |
| Teaching | 1.05 | | 1.66 | | 2.46 | | 1.91 | |
| Nursing | 0.03 | | 0.03 | | 0.17 | | 0.29 | |
| Other professional | 0.10 | | 0.26 | | 0.52 | | 0.69 | |
| Commercial | ~ | | 0.03 | | 0.41 | | 2.39 | |
| Retail* | 0.81 | | 1.73 | | 2.41 | | 3.83 | |
| Conveyance | 0.16 | | 0.22 | | 0.22 | | 0.35 | |
| Board and lodging | 0.04 | 2.20 | 27.08 0.10 | 4.10 35.82 | 0.10 | 6.44 36.64 | 0.46 | 10.43 35.86 |
| Undefined | 0.12 | | 1.01 | | 0.83 | | 0.35 | |
| Unoccupied | 43.48 | | 38.76 | | 36.64 | | 34.60 | |

*  This figure is an underestimate. It is composed only of those returned as druggist, draper, hosier, haberdasher, bookseller, stationer, ironmonger, as selling china and glass, food and drink, trader, dealer, hawker, huckster, shopkeeper, shopwoman. Others in the retail trade, e.g. jewellery, were included with 'workers' in the census, and the numbers involved on the retail side cannot be distinguished from the rest.

*Table 4.3* Percentage of women aged 15–24 in occupations usually regarded as middle class and working class in 1851, 1871, 1891 and 1911

| Census year | 1851 | 1871 | 1891 | 1911 |
|---|---|---|---|---|
| Middle class occupations | | | | |
| Dressmaking | 6.70 | 5.79 | 7.32 | 6.37 |
| Non-personal service | 2.20 | 4.10 | 6.44 | 10.38 |
| | 8.90 | 9.89 | 13.76 | 16.75 |
| Working class occupations | | | | |
| Agriculture | 4.59 | 1.13 | 0.37 | 1.11 |
| Other dress | 3.94 | 3.57 | 3.98 | 4.73 |
| Textiles | 11.36 | 10.88 | 9.69 | 9.14 |
| Other manufacture | 2.73 | 3.04 | 4.53 | 7.83 |
| Personal service | 24.88 | 31.72 | 30.20 | 25.43 |
| Undefined | 0.12 | 1.01 | 0.83 | 0.35 |
| | 47.62 | 51.35 | 49.60 | 48.59 |

*Table 4.4* Number of women in selected occupations 1841–1911 with percentage of total number in each occupation

| Occupation | 1841 | 1851 | 1861 | 1871 |
|---|---|---|---|---|
| Physician, surgeon, registered practitioner | — | — | — | — |
| Nurse, midwife | 13,855 (99.5%) | 25,772 (100%) | 26,734 (100%) | 30,632 (100%) |
| Druggist, chemist | 161 (1.6%) | 268 (1.9%) | 388 (2.4%) | 494 (2.5%) |
| Teacher | 30,019 (61.5%) | 64,613 (72.0%) | 80,017 (72.5%) | 89,239 (73.1%) |
| Author, editor, journalist | 15 (9%) | 109 (4.1%) | 145 (8.7%) | 255 (10.6%) |
| Painter, sculptor, engraver | 278 (6.9%) | 527 (9.3%) | 901 (8.3%) | 1,140 (8.6%) |
| Musician, music teacher | 955 (15.1%) | 3,129 (27.9%) | 4,721 (31.4%) | 7,056 (37.9%) |
| Photographer | — | — | 168 (6.6%) | 694 (14.7%) |
| Telegraph | — | — | 213 (8.2%) | 222 (7.6%) |
| Civil srvice: officers and clerks | — | — | — | — |
| Commercial clerks | 164 (0.34%) | — | 274 (0.5%) | 1,412 (1.6%) |
| Other clerks | — | — | — | — |
| Milliner, dressmaker, staymaker | 96,979 (100%) | 245,612 (100%) | 296,896 (99.4%) | 308,347 (99.2%) |

*Table 4.4* (continued)

| Occupation | 1841 | 1851 | 1861 | 1871 |
|---|---|---|---|---|
| Haidresser, wigmaker | 249 (2.6%) | — | 412 (3.7%) | 1,240 (9.4%) |
| Draper | 2,684 (10.2%) | 6,134 (15.3%) | 11,903 (20.6%) | 19,112 (25.7%) |
| Bookseller, publisher, librarian | — | 858 (12.4%) | 1,065 (12.2%) | 1,077 (12,9%) |
| Retail food | — | 40,746 (15.3%) | 49.728 (16.5%) | 54,697 (15.9%) |

| | 1881 | 1891 | 1901 | 1911 |
|---|---|---|---|---|
| Physician, surgeon, registered practitioner | 25 (0.2%) | 101 (0.5%) | 212 (0.9%) | 477 (2.0%) |
| Nurse, midwife | — | 53,057 (98.9%) | 67,269 (19.4%) | 83,662 (98.5%) |
| Druggist, chemist | 631 (3.3%) | 1,340 (6.1%) | 3,105 (10.9%) | 5,390 (16.7%) |
| Teacher | 122,846 (72.7%) | 144,393 (74.0%) | 171,670 (74.5%) | 183,298 (72.7%) |
| Author, editor, journalist | 452 (13.2%) | 660 (11.4%) | 1,249 (11.3%) | 1,756 (12.7%) |
| Painter, sculptor, engraver | 1,960 (17.7%) | 3,032 (24.7%) | 3,699 (26.5%) | 4,355 (26.0%) |
| Musician, music teacher | 11,376 (44.5%) | 19,111 (49.5%) | 22,644 (52.4%) | 24,272 (51.5%) |
| Photographer | 1,309 (19.7%) | 2,469 (23.0%) | 3,851 (25.7%) | 5,016 (29.7%) |
| Telegraph | 2,228 (23.6%) | 4,356 (29.1%) | 9,256 (40.6%) | 14,308 (52.2%) |
| Civil srvice: officers and clerks | 3,216 (12.6%) | 8,546 (21.3%) | 14,312 (25.2%) | 22,034 (26.5%) |
| Commercial clerks | 5,989 (3.3%) | 17,859 (7.2%) | 55,784 (15.3%) | 117,057 (24.5%) |
| Other clerks | — | 1,085 (0.9%) | 1,952 (1.3%) | 7,805 (3.7%) |
| Milliner, dressmaker, staymaker | 357,995 (99.2%) | 415,961 (98.9%) | 401,614 (99.4%) | 419,167 (98.7%) |
| Haidresser, wigmaker | 768 (5.1%) | 1,274 (5.0%) | 1,745 (4.9%) | 4,687 (9.6%) |
| Draper | 28,781 (34.9%) | 46,347 (43.3%) | 68,487 (50.4%) | 84,606 (56.0%) |
| Bookseller, publisher, librarian | 1,438 (14,5%) | 2,240 (16.5%) | 2,553 (17.3%) | 3,366 (20.0%) |
| Retail food | 65,816 (19.4%) | 111,850 (20.9%) | 114,581 (21.2%) | 178,979 (26.4%) |

*Table 4.5:* Number of women aged 15-24 in selected occupations 1851–1911 with percentage of age group in each occupation

| Occupation | 1851 | 1861 | 1871 | 1881 |
|---|---|---|---|---|
| Physician, surgeon, registered practitioner | — | — | — | — |
| Nurse, midwife | 534 (0.03%) | 1,009 (0.05%) | 731 (0.03%) | — |
| Druggist, chemist | 22 (0.001%) | 48 (0.002%) | 81 (0.004%) | 233 (0.010%) |
| Teacher | 18,274 (1.04%) | 29,125 (1.50%) | 35,692 (1.66%) | 62,265 (2.60%) |
| Author, editor, journalist | 15 (0.001%) | 21 (0.001%) | 20 (0.001%) | 54 (0.002%) |
| Painter, sculptor, engraver | 165 (0.01%) | 295 (0.02%) | 367 (0.02%) | 682 (0.03%) |
| Musician, music teacher | 1,207 (0.07%) | 2,062 (0.11%) | 2,993 (0.14%) | 4,757 (0.20%) |
| Photographer | — | 65 (0.003%) | 324 (0.02%) | 748 (0.03%) |
| Telegraph | — | 161 (0.01%) | 167 (0.01%) | 1,455 (0.06%) |
| Civil service: officers and clerks | — | — | — (0.04%) | 1,065 |
| Commercial clerks | — | 118 (0.01%) | 708 (0.03%) | 3,297 (0.14%) |
| Other clerks | — | — | — | 206 (0.01%) |
| Milliner, dressmaker, staymaker | 117,578 (6.7%) | 128,697 (6.6%) | 124,425 (5.8%) | 160,241 (6.7%) |
| Hairdresser, wigmaker | — | 126 (0.01%) | 544 (0.03%) | 291 (0.01%) |
| Draper | 2,750 (0.16%) | 6,246 (0.32%) | 10,458 (0.49%) | 16,628 (0.69%) |
| Bookseller, publisher, librarian | 199 (0.01%) | 215 (0.01%) | 310 (0.01%) | 489 (0.02%) |
| Retail food | 5,227 (0.30%) | 7,770 (0.40%) | 9,837 (0.46%) | 16,989 (0.70%) |

after 1890 described a far wider range of occupations. In 1894 A. Amy Bulley and Margaret Whitely's *Women's Work* saw women's professional occupations as including literature, journalism, music, art, the stage, teaching, nursing, medicine, pharmacy, dentistry, accountancy and legal conveyancing, while under the heading 'Clerical and Commercial' they dealt with the occupations of typist, shorthand writer, secretary, clerk, book-keeper, telegraph

| Occupation | 1891 | 1901 | 1911 |
|---|---|---|---|
| Physician, surgeon, registered practitioner | 13 | 8 | 7 |
| Nurse, midwife | 4,983 (0.17%) | 7,140 (2.60%) | 9,806 (0.29%) |
| Druggist, chemist | 689 (0.02%) | 1,955 (0.06%) | 3,305 (0.10%) |
| Teacher | 70,742 (2.45%) | 85,410 (2.60%) | 64,241 (1.91%) |
| Author, editor, journalist | 71 (0.002%) | 149 (0.005%) | 151 (0.005%) |
| Painter, sculptor, engraver | 895 (0.03%) | 826 (0.03%) | 897 (0.03%) |
| Musician, music teacher | 7,727 (0.26%) | 8,406 (0.26%) | 7,216 (0.22%) |
| Photographer | 1,468 (0.05%) | 2,353 (0.07%) | 2,724 (0.08%) |
| Telegraph | 3,048 (0.11%) | 6,792 (0.21%) | 9,688 (0.29%) |
| Civil service: officers and clerks | 3,089 (0.11%) | 6,256 (0.19%) | 8,637 (0.26%) |
| Commercial clerks | 10,924 (0.38%) | 37,184 (1.13%) | 76,373 (2.30%) |
| Other clerks | 433 (0.02%) | 1,023 (0.03%) | 4,736 (0.14%) |
| Milliner, dressmaker, staymaker | 211,171 (7.3%) | 203,874 (6.2%) | 213,563 (6.4%) |
| Hairdresser, wigmaker | 539 (0.02% | 849 (0.03%) | 2,437 (0.07%) |
| Draper | 25,418 (0.88%) | 40,658 (1.24%) | 44,474 (1.33%) |
| Bookseller, publisher, librarian | 773 (0.03%) | 1,127 (0.03%) | 1,450 (0.04%) |
| Retail food | 30,135 (1.08%) | 30,343 (0.92%) | 45,805 (1.37%) |

operator and telephonist, as well as assistant in shops of all kinds (Bulley and Whitley 1894: 1–50). M. Mostyn Bird, writing in 1911, dealt with a similar range of occupations for middle-class girls (Bird 1911: 126–42). It seems that employers' 'knowledge' of the appropriate division of labour between the sexes and the age groups had been modified.

This entry of women into areas previously seen as appropriate only to men

*Table* 4.6: Number of women aged 15–24 in selected occupations 1851–1911 expressed as a percentage of the total number of women in each occupation

| Occupation | 1851 | 1861 | 1871 | 1881 | 1891 | 1901 | 1911 |
|---|---|---|---|---|---|---|---|
| *Physician, surgeon, registered practitioner* | — | — | | — | 12.9 | 3.8 | 1.5 |
| *Nurse, midwife* | 2.1 | 3.8 | 2.4 | — | 9.4 | 10.6 | 11.7 |
| *Druggist, chemist* | 8.2 | 12.4 | 16.4 | 36.9 | 51.4 | 63.0 | 61.3 |
| *Teacher* | 28.3 | 36.4 | 40.0 | 50.7 | 49.0 | 49.8 | 35.0 |
| *Author, editor, journalist* | 13.8 | 14.5 | 7.8 | 11.9 | 10.8 | 11.9 | 8.6 |
| *Painter, sculptor, engraver* | 31.3 | 32.7 | 32.2 | 34.8 | 29.5 | 22.3 | 20.6 |
| *Musician, music teacher* | 38.6 | 43.7 | 42.4 | 41.8 | 40.4 | 37.1 | 29.7 |
| *Photographer* | — | 38.7 | 46.7 | 57.1 | 59.5 | 61.1 | 54.3 |
| *Telegraph* | — | 75.6 | 75.2 | 65.3 | 70.0 | 73.4 | 67.7 |
| *Civil service: officers and clerks* | — | — | — | 33.1 | 36.1 | 43.7 | 39.2 |
| *Commercial clerks* | — | 43.1 | 50.1 | 55.1 | 61.2 | 66.7 | 65.2 |
| *Other clerks* | — | — | — | 22.7 | 39.9 | 52.4 | 60.7 |
| *Milliner, dressmaker, staymaker* | 49.9 | 43.3 | 40.4 | 44.8 | 50.8 | 50.8 | 50.9 |
| *Hairdresser, wigmaker* | — | 30.6 | 43.9 | 37.9 | 42.3 | 48.7 | 52.0 |
| *Draper* | 44.8 | 52.5 | 54.7 | 57.8 | 54.8 | 59.4 | 52.6 |
| *Bookseller, publisher, librarian* | 23.2 | 20.2 | 28.8 | 34.0 | 34.5 | 44.1 | 43.1 |
| *Retail food* | 12.8 | 15.6 | 18.0 | 25.8 | 26.9 | 26.5 | 25.6 |

seems to have been accompanied by a relaxation of the patriarchal constraints on working girls. This had happened, it was pointed out in the previous section, in elementary schoolteaching. There is no suggestion anywhere in the literature that female clerks, either in the civil service or in private firms, ought to be boarded by their employers, and independent professionals in medicine, literature, and the fine arts could scarcely have worked under such conditions. Even in the traditional female areas the custom of living-in was becoming less common. By the 1890s dressmaking establishments were increasingly employing outdoor hands while middle-class girls' education was taking place in day schools rather than under governesses at home, and thus many teachers must have lived away from the school (PP 1893–94, vol. 37: 10, 91; Boucherett 1884: 105). Living-in conditions continued in retail work, but they had become a grievance by the end of the century, with employers being accused of insisting on them because they made a profit out of them (Bird 1911: 68–73; Bulley and Whitley 1894: 58–60). Only in domestic service and nursing were such conditions the rule rather than the exception by 1911.

These new occupations fell far short of providing equal opportunities for men and women. Though women were flocking into clerical work they were, as is well known, confined to the lower levels, and denied the promotion to minor managerial posts that was still available to men who began their working lives as clerks (Jordan 1996: 74–5; Lockwood 1989: 23–8). Moreover almost all the skilled trades available to lower-middle-class men were still closed to women. Even by the end of the first decade of the twentieth century only three new occupations entered by apprenticeship had been added to the traditional dressmaking and millinery: hairdressing, pharmacy and work as a florist (Spencer 1909: 48–51, 132–3, 46–7). Whereas a man who had had a secondary education could look forward to living in a semi-detached house in the suburbs, filled with his own carefully chosen furniture, and to being able to support a wife and bring up a family, an unmarried woman with the same education, unless she was very lucky, could expect little more than a furnished bedsitter with a gas ring on the hearth (Collet 1902a: 71–89).

The books on women's work written in the 1890s and 1900s nevertheless give the impression that the extension of work had diminished the problem of low wages caused by overstocking. Whereas accounts of women's work in the late 1840s, 1850s, and 1860s were largely a catalogue of misery, poverty, and exploitation, the writings of the 1890s and later had a different tone. In Bulley and Whitley's *Women's Work* there was overall criticism that women were underpaid when the cost of their training was taken into account, but it was only when writing of shop assistants that their account was, as they said, 'little else than a recital of their grievances' (Bulley and Whitley 1894: 49). M. Mostyn Bird put much of the blame for unsatisfactory conditions on women's failure to take advantage of the opportunities for training and promotion available (Bird 1911: 4–11). Unmarried women, it seems, though still far from equal with their brothers, no longer had to work for 'pin money' wages. They were therefore not necessarily bound to live at home under parental control or be supervised by their employers out of working hours. They were thus almost in the position, economically, of the 'free, flippant, uncontrolled' factory girls of the textile towns whose independence had so shocked Margaret Oliphant.

This new freedom does not appear to have been restricted to those women whose family circumstances made it essential for them to work outside the home. The literary evidence suggests that between 1870 and 1890 the idea of girls as primarily part of a family group with their working life determined by the group's needs whether for money or status, was beginning to be supplanted by the idea that girls ought to have an occupation of their own, regardless of the family's finances. Many girls at least took this view. 'Straining at the leash, I am. Straining at the leash,' one much indulged tradesman's daughter told Flora Thompson in the 1890s (Thompson 1931: 572). In 1911 M. Mostyn Bird was writing of the girl 'who demands freedom from home duties to work at her profession' as a common phenomenon (Bird 1911: 5).

The books of advice on women's occupations suggest that this change in attitude had spread quite widely through the lower middle class and was beginning to affect the upper middle class. The first chapter of Bulley and Whitley's *Women's Work* is scattered with references to 'ladies' and 'women of education' as likely to be found in the occupations being discussed (Bulley and Whitley 1894: 1–30). In the 1890s the High Church magazine for girls, *The Monthly Packet*, ran a series of articles on work for upper-middle-class women which were collected and published under the title *Ladies at Work: Papers on paid employments for ladies* (Jeune 1893). (The occupations discussed were journalism, art, music, authorship, the stage, medicine, teaching, nursing, and rent-collecting.) All the authors assumed that work was desirable as a secular vocation rather than as something imposed by dire financial circumstances. By 1911 the idea of unmarried women working at a paid profession was so well established that M. Mostyn Bird devoted most of the introduction to *Woman at Work* to bewailing the fact that the prospect of marriage diminished the seriousness with which women approached their occupations (Bird 1911: 3–7).

It would seem that many of the sort of girls who, in 1850, believed that to leave their homes to work for money would destroy their status as ladies and unsex them as women were happily training for occupations and earning a living at them. Middle-class girls, after almost a century of striving to be ladies on the upper-class pattern, turned about in the 1880s and began to see work for wages, previously a distinguishing mark of the working-class girl, as not incompatible with 'gentle' status (Mitchell 1995: 23–30).

It will be argued in the chapters which follow that these changes can only be explained as resulting from changes in the society's gender beliefs. Two sets of women, with different ideological allegiances but similar dissatisfactions with the conditions prescribed by the domestic ideology, began to challenge first the definition of women as 'relative creatures' and then the doctrine of separate spheres, transforming them from doxa to orthodoxies. In consequence, employers' 'knowledge' of what constituted women's work was modified, and the status requirements for being a lady were redefined to include paid work for unmarried women. Both groups used the same strategy of pointing out the logical incompatibility of the definition of women's place as confined to the domestic sphere with broadly held beliefs within other cultural fields. The first group demonstrated the incompatibility of the definition of women as 'relative creatures' with accepted religious beliefs about the individual's direct relation to God, and the second group used political and economic liberalism to argue against the gendering of the public/private divide. Both heterodoxies thus contributed to making the case that young, unmarried, middle-class women should work outside the home, and to opening new occupations to them.

# Part III

# STRONG-MINDED WOMEN

# 5

# BLUESTOCKINGS, PHILANTHROPISTS AND THE RELIGIOUS HETERODOXY

Throughout much of the nineteenth century and right up to the first World War, an unflattering stereotype existed of the woman who earned money by her pen or engaged in philanthropic activities of a public sort. Numerous examples exist in the fiction of the period. Thackeray, for example, produced a brief sketch in Lady Emily Sheepshanks 'who took considerable rank in the serious world' as author of some 'delightful tracts' and 'and of many hymns and spiritual pieces.'[1] The description of her continues:

> A mature spinster, and having but faint ideas of marriage, her love for the blacks occupied almost all her feelings . . . She had correspondences with clerical gentlemen in most of our East and West India possessions; and was secretly attached to the Reverend Silas Hornblower, who was tattooed in the South Sea Islands.
>
> (Thackeray 1847: 328)

Fuller portraits of women further down the social scale are Miss Carberry in Charlotte Bronte's *Shirley* (1849), and Miss Clack in Wilkie Collins's *The Moonstone* (1868). The strong-minded woman was usually depicted as a sexually unattractive spinster (Dickens's Mrs Jellyby was an exception), although in fact most of the women who made their names in such activities were married when they began or later married.

At the beginning of the century the most usual term for such women was 'bluestocking' or 'blue' (Theobald 1996: 21–2) and in the latter part of the period the stereotype was transferred to the 'new woman' and the suffragette, but from the 1830s to the 1890s it was labelled the 'strong-minded woman'. According to one writer men had such 'a general horror of any womanly trespass on their studies, their pursuits, or their prerogatives' that they 'raised a bugbear with which to frighten male and female children of a larger growth'.

Selecting some of the least attractive of the weaker sex – remarkable,
be sure, for sternness of countenance and angularity of outline; the
very heroines, indeed, most calculated to strike terror into friend and
foe – they have tied them together, so to speak, in one forbidding
bunch, and labelled it 'Strong-minded Women'.

(Whyte-Melville 1863: 668–9)

This caricature figure's ungainliness and unattractiveness were seen as
having been caused by her intellectual and philanthropic activities. They
'unsexed' her (Greenwell 1862: 69), and turned a woman's 'powerful and
earnest capability and desire for direct personal influence into a weak and
sentimental taste for ameliorating the condition of her race' (Patmore 1851:
525). Such women lost all power to charm. In 1848 an article in the
*Westminster Review* described the women who, disgusted by most women's
frivolity, 'incline to make the character of a man the standard by which to
form their own'.

But it will not do; industry and holy definite purpose mark their
career. If they could become men we should accept them for that,
and love and respect them as such; but they do not; are neither man
nor woman, and do not act finely on those around them, ever
winning by their work and life more respect than love; for we may
respect where we cannot love, while love necessitates respect.

(Adams 1849: 354)

One of Charlotte M. Yonge's heroines 'thought of herself as a strong-
minded woman, who could never be loved, and who could only suffer
through her woman's heart', though the novel then demonstrates that she
was wrong in this estimate of her attractions (Yonge 1854: 167).

In this chapter it will be argued that the women who led to the creation of
this stereotype were engaged in addressing some of the problems faced by
middle-class women. On the one hand they were reacting against the inactivity
and boredom that the pressures of gentility and femininity had created, and in
their search for 'something to do' to fill their idle hours they gradually established for the women who came after them a range of acceptable activities not
focused solely on the family and its welfare, while on the other hand, by establishing a heterodox discourse that began the transformation of the belief that
women were 'relative creatures' into an orthodoxy, they began the process of
challenging the 'knowledge' that had created the overstocking in teaching and
dressmaking, and by so doing opened two new paid occupations, nursing and
social work, to young middle-class women. Furthermore they ensured that the
transition of adolescent education from private to public institutions encompassed girls as well as boys, with the consequence that their teachers, too,
enjoyed the more stable conditions this implied.

## Borderlands

The strong-minded woman was accused of being unfeminine because in the eyes of her critics she had invaded the public sphere, which in the binary oppositions then operating as doxa, was paralleled by the masculine/feminine opposition. Yet it was only a very limited part of that public sphere that was involved: primarily the practice of literature and involvement in philanthropy, both of which could also be defended as sufficiently 'private' to be appropriate for women. Ann Digby has suggested that the psychiatric term 'borderlands'could be extended to describe such liminal areas.[2] She argues that at a time of unprecedented social, political and economic change, new areas of social action and interaction (what in Bourdieu's terminology could be termed social fields) were opening which had not yet been firmly defined within the binary oppositions that structured contemporary thinking, and that these could be penetrated by women. Such areas are, she writes: 'peopled by "doubtful cases" whose "peculiarities of thought or feeling or character make them objects of remark among their fellows".' She goes on:

> There were risks for women in establishing frontier posts within this social borderland, and these varied according to the behaviour of the colonists. Those who, in demeanour as well as activity, flouted traditional gender conventions might find themselves designated as occupying not only a social borderland but a psychiatric one also. What both social and psychiatric borderlands had in common, however, was their shadowy, shifting, indeterminate, and ambiguous character.
>
> (Digby 1992: 198)

The strong-minded woman would seem to fit this characterization, on occasion socially condemned and yet by no means totally ostracised, and in fact playing a significant part in giving a more stable definition to these newly emerging social fields.

In the earlier part of the century an ideological struggle took place between those to whom these new social fields seemed to be 'public' and therefore 'male', and those, predominantly but by no means exclusively women, who believed that they could be part of an area common to both sexes. Since many of the women concerned were socially of a higher class than those who condemned them, they possessed the symbolic capital which, Bourdieu assures us, allows people to push the rules within a social field to the limit, particularly if they are what he calls 'virtuosi', those who can devise strategies for gaining what they want while avoiding transgressing the rules so obviously as to provoke social retribution (Bourdieu 1990a: 11–12). These women, I shall argue, achieved this by using the strategy described by Phillipa Levine as 'rewriting the political script' by capitalizing 'on inconsistencies and confusions in their society' (Levine 1990: 178).

The inconsistencies and confusions on which they focused were those raised by the evangelical religion of the late eighteenth and early nineteenth centuries, which on the one hand saw women as Christians in a personal and responsible relationship with God which would determine their fate in the afterlife, and on the other, as bound by their religion to obedience to the head of the patriarchal household in which they lived. In so doing they created a discourse which made it impossible for the borderlands of the arts and philanthropy to be defined as exclusively male, for this to become doxa. This discourse, which I have chosen to call the 'religious heterodoxy', ensured that claims by their critics that women who engaged in such activities were unfeminine became an orthodoxy rather than doxa, accepted perhaps by the majority, but disputed by the women themselves, who were able to defend their actions in terms of a heterodox discourse which shared the religious premises of the orthodoxy, but argued from them for a very different set of God-ordained practices.

The religious heterodoxy, it will be argued, was the outcome of an encounter between the tradition of the learned lady which had in the seventeenth century established a place for women in the borderland of enlightenment thought, and the revival of religious 'enthusiasm' in the late eighteenth century which created a new borderland of voluntary charity. Furthermore, the resulting discourse proved so successful in establishing these borderlands as feminine, that by mid-century it had almost ceased to appear heterodox, and historians of the latter part of the century refer to women invoking it at that date as 'conservative' (Delamont 1978a; Digby 1992; Pederson 1981).

The foundations were laid by the 'learned ladies' of the seventeenth century. Ruth Perry has argued that women were by no means excluded from the intellectual revolution of the seventeenth and eighteenth centuries. She writes:

> The 'new philosophy,' whether the rationalism of Descartes or the empiricism of Bacon, did women the incalculable service of taking formal thought out of the schools, from which women, even the most aristocratic, had always been excluded. The new philosophical practice did not require formal education or even familiarity with classical texts; anyone who could meditate and think logically about that meditation, might contribute to knowledge. Descartes himself made it clear that an old-fashioned classical education was irrelevant to the most profound questions of philosophy – questions about the nature of knowledge itself. Poullain de la Barre, a feminist disciple of Descartes, held that since men and women had the same physiological equipment for receiving and registering sensations – the same bundles of nerve fibers – they therefore had the same potential for finding their way to Truth. Once put on this experiential basis,

philosophy became the common intellectual ground on which men and women might meet to discuss the nature of thought and of physical matter.

(Perry 1985: 475–6)

Intellectual life, by moving away from the church and the universities, had become a new social field, and thus a 'borderland' into which women could penetrate. Aristocratic women could become patrons of notable male intellectuals and they could and did correspond with leading figures. It would seem that many philosophers were happy to enter into such relations with women (the fact that the women were usually of a higher social status than the men in such relationships may have balanced the inequalities that could be presumed to come from difference in sex), and a number of the women, the main representative in Britain being Margaret Cavendish, Duchess of Newcastle, later published works based on this correspondence (Perry 1985: 479–81). Women were, therefore, creating for themselves a presence in this new borderland of rationality and enlightenment, a borderland which had no necessary connection with any of the entrenched public institutions of their society.

Their presence there was resented and contested by many of the male participants. A number of feminizt historians have shown how determinedly some philosophers strove to have the rational/emotional opposition equated with the male/female, and there was considerable public mocking of these ancestors of the strong-minded woman. In France Molière caricatured them as *les précieuses* in *Les Femmes Savantes*, and the Duchess of Newcastle was labelled 'Mad Madge' by those outside her circle (Perry 1985: 474–5, 479, 481). Many of the women involved, because of their high social status, had enough symbolic capital to resist these attempts to exclude them. Lady amateurs had some of the same freedom as gentleman amateurs to engage in the same manner as professionals in any area of the arts and sciences, and be welcomed by more humble participants for the money and prestige they contributed to the area. Thus enlightenment philosophy and science remained a contested area, with a number of women determinedly maintaining their claim to be rational beings without losing either their femininity or their position in society.

This borderland included fiction and poetry, and by the early nineteenth century both female amateurs from among the gentry like Maria Edgeworth and Jane Austen and professionals from the middle ranks like Fanny Burney and Hannah More had demonstrated that women could engage in authorship without compromising their femininity or the gentility of their families. This was, of course, work that could be done at home and the actual performance of the work did no more to bring them under a public gaze than exclusively feminine activities like embroidery or sewing, so whether their studying and writing was done for private consumption or for sale it could, like the work approved by Sarah Trimmer for the lower classes, be done by a woman 'sitting down in peace and quietness in her own little neat apartment, surrounded by playful innocents' (Trimmer 1787: 66). A number of the female authors from the turn of the century stressed this aspect of their femininity by publishing as Mrs Barbauld, Mrs Trimmer, or Mrs Hemans.

Authorship was thus established as feminine before the separation of home and work and the domestic ideology narrowed the definition of femininity, and placed an embargo on women's contributing to the family income except in cases of dire necessity. Consequently, with the press open to them, it was possible for women in the learned lady tradition to contest the attempts of philosophers and moralists to establish the work of the intellect as public and masculine.

## Bluestockings and evangelicals

In the late eighteenth century in Britain the tradition of the learned lady was continued by the 'bluestockings', the group of literary hostesses, Mrs Montague, Mrs Vesey, Mrs Boscawen, who prided themselves on their intellectual evening parties and their superiority to an interest in dress and cards. Their intellectual world was, however, increasingly influenced by the revival of religion that characterised the period from the time of John Wesley onwards. For intellectuals like Dr Johnson, religion was seen as compatible with enlightenment thought, and the moral autonomy so prized by evangelicalism, the personal guidance given by God to each individual through prayer and inspiration, was linked with rationality and education. Educated Christians must fit themselves by the 'cultivation of the mind' to make their own moral judgements. By claiming that women, too, were called on to exercise their reason as part of their Christian duty, women in the bluestocking circle could situate their desire for education within the ungendered borderland of the soul's relation to God.

It was suggested in Chapter 3 that one of the reasons women so willingly internalised the Angel in the House myth was that it gave them a sense of mission, a justification for the life of idleness forced on them by the status needs of their families. However, though it may have been the moral imperatives of evangelicalism which made women like Hannah More feel the need for a mission, the myth endorsed aspects of the domestic ideology that were not congruent with other parts of the evangelical creed. Though evangelicalism supported patriarchal control of women, and in particular their obligation to obey their husbands, on biblical grounds, it did not assume, as the Angel in the House myth as finally elaborated by Comte and Ruskin did, that woman's only purpose was to inspire and minister to the needs of particular men (Comte 1865: 276; Ruskin 1865: 119).

In the more intense religious sects this led to women being given a status more similar to men's than in society as a whole. The Quakers were well known for this and Methodism in its early days had some powerful female preachers (Atkinson 1861: 471; Cobbe 1869: 25). Moralists held that the duty to obey husbands did not come before that to obey God, and even John Wesley's saintly mother defied her husband on matters of principle. The moral imperatives of Christianity were felt to be equally binding on men and women (Harmon 1968: 47, 79–80; Pennington 1761: 90; Yonge 1877: 179–80).

Thus the 'relative creatures' view of women ('He for God only/She for God in him'), in its denial of a direct relationship between the woman and God, created an uneasiness in intellectual, religious women throughout the nineteenth century. It conflicted with what their religion laid down as their highest duty of all: serving God and fitting their souls for Heaven. Women with intellectual leanings began to argue that women, as well as men, should be morally autonomous, able to make their own moral judgments. Only a tiny group of protofeminists, mostly connected, like Mary Wollstonecraft, to the broader radical movements, extended this demand to political and economic autonomy (Rowbotham 1975: 39–46; Taylor 1983: 57–82), but there was a considerably larger group of upper middle-class women prepared to criticize the position, and particularly the education, of women from the standpoint of the need to develop their full spiritual potential.

The heterodox nature of this view can be seen if one contrasts a standard book of advice for women written by a man, Dr Gregory's *A Father's Legacy to His Daughters*, with an equivalent book written by a member of the blue-stocking circle, Hester Chapone's *Letters on the Improvement of the Mind*. The difference between the man, who saw women's main object as making them-selves pleasing to men, and the woman, who saw it as improving their minds and saving their immortal souls, is striking. Dr Gregory could not even finish his chapter on religion without throwing in a reference to its useful-ness in getting a husband:

> Women are greatly deceived, when they think they recommend themselves to *our* sex by their indifference about religion. Even those men who are themselves unbelievers, dislike infidelity in *you*. Every *man* who knows human nature, connects a religious taste in *your* sex, with softness and sensibility of heart ... Besides, *men* consider *your* religion as one of their principal securities for that female virtue in which *they* are most interested. If a gentleman pretend an attachment to any of *you*, and endeavour to shake your religious principles, be assured he is either a fool, or has designs on you which he dares not openly avow.
>
> (Gregory 1774: 12)

Hester Chapone did not see it this way. The closest her chapter on religion came to these sentiments was this passage:

[B]e assured, that the more you increase in love to [God], and delight in his laws, the more you will increase in happiness, in excellence, and honour: that in proportion as you improve in true piety, you will become dear and amiable to your fellow-creatures.

(Chapone 1773: 7)

The difference in their estimate of female intellectual power is also marked. Dr Gregory wrote:

Religion is rather a matter of sentiment than reasoning. The important and interesting articles of faith are sufficiently plain. Fix your attention on these, and do not meddle with controversy.

(Gregory 1774: 9)

For Hester Chapone, however, religion was a matter of intellectual striving:

If you desire to live in peace and honour, in favour with God and man, and to die in the glorious hope of rising from the grave to a life of endless happiness, – if these things appear worthy your ambition, you must set out in earnest in the pursuit of them. Virtue and happiness are not attained by chance, nor by a cold and languid approbation; they must be sought with ardour, attended to with diligence, and every assistance must be eagerly embraced that may enable you to attain them.

(Chapone 1773: 2)

This diligence she implied would involve serious study:

As you advance in years and understanding, I hope you will be able to examine for yourself the evidences of the Christian Religion, and be convinced, on rational grounds, of its divine authority.

(ibid.: 8)

A quarter of her book was devoted to giving guidance on the serious study of Geography, Chronology and History.

Hannah More, a younger, more evangelical member of the bluestocking group, also argued that education was necessary to lead a religious life:

A lady studies, not that she may qualify herself to become an orator or a pleader; not that she may learn to debate, but to act. She is to read the best books, not so much to enable her to talk of them, as to bring the improvement which they furnish, to the rectification of her principles and the formation of her habits. The great uses of study to a woman are to regulate her own mind, and to be instrumental to the good of others.

(More 1799, vol. 2: 1–2).

She too devoted much of her *Strictures on the Modern System of Female Education* to chapters with titles like 'On the religious and moral use of history and geography'.

Mary Wollstonecraft, politically the antithesis of the bluestockings, used the same arguments in her *Vindication of the Rights of Women*, though unlike the bluestockings, she was prepared to argue explicitly that female education should be the same as male:

> I hope I shall not be misunderstood when I say, that religion will not have this condensing energy, unless it be founded on reason. If it be merely the refuge of weakness or wild fanaticism, and not a governing principle of conduct, drawn from self-knowledge, and a rational opinion respecting the attributes of God, what can it be expected to produce.
>
> To render mankind more virtuous, and happier of course, both sexes must act from the same principle; but how can that be expected when only one is allowed to see the reasonableness of it? To render also the social compact truly equitable, and in order to spread those enlightening principles, which alone can ameliorate the fate of man, women must be allowed to found their virtue on knowledge, which is scarcely possible unless they be educated by the same pursuits as men.
>
> (Wollstonecraft 1792: 125, 192)

As the domestic ideology gained a firmer hold, this demand for moral autonomy began to seem at odds with the belief that a woman should be a 'natural second' dependent on her husband for advice and direction. Yet advocates of intellectual education for women found a way to justify their demands in terms of certain aspects of the emerging Angel in the House myth, in particular the belief that women's primary function was to make of the home a holy sanctum where, under the influence of their purity and piety, men's moral nature would be refreshed and refurbished (Houghton 1957: 343–8). The bluestockings' identification of intellectual education with moral excellence made possible the development of a rather neat syllogism justifying intellectual education in terms of the Angel in the House myth: the main role of wives and mothers was to influence their husbands and children for good, but only an intellectual education made a woman truly moral. Therefore an intellectual education made women better wives and mothers.

## The bluestocking syllogism and the intellectual woman

The origins of this argument can be found in Hannah More's work. Her *Strictures on the Modern System of Female Education* began with this 'address to women of rank and fortune':

Among the talents for the application of which women of the higher class will be peculiarly accountable, there is one, the importance of which they can scarcely rate too highly. This talent is influence. We read of the greater orator of antiquity, that the wisest plans which it had cost him years to frame, a woman would overturn in a single day; and when we consider the variety of mischiefs which an ill-directed influence has been know to produce, we are led to reflect with the most sanguine hope on the beneficial effects to be expected from the same powerful force when exerted in its true direction.

(More 1799, vol. 2: 1–2)

It was for this reason, above all others, she argued, that women's education was so vitally important and that 'the present erroneous system' was so deeply to be deplored.

As the Angel in the House myth grew in strength and intensity, the blue-stocking syllogism grew along with it. Believers in the Angel in the House myth were by no means all advocates of rigorous intellectual training for women, but the strength of the belief in 'influence' could be harnessed, by means of the bluestocking syllogism, to its support, and for some of its leading exponents it was an integral part of the myth. The syllogism was, for example, implicit in Sarah Lewis's *Woman's Mission*:

A simple question will . . . place this subject in a stronger light: 'Are women qualified to educate men?' if they are not, no available progress has been made. In the very heart of civilized Europe are women what they ought to be? . . . Is it possible to believe, that upon their training depends the happiness of families; the well-being of nations? The selfishness, political and social; the forget-fulness of patriotism; the unregulated tempers and low ambition of the one sex, testify but too clearly, how little has been done by the vaunted education of the other. For education is useless, or at least neutral, if it do not bear upon duty, as well as upon cultivation, if it do not expand the soul, while it enlightens the intellect.

(Lewis 1839: 56)

On a less exalted plane it was argued that an educated woman made the most companionable wife. The Angel in the House myth had developed the idea that the wife was now a friend, a companion, a 'helpmate' to her husband. Educated men, it therefore followed, must have educated wives (Lister 1841: 191; Milne 1857). Once again Hannah More had shown the way. In her novel, *Coelebs in Search of a Wife*, a leading character argued:

A man of taste who has an ignorant wife, cannot in her company, think his own thoughts, nor speak his own language; his thoughts he will suppress; his language he will debase, the one from hopelessness, the other from compassion. He must be continually lowering and diluting his meaning, in order to make himself intelligible. This he will do for the woman he loves, but in doing it he will not be happy. She, who cannot be entertained by his conversation, will not be convinced by his reasoning; and at length he will find out, that it is less trouble to lower his standard to hers, than to exhaust himself in the vain attempt to raise hers.

(More 1809, vol. 2: 234)

In 1843 Mrs Ellis was arguing in *Wives of England* that a wife must be educated so that she could be 'a companion who will raise the tone of his mind . . . from low anxieties and vulgar cares' (Turner 1974: 85 quoted), while in 1859 Emily Shirreff suggested in *Intellectual Education* that a wife's 'sphere of enjoyment and influence is increased by extending to man's intellectual life the power of sympathy she exercises so strongly within the range of feelings and affections.' (Shirreff 1858: 19)

To be an adequate mother, too, it was averred, the woman must be educated. One of the first to produce this argument was Mary Wollstonecraft:

As the care of children in their infancy is one of the grand duties annexed to the female character by nature, this duty would afford many forcible arguments for strengthening the female understanding, if it were properly considered.

(Wollstonecraft 1792: 166)

Forty years later Sarah Lewis was using the same argument:

The combination of high mental power with feminine purity and unselfishness gives a dignity to intellectual maternity which really overawes the youthful mind and . . . has a tendency to stamp it indelibly with virtuous sentiments, and with those high views of the feminine character which are so essential to man's happiness and goodness.

(Lewis 1839: 35)

The bluestocking syllogism thus became part of the rhetoric of those arguing that girls' education should have an intellectual dimension.

The influence of these ideas on the curriculum in girls' schools will be considered in the next chapter, but the general argument that women should develop and make use of their God-given intellectual abilities served to legitimize the growth of female authorship. Women confined to the home by the changes in household structure, could devote their ample spare time to study and to writing. Female novelists, dramatists, poets and essayists found a ready market for their works from the end of the eighteenth century onwards, though their presence there was ignored or contested by many men in the same profession (Johnston 1997: 14–18).[3] Female novelists and poets included not only those like Margaret Oliphant and George Eliot who needed to earn a living, but upper-middle-class women like Elizabeth Barrett Browning and Elizabeth Gaskell. Women were also, as Judith Johnston points out, 'both enormously productive and highly successful, as translators, biographers, historians, philosophers, critics and editors' (Johnston 1997: 17). Mrs Somerville, Mrs Marcet and Harriet Martineau, for example, popularized the latest views in science and economics and found a lucrative market for their work. Women also edited journals and magazines. It is well known that in the 1840s George Eliot was editor in all but name of the *Westminster Review*, while in the same decade, but at a rather different intellectual level, Anne Mozley edited the *Magazine for the Young*, also without her name appearing anywhere. Furthermore, quite a number of women combined this work with marriage and maternity, even turning it into a family business. Jane Austen's niece, Anna Lefroy, and her daughters produced dozens of little books for the juvenile market for the publisher James Burns, while a rather more distinguished mother and daughter were Margaret Gatty and Juliana Horatia Ewing who produced the notable *Aunt Judy's Magazine*, and in the first case more than twenty and in the second almost forty separate publications (Maxwell 1949, Alderson 1994).

## 'Something to do' and philanthropy

Intellectual and literary pursuits, however available, could not fill the needs of all leisured women. There were intelligent, energetic women who needed a rather different field of activity, and many of them found this by gaining a place for themselves in the new borderland of voluntary charity. Indeed, for some of them, this was the purpose of their education. A reviewer of Emily Shirreff's *Intellectual Education* in the *English Woman's Journal* in 1858 wrote:

> The stranger within our gates and the neighbour just outside them, have upon all women in comfortable circumstances a sacred claim; a claim not incompatible with a large amount of self culture, but wholly precluding it as a main occupation.
>
> (EWJ July 1858: 346)

As Ann Summers has pointed out, it would be trivializing the motives of these women to see them as coming simply from 'boredom'. Their charitable work, she argues, began as 'an engagement of the self which involved the sacrifice of leisure and the development of expertise', and it led to informal groupings of women 'which exercised significant political and social pressure on the direction and administration of official policies towards the poor' (Summers 1979: 33).

There were many men, both leisured and professionally or commercially occupied, who devoted themselves to the public good by serving on public bodies from parliament through the magistracy to the parish vestry, and who also served on the committees and councils of the new voluntary charities (Summers 1979: 38). Popular 'knowledge', which increasingly accepted the binary opposition that equated public with male, made it impossible for women to take on responsibilities in the first social field, but voluntary charity as it emerged in the late eighteenth and nineteenth centuries was still a borderland, and one where, it will be argued, the religious heterodoxy made possible what Ann Digby has described as the 'unofficial female colonisation of the borderland' where 'women successfully occupied, and extended, their space' (Digby 1992: 198).

It has long been recognized by historians that one of the major effects of the evangelical movement on nineteenth century society was the expansion of the idea of Christian charity into that of philanthropy. It had always been part of the *noblesse oblige* justification of the wealth and leisure of the upper class that ladies and gentlemen looked after the poor of their parishes, but evangelicalism took this a good deal further. It was no longer felt that it was enough to cultivate one's own garden. To neglect a general social evil because it was not part of one's traditional duty was the equivalent of passing by on the other side, and it was not just men but women too who felt called upon to play the good Samaritan in a wider, even a national, sphere (Prochaska 1988: 21–2).

Women's occupation of this borderland did not happen automatically. It was the outcome of the actions of countless individuals, most of whom would, if pressed, have defended their actions in terms of some version of the religious heterodoxy. The Christian moral imperative to love one's neighbour as oneself applied, they believed, to women as well as men, and so women too had a duty to redress what seemed to be crying social evils. An early example of this process at work can be seen in the life of Sarah Trimmer, one of the women whose practice in the late eighteenth century had contributed to authorship becoming an acceptable occupation for middle-class married women. In 1786 she published a book urging women, particularly those 'in the middling situations of life', to take part in the Sunday school movement initiated a few years earlier by Robert Raikes (Purvis 1991: 15). The general purpose of the movement she saw as coping with the problems created by increasing urbanization and the growing gap between rich and poor, and she argued the case for dealing with the social problems created using enlightenment appeals to rationality to defend a basically conservative vision of a God-ordained hierarchical social order:

It is obvious to common sense that a want of concord among the various orders of people must be prejudicial to a nation at large; for, in appointing different ranks among mankind our all-wise and beneficent CREATOR undoubtedly intended the good of the whole. 'He regardeth not the rich any more than the poor; they are all the work of his hand:' and, that a proper agreement might be kept up among them, he has made their welfare and happiness to depend in a great measure on their mutual interchange of good offices, and has ordained to each peculiar duties; to all in superior stations, justice, humanity, condescension and charity: to the poor, honesty, diligence, humility and gratitude. The general practice of these duties is essentially requisite to produce the unanimity which ought to subsist among a race of rational beings, and particularly among the professors of a holy religion which so strongly inculcates universal benevolence. It is evident that unanimity does not at present subsist in this country and the consequences are dreadful to society; it is therefore incumbent on all its members to use every means in their power towards a restoration of that harmony, without which there cannot be either safety or tranquillity: and surely it is perfectly consistent with the female character for ladies to exert their endeavours towards reconciling these unhappy differences, and effecting that mutual good understanding which the practice of reciprocal benevolence and gratitude would naturally produce, which Christianity requires, and which has subsisted in the nation in former ages of the world.

(Trimmer 1787: 3–4)

The Sunday school movement was, she believed, effective primarily because men of the upper ranks were themselves engaged in the teaching, giving the poor children the benefit of their example and of their educated understanding of religion.

Can ladies view these noble exertions of the other sex, and not be inspired with emulation to join with equal ardour in an undertaking which has for its object the reformation of so considerable a part of the kingdom; and which, in the end, may lead to a general reformation?

What can be a greater act of charity than to contribute to the success of an institution like this? What more suited to the tenderness which is allowed to be natural to our sex? Can a woman, accustomed to the exercise of maternal affection towards her own beloved offspring, be indifferent to the happiness of poor children, who have no means of learning their duty but what these schools afford? Can she think of multitudes being devoted to ignorance, vice, and perhaps eternal misery, and not reach forth a ready hand to snatch them from so dreadful a fate? Will she not afford every assistance in her power towards the success of an establishment which is calculated to obviate these evils; to inculcate useful knowledge; adorn the mind with Christian graces; and procure for those, who are doomed to suffer the miseries of this life, eternal happiness in a future state?

(ibid.: 19–20)

Here again one can see the tactic of capitalizing 'on inconsistencies and confusions in their society' (Levine 1990: 178) at work, using the accepted view of the nature of women to argue for their admission to a new social field.[4]

Sunday school teaching was a field in which lay men and women participated equally, and recruits were drawn from all levels of the middle class. There was another area, however, of religious intervention where women, predominantly from the upper middle class, seem to have taken on work which was traditionally reserved for the clergy alone. This was district visiting. The religious revival had convinced many of the clergy that their mission included pastoral care of their parishioners, which in the case of the poor combined the provision of material comforts with spiritual guidance and exhortation. By the 1840s in a great many parishes much of this work was being undertaken by lady parishioners acting as the clergyman's deputy (Prochaska 1980: 43–48; Summers 1979: 39–42). The parish was divided into 'districts' and each lady visitor had her own.

A considerable literature grew up outlining the lady visitor's duties. She was to call on the residents in her district regularly, in a neighbourly fashion, and though she might often give material help, hers was to be primarily a spiritual mission, but one exercised through sympathy rather than exhortation. As one London parson wrote:

Now, as it is made a main part of a Visitor's business, in London especially, to relieve distress by tickets for bread and groceries, and other necessaries, it happens too often that the Visitor subsides into this office alone. With reference to this danger, it is especially needful to cherish that reverence for the poor as fellow-creatures and spiritual beings, which is implied in the act of claiming fellowship with them. Nothing is more revolting and insulting than the tone of language which may sometimes be heard from professed philanthropists about feeding and clothing the poor. If we *put ourselves* in the place of the needy, we shall feel what a shock it would give to our self-respect, to our sense of honour, to receive a dole of relief. Surely all almsgiving should be done with the greatest delicacy, and if possible secrecy. We must not help to turn any poor persons into hungry animals.

(Davies 1855: 130)

The novelist Charles Kingsley, writing on 'Country parishes' in the same volume, stressed the relation of this work to the 'influence' seen as so important by the Angel in the House myth:

> You wish for personal contact with the poor round you, for the pure enjoyment of doing good to them with your own hands. How are you to set about it? First, there are clubs, – clothing-clubs, shoe-clubs, maternal-clubs; all very good in their way. But do not fancy that they are the greater part of your parish work. Rather watch and fear lest they become substitutes for your real parish work; lest the bustle and amusement of playing at shopkeeper, or penny-collector, once a week, should blind you to your real power – your real treasure, by spending which you become all the richer. What you have to do is to ennoble and purify the *womanhood* of these poor women; to make them better daughters, sisters wives, mothers: and all the clubs in the world will not do that.
>
> (Kingsley 1855: 57)

This personal ministry gradually extended to visiting in public institutions like prisons, workhouses and hospitals (Prochaska 1980: 138–81). Some of the pioneers in such work were raised to the status of 'heroines', women who acted in a manner contrary to the timid, retiring, modest aspects of women's nature, because they were driven by their womanly sympathies: Hannah More (an Anglican), for example, for her work in establishing a system of schools in Cheddar, Elizabeth Fry (a Quaker) for her work among women prisoners, and Caroline Chisholm (a Roman Catholic) among female emigrants (Boucherett 1863: 89–90; Vicinus 1994: 53–7; Yonge 1888b: 78–100). By the 1870s such women were being included among those whose formulaic biographies were published in gift book editions of *Noble Heroines* (Vicinus 1994: 53–5). As Anne Summers has shown, the phrase 'woman's mission', first used by Sarah Lewis to justify women's confinement within the home, was rapidly extended to describe instead this commitment to philanthropic activities outside it (Summers 1990: 125).

Women were also joining actively in the notable development identified by Frank Prochaska as characteristic of nineteenth century charity: the emergence of the charitable society whose work was supported by voluntary subscriptions, rather than the endowed trust, as the main vehicle for charitable work. Once again, a new borderland had emerged, and there was, as he notes, 'an explosion of societies run by women' throughout the period while there were many others ostensibly run by men in which they played a significant part (Prochaska 1980: 22–9, 242–5). An example of the range can be seen in those mentioned in a list of pamphlets, reports and prospectuses received by the *English Woman's Journal* in April, 1860: the Workhouse Visiting Society, St Joseph's Industrial Institute, the British Ladies' Female Emigrant Society, the Red Lodge Girls' Reformatory School, Bristol, the Bristol Ragged School on St James' Back, the Association for Promoting the General Welfare of the Blind, the Royal Maternity Charity, the Jenny Lind Infirmary for Sick Children, the Norwich Lying-in Charity, the National Society's Training Institution for Schoolmistresses (EWJ April 1860: 131–2). Some societies had all-male councils (for example St John's House, founded 1848), some had all-female councils (the Institution of Nursing Sisters, founded 1840), and some had mixed advisory committees (the Ranyard Mission, founded 1859) (Prochaska 1980: 243–5). There was also a widespread pattern of establishing Ladies' Auxiliaries whose primary purpose was supposed to be fundraising, but which increasingly gave advice on policy often to the discomfiture of the men (ibid.: 23–8).[5]

Service on such committees must have meant considerable training in business methods for the women involved. The committees were accountable to subscribers and felt bound to keep proper records of decisions and expenditure, and indeed seem to have modelled their practices on those of limited liability companies. Having spent time examining both the minutes of commercial institutions like the Society of Apothecaries and the Prudential Insurance Company and those of voluntary charities, I have been struck by the similarities and also by the competence of the women involved. The all-female Institution of Nursing Sisters, where minutes and accounts were kept by unpaid female committee members, reveal notable efficiency, and an unblemished record, unlike St John's House and the Ranyard Mission, which had to cope with the scandal of paid secretaries (both clergymen) absconding with some of the funds.

Beyond serving on committees, these organizations involved women in fundraising, and bazaars where objects made by the whole range of women, from little girls to old ladies, were on sale, were a notable feature of the social life of the period. Fictional accounts of the excitements, embarrassments and jealousies of these occasions can be found in Charlotte Yonge's *The Daisy Chain* (1856), George Eliot's *The Mill on the Floss* (1860), and Anthony Trollope's *Miss Mackenzie* (1865). An 1857 painting by James Collinson called *The Empty Purse: At the Bazaar* portrays the scene (Casteras 1987), and Frank Prochaska (1980: 47–72) has given a scholarly account of the emergence and proliferation of the practice.[6]

By the middle of the century the use of women by clergy and philanthropic groups was so well-established that L. F. M. Phillips could write that it was 'now spoken of . . . as though it were to be the panacea for all our ills; and whenever negligence and imperfection is found in any of our charitable or social institutions in connection with the uneducated, there is a call made for our help' (Phillips 1861: 13–14).

Yet throughout this period the legitimacy of women's participation in philanthropic activity was still being 'discussed and disputed'. There were those prepared to argue that this was public sphere activity and women had no place there, that their 'mission' should be restricted to doing good in their own households. A writer in the *Edinburgh Review* in 1833 roundly declared:

> The less women usually meddle with any thing which can be called public life out of their village, we are sure the better for all parties. A deep sympathy with the precarious situation of their poorer neighbours and an active benevolence in relieving the distressed, and in encouraging the virtuous, furnish them with a circle wide enough. These are cares which may well satisfy any reasonable personal ambition; while they are identified with the best ornaments of the female character and the real out of door duties of female life.
>
> (Empson 1833: 3)

Even these works were expected to give way to women's 'little home duties', and what Emily Shirreff was to call the 'shirt button and slipper' argument (Grey 1884: 61) was used against women who sought a wider role. The *Christian Remembrancer* noted:

> Every man finds the convenience of a wife and daughters being able to leave what they are about, and take up his interests, do his errands, carry out his plans at a moment's notice. His home would not be a happier one if his own rule of never being interrupted were adopted by the ladies of his family.
>
> (Phillips 1861: 27 quoted)

Such arguments were even used to forbid women taking part in any charitable work. The same paper said:

> When a father has given his daughter the education of a lady, it cannot be just to him or to society for her to spend her whole energies in the duties of a common hired attendant in a labourer's family.
>
> (ibid.: 30 quoted)

However in the period before 1850 the religious heterodoxy had its effect and provided a justification for wider interests which must have given some upper-middle-class women alternative activities with which to occupy their too ample leisure. Women who obtruded their participation in these border-lands too forcefully may have had to bear the label in their circles of being 'blue' or 'strong-minded', but such forms of deviance seem to have been sufficiently widespread and supported by a heterodoxy which was sufficiently congruent with orthodox religious and political opinion not to lead to social ostracism, particularly when the practitioners possessed, as a great many did, the symbolic capital of unimpeachable gentility, and when they did not violate too obtrusively what Bourdieu has called 'the rules of the game'.

## Consolidation

The extent to which the borderlands of self-culture and philanthropy had been colonised by women can be seen in the novels of Charlotte M. Yonge, a high Anglican, rather than an evangelical, but a passionate adherent of the religious heterodoxy. Although she accepted much of the Angel in the House definition of women's role, she also believed fervently in both the need for women to make use of their intelligence and to undertake philanthropic work. In her most widely read novel, *The Daisy Chain* (1856), the heroine, Ethel May, was an eager, intellectual girl who kept up with her brother in his classical and mathematical studies, spent endless time and enthusiasm on the running of a school for quarry workers' children she and her sisters had established in their teens, and acted as the unconventional housekeeper for her widowed father and her younger brothers and sisters.

Charlotte Yonge saw home, philanthropy and intellectual interests as fulfilling the main needs of a woman, and since her books were enormously popular, stayed in print until World War I, and were read by almost all religious girls who read novels at all, her views can be taken as both representative of those of holders of the religious heterodoxy and influential, since she was apparently regarded as something of an oracle by many of her readers (Battiscombe 1943: 107–7, Coleridge 1903: 149, 292). Her books also provide a very interesting picture of the reactions of a holder of the religious heterodoxy to the more thoroughgoing Women's Movement in the years after 1860.

The religious heterodoxy, though it established that the borderlands of philanthropy and the practice of the arts were social fields where middle-class women could operate without sacrificing their claims to gentility and femininity, never attacked the patriarchalism inherent in the domestic ideology. It was in no way an attack on the duty of obedience to parents, and the reason for this lay in the wider ideological allegiance of the mainstream religious groups. Both evangelicals and high Anglicans, by and large, subscribed to what Harold Perkin has named the aristocratic ideal (Perkin 1969: 237–52). The church catechism laid down that it was everyone's duty 'to submit myself to all my governors, teachers, spiritual pastors and masters' and 'to do my duty in that state of life, unto which it shall please God to call me.' Thus, though holders of the religious heterodoxy believed that Christian morality was the same for men and women, they also believed that the 'state of life' of each individual was determined by God, and that it was everyone's duty to submit and not rebel. God had selected certain people – in some cases women – to have power over others and chosen others to remain under authority. It was the duty of all to accept their God-ordained spheres and tasks. A more refined morality might impel the masters to change the conditions they imposed, but it could never justify rebellion by those under them. Furthermore there was no real challenge to the belief in separate spheres. The attempt was only to modify somewhat the generally held definition of women's sphere to include intellectual pursuits and philanthropic work where this did not involve disobedience or interfere with home duties.

Nevertheless, the religious heterodoxy was not mobilised only to justify women with 'nothing to do' engaging in study and philanthropy. The need for relief from the burden of enforced leisure was such that, given the support of the religious heterodoxy, it became a dynamic force for change in society, leading, as the next two chapters will argue, to opening new professions to women and thus relieving to some extent the 'overstocking' in teaching and dressmaking. In the late 1840s it became possible for them to train as professional artists and musicians at publicly funded art and music schools, in the 1850s the new occupation of secondary school teacher in public schools began to open, and in the 1860s hospital nursing was reorganized and offered conditions middle-class women found appropriate. It also, though this development was to come after the period considered here, played a major part in developing social work as an occupation for middle-class women.

# 6

# DETERMINING GIRLS' EDUCATION

## Governesses and the ladies' colleges

From the 1850s on, a change occurred in the education of girls which ultimately took it out of the hands of the governess and the tiny private school and transferred it to salaried high school teachers working in 'public' schools (so-called because they were run, not by a 'private' individual to make a profit, but by a board whose activities were open to scrutiny). The ultimate outcome was that teachers of middle-class girls became, like those in elementary schools, free wage labourers, with similar conditions to, though lower salaries than, their male counterparts. During the same period women were admitted to the new publicly-funded music and art schools, and an increasing number of women began to earn their livings not just as art and music teachers, but as professional practitioners of these arts, again with the same economic constraints and opportunities that applied to men in these fields. This chapter will examine the origins of these changes and argue that they were the outcome of actions taken by men and women who accepted the revised definitions of gentility and femininity promulgated by holders of the religious heterodoxy.

Margaret Bryant (1979: 76, 106) has argued that the change in girls' education which made the occupation of female high school teacher possible was part of a wider change in middle-class education, that the movement of education from private to public schools encompassed both sexes more or less equally. Yet there were differences that need explaining. In the first place the establishment of public schools for girls lagged at least thirty years behind that of boys. J. A. Banks, using the *Year Books* of girls' and boys' schools from the late 1940s, has shown that between 1840 and 1890 sixty-nine new or reorganized public schools for boys were opened, and seventy-eight new schools for girls. But while thirty-five of the schools for boys were opened before 1870, only nine of the new schools for girls opened during this period (Banks 1954: 228–30).[1] Furthermore, there was a considerable difference in the curriculum. While the boys' public schools continued with the Renaissance classical curriculum (Young 1953: 96–9), the girls' schools offered a curriculum that had much more in common with the high school syllabuses of the twentieth century, and gave far more emphasis to the arts (Theobald 1988: 22-4).

## The bluestocking syllogism and girls' education

The curriculum established in these new girls' schools owed much to the campaign for women's intellectual education waged by the bluestockings and their evangelical successors. From the end of the eighteenth century onwards, a stream of publications by women writers appeared attacking the kind of education offered by governesses and private girls' schools. The criticisms differed little between 1787 when Mary Wollstonecraft published her *Thoughts on the Education of Daughters* and 1868 when the Taunton Royal Commission delivered its report. The Royal Commission summed up its findings thus:

> The general deficiency in girls' education is stated with the utmost confidence, and with entire agreement, with whatever difference of words by many witnesses of authority. Want of thoroughness and foundation; want of system; slovenliness and showy superficiality; inattention to rudiments; undue time given to accomplishments and those not taught intelligently or in any scientific manner; want of organization – these may sufficiently indicate the character of the complaints we have received, in their most general aspect.
>
> (PP 1867–68 vol. 28: 548–9)

All the stress, these critics insisted, was on preparing the girls to catch a husband by displaying showy accomplishments, rather than on training them for their future roles as wives and mothers. (Delamont 1978a: 136–8; Kamm 1965: 166–71; Percival 1939: 78–121). Yet the recommendation was not, as might have been assumed, that women should be trained in the housewifely arts. Instead it was forcibly argued that the education should take the form suggested by the bluestocking educational reformers and justified by what I have called the bluestocking syllogism.

The bluestockings had been clear on what they saw as an appropriate education for women, and, as with the arguments defending it, the same themes can be found running through books written throughout the nineteenth century. The ideal curriculum can be found described in books ranging from Hannah More's *Strictures on the Modern System of Female Education* of 1799 to Charlotte M. Yonge's *Womankind* of 1877, and is implicit in other works recommending intellectual education like Maria Edgeworth's 'The Good French Governess' (1801) and Maria Grey and Emily Shirreff's *Thoughts on Self Culture Addressed to Women* (1850). They did not take the classical education still offered to boys in the new and reformed public schools as their model. Their inspiration came from the enlightenment break with tradition which, as described in Chapter 5, had allowed women into a new borderland of thought not connected with the universities or the church. The kind of education they had in mind was intended to create a literate, cultivated woman who might not necessarily have the proficiency in the classical languages provided by the boys' public schools and the universities, but who would probably have a better knowledge of more recent literature, both English and European, and of history, geography and natural science (Edgeworth 1801; Grey and Shirreff 1850; More 1799; Theobald 1988: 22–4; Yonge 1877).

Though the content of the education was important to these women, even more important for them was the development of habits of independent thought. In particular, the ability to reason was stressed. This was, as Mrs. Chapone's writing shows, seen as an integral part of developing religious autonomy. It was given a more secular turn in the writings of Maria Edgeworth. She describes how her 'Good French Governess':

> discouraged, in Isabella, the vain desire to load her memory with historical and chronological facts, merely for the purpose of ostentation. She gradually excited her to read books of reasoning, and began with those in which reasoning and amusement are mixed. . . . It was an easier task to direct the activity of Isabella's mind, than to excite Matilda's dormant powers. . . . Mad. de Rosier took the greatest care in conversing with Matilda, to make her feel her own powers: whenever she used good arguments, they were immediately attended to; and when Matilda perceived that a prodigious memory was not essential to success, she was inspired with courage to converse unreservedly.
>
> (Edgeworth 1801: 305)

In 1858 Emily Shirreff was still laying stress on the moral importance of a training in reasoning:

> Selfishness is generally at the root of the injustice of men, ignorance and impulsive feeling of that of women; thus the former are mostly unjust in action, the latter in judgment. They are not trained to reason upon what touches their feelings, and we must remember that in the narrow experience of women it is mostly on points more or less personally interesting that their judgments are called for. . . . This view of the character of injustice in women points out the course of training required to preserve the young mind from the error. The *intellectual capacity for being just*, must be cultivated no less than the love of moral justice; and that can be done only by strengthening the reasoning power, to counterbalance the natural predominance of feeling; and by forming habits of accuracy and

discrimination in all matters of opinion. The necessity of the invigorating influence of severer mental training is thus felt at every step of female education.

(Shirreff 1858: 75–6)

The impact of these ideas has, Marjorie Theobald (1996: 29–54) argues, been considerably underestimated by historians. The female educational writers succeeded, she has shown, to a very considerable degree, in having their suggestions made the basis for the standard 'English' curriculum taught by governesses and offered in the private schools (Theobald 1988: 22–4). The continuing barrage of criticism suggests that, though the ideal may not have been always fulfilled, the pressure on teachers and parents to subscribe to it was continuous. These critics had, moreover, the advantage of being the only group proposing an articulated philosophy of girls's education in an era when other social pressures ensured that most middle-class parents were prepared to pay for an education for their daughters well into their teens.

There is ample literary evidence that at the beginning of the century there were already a great many governesses employed in private families and large numbers of privately owned girls' schools catering for different levels of the middle class, while the census figures quoted in Chapter 3 show that during the latter part of the century between 8 per cent and 14 per cent of families with teenage girls were paying for some sort of education for their daughters. This trend, it was argued in Chapter 2, was a consequence of the middle class's aspiration to gentility, to living as far as possible as the gentry did.

One way for a family to demonstrate its status was to have the daughters educated in a manner which imitated as far as possible the education of the women of the aristocracy. What parents expected of the schools, therefore, was a reproduction of the status and gender order of middle-class society. The schools were expected to produce a girl who bore the marks of her middle-class status in her manners and deportment, who fulfilled the ideal of femininity defined by the domestic ideology, and who would thus be a credit to her family and enhance its status, and appear to be, after a number of years spent living as a young lady at home, a suitable marriage partner for a man of the same social rank (Dyhouse 1981: 51–5; Pinchbeck 1930: 34–7; Theobald 1988: 25).

The primary demand made on the schools by parents was, therefore, that they preserve the purity and chastity on which the girl's reputation and the respectability of her family depended. Most schools seem to have interpreted this as meaning that the pupils must not be allowed to think about men or sex. The constant supervision in these schools, sometimes criticized as a form of spying, grew out of a fear that the girls might corrupt one another's minds, while much of the secretiveness and deceit which the educational reformers deplored came from bored and excitable girls trying to make some contact, however brief, with any young men they might see at church or on their

110

walks (Burstall 1907: 175; HW 1855: 40–1; HW 1856: 314; Theobald 1996: 51; Yonge 1857: 8; Yonge 1885: 132–3, 278).

The second offering of the schools was a curriculum which defined both status and gender. An almost identical syllabus, Marjorie Theobald (1996: 14–5) has pointed out, was offered in schools all over the country. It combined a series of subjects which have since become academic disciplines (though not at that date defined as such by the universities) with artistic 'accomplishments' I would suggest, however, that it was not the content of the curriculum that was important to many parents, but the fact that it differed from the education offered to boys and to the working class. It defined status by giving middle-class women artistic expertise which they shared with the aristocracy, but which was unknown in the working class, and defined gender by ensuring that their knowledge and talents would be different from those acquired by boys.

As I have argued elsewhere, the early educational reformers were therefore faced with a situation which it was possible to manipulate for their own ends. Parents were prepared to pay for an education for their daughters, but many cared very little about its content so long as it guaranteed gentility and femininity. The bluestocking syllogism could thus be used to appropriate the definition of femininity: to take from the domestic ideology the notion that women's sphere was the home and their vocation being wives and mothers, and then to argue that only women educated in the way they favoured could become good wives and mothers and therefore truly feminine (Jordan 1991: 446–50).

The educational writers' tactic of spreading their ideas through highly coloured pictures of the worst contemporary examples has led many histo-rians to take these pictures as a balanced description of the norm, and to overlook the fact that many schools and governesses tried to implement the ideal. Thus until very recently historians of girls' education have assumed that these ideas had little impact before the emergence of the public girls' schools in the second half of the century. Furthermore, they have echoed the claims made by the apologists for this change who wrote and spoke as though the pre-1850 criticisms made of the private education of girls, whether by governesses or in the various ladies' academies, were without influence, and that serious academic study was not available to women before the advent of the high schools. Marjorie Theobald notes:

> On the basis of very little research, they have concluded that educational provision for middle-class women until the last quarter of the nineteenth century was meretricious and misguided. Parents cared little about the education of their daughters. The governess in the private home, the lady principal in her female academy and the ubiquitous music master presided over a nether-world of education which was costly, pretentious and haphazard, teaching a smattering

of 'ladylike' accomplishments to groom daughters for the marriage market. In this view, girls were educated by default or not at all.
(Theobald 1996: 29)

Yet, as she has shown, many of the women who ran these ladies' academies had a very clear idea of their aims. One advertisement of 1823 announced that the school offered 'all the essentially useful and solid acquirements with the more feminine and ornamental accomplishments, so as to ensure to those entrusted to their care an opportunity of acquiring all that is necessary to form and adorn the female character'. In 1857 another described the 'objects of the institution' as being: 'To impart a solid and superior education . . . comprehending the development of the Intellectual Faculties and high Moral and Religious Training (and) those graceful accomplishments proper to ladies' (Theobald 1996: 35, 45 quoted). Theobald has also shown that these 'solid' acquirements were those advocated by educational writers from the bluestockings on as developing rationality and autonomous morality.

Obviously many schools and homes did not rise to the ideals set – what system of education is ever universally successful? – and many no doubt fell disastrously short of the mark.[2] Nevertheless, there are notable examples of successful women educated in this tradition. George Eliot and Frances Power Cobbe made their mark on serious journalism while still in their twenties, and one cannot read their writings without coming to the conclusion that some women, at least, had acquired a broad background of knowledge and the ability to present a logical argument. Marjorie Theobald (ibid.: 39) has reached the same conclusion after reading the letters of some of the women who established ladies' schools in Australia.

Girls' education of this sort was by no means cut of from the main intellectual traditions of the day. Women in intellectual families had the benefit of contact with fathers and brothers who had been at the universities, and some of the schoolmistresses came themselves from such families. The novelist Elizabeth Sewell (1815-1906), who for many years ran a school on the Isle of Wight and wrote a number of articles and books on girls' education, had such a background (Todd 1991: 603). Furthermore, as girls grew older, much of their instruction came from 'masters' and these could be well-educated men or practising artists adding to their incomes in this way (Theobald 1996: 16; Young 1953: 90). Families belonging to the commercial elite as well as professionals employed such men for their daughters. Anne Mozley, the daughter of a printer in Derby and in her middle years a frequent contributor to the serious press of the 1860s and 1870s, was taught mathematics by a master who was a 'thinker . . . of the school of Dr. Erasmus Darwin (who founded a Philosophical Society in Derby)' (Mozley 1888: xv).

Masters were also much employed in teaching 'those graceful accomplishments proper to ladies' which would 'adorn the female character'. Though there was much criticism of the triviality of some of the activities defined as 'accomplishments' (readers of *Pride and Prejudice* will remember Mr Bingley's account of the young ladies who 'paint tables, cover skreens and net purses'), the term could also cover Miss Bingley's alternative definition of 'a thorough knowledge of music, singing, drawing, dancing and the modern languages' (Austen 1813: 41–2). Once again, many of the teachers of these arts were themselves professional artists and musicians supplementing their income in this way (*Fraser's* 1836: 311), and their most gifted pupils were in a position to become lady amateurs. By the late eighteenth century such women were sending paintings to the exhibitions of the Society of Artists, the Free Society and the Royal Academy and this continued into the early years of the nineteenth, with the demand for training being great enough by the 1840s for one of the major private arts schools, that run by James Mathews Leigh in Newman Street, London, to offer separate female classes (Burton 1949: 29; Butler 1868: 24; Greer 1979: 277-9, 283–91).

## Employment in the arts

The practice of the arts therefore became another of the contested borderlands which some believed were public and male, and others appropriate for women. The Angel in the House myth could be invoked to defend girls being trained in music and art as accomplishments which would allow them to embellish their homes and entertain their husbands, children and friends. Thus, there could be nothing intrinsically wrong with them since they could be practised within the home and advanced woman's mission of service to male relatives. Furthermore accomplished women in need of money could earn it by teaching these arts to others, teaching being *the* acceptable resource for women in this predicament. It was therefore only a small step to equating music and art with literature as a borderland which might be opened to women as well as men.

A significant outcome of this contestation, and partial victory for women artists, was the fact that when the state began to organize and subsidise art and music schools, women participated almost from the beginning. In 1837 a School of Design was established by the Board of Trade in Somerset House, and in 1842 a Female School of Design was added. When the Central Training School was set up in 1852 it also took female pupils as did most of the provincial Schools of Design (Brown 1912: 1–2; *Athenaeum* 1845: 550; 1846: 226, 227). The first secular music school, the Royal Academy of Music founded in 1822, began with the intention of taking half girls and half boys, and when other music colleges were founded women's participation seems to have been accepted as a matter of course (Sadie 1980 vol 11: 212).

Some of the women trained in these schools became teachers, and during the second half of the century the proportion of women doing this work increased, probably because they were, as always, prepared to undersell the men. The census figures for music teachers (art teachers were not listed separately) demonstrate this increase. The proportion of female music teachers rose from 24.3 per cent of the category in 1841 to 55.9 per cent in 1861, and though musicians and music teachers were recorded together thereafter, the female representation still rose from 31.4 per cent in 1861 to 51.5 per cent in 1911.

Women were also increasingly entering the fields of art and music as practitioners in their own right. In 1841 there were 264 female musicians returned in the census, rising to 1,618 in 1861 and from 7.3 per cent to 17.1 per cent of the number in the occupation in the same period. The number of women returned as occupied in painting, sculpture and engraving also increased. In 1851 women were 5 per cent of this category, 8.3 per cent in 1861, 9.2 per cent in 1871, 24.7 per cent in 1891, 26.5 per cent in 1901, and 26 per cent in 1911. They also began to figure significantly among the photographers, though mostly as tinters of photographs (Boucherett 1863: 29; Kaye 1857: 330; Warren 1865b: 86, 97), rising in numbers from 168 in the 1861 census to 1,301 in 1881, and from 6.6 per cent to 19.6 per cent of the total number in the occupation in the same period. Though women entering these fields may have encountered some male prejudice and jealousy (there seems to have been some opposition to the Female School of Design (Jameson 1843: 259)), the actual activities were already defined as both feminine and genteel. What was involved was not a radical change in 'knowledge', but a contest over their right to enter a new borderland.[3]

As with literature, women gradually began to take their place among professional artists. The examples of the two Thompson sisters (later Alice Meynell and Lady Butler) show that for women born in the 1840s art as well as literature had become available as a career. They were the daughters of a Cambridge graduate with private means and his wife, a former concert pianist. The career of the literary sister, Alice (1847-1922), followed a pattern well established for female authors. She gained praise for her first book of poems published in 1875, and in 1877 married a journalist and combined literature with marriage and maternity for the rest of her life, publishing a large body of poetry, essays and reviews (Meynell 1929). Her sister Elizabeth took advantage of the new availability of public art schools to undertake a parallel career as a painter. She began her art training in 1861 at the age of fifteen at the South Kensington art school. The next year she transferred to the school at Boston in Lincolnshire, where she won prizes each year. She returned to South Kensington in 1866 and continued working there until 1870, when she went abroad for further study. In 1874 her painting *Reading the Roll Call after a Battle in the Crimea* was exhibited at the Royal Academy and attracted such attention that *Queen* magazine referred to her as 'the artistic heroine of the day'. She married and had a number of children, but continued with her profession, painting battle pictures until the end of the 1920s (EWR 1874: 226; 1874: 293; Usherwood and Spencer-Smith 1987: 13–43, 69–73, 138–41).

## Governesses

It was women's claim to the borderland of enlightenment thought that was largely responsible for the form their education took, but it was the more general philanthropic pressure of the age which began the process which resulted in the transformation of the governess into the high school teacher. In 1841 a charity had been founded which became known as the Governesses' Benevolent Institution. Charitable societies aiming to help middle-class groups in difficulties were common at this period (Prochaska 1988: 38–9), and the Governesses' Benevolent Institution seems to have been the product of such an impulse to help indigent gentlefolk.

The Institution began with considerable panache at a public meeting chaired by the Duke of Cambridge, an uncle of the Queen, and after nine months had over 600 subscribers. The subscriptions seem to have been put to little use, however, until March 1843, when the Rev. David Laing became secretary. He first established a ladies' committee for 'offering assistance privately and delicately to ladies in temporary distress' (Parkes 1858: 2). Then a home was set up where governesses could stay between situations or while seeking new ones, a Provident Fund for their old age was established, a free registry office set up, and annuities were offered to governesses too old to work any longer (*James's* 1862: 502–3). The offer of annuities, as the case histories quoted in Chapter 1 show, revealed something of the extent of the problem of these elderly governesses, and it was the reports of the society which provided the information on which the articles on governesses in the serious reviews were based.

The public response to these revelations seems to have prompted David Laing to devise new and more radical initiatives for dealing with the problems of governesses. All the writers on this subject agreed that governesses were trapped by the overstocking of their profession. Those who could genuinely offer something superior were undercut by those who professed to offer the same thing for a lower price, and parents had no way of distinguishing between the genuine and the bogus. It was, wrote Sarah Lewis in 1848, 'the only profession which offers no premium to distinguished abilities' (*Fraser's* 1844: 583; Craik 1858: 46, 48; Lewis 1848: 412). Laing devised a scheme to address this problem.

At this date, the mid-1840s, the movement towards accreditation through examination was well-established in the older professions, and male teachers were taking some tentative steps in the direction shown by lawyers and doctors. In 1846 the College of Preceptors, which offered a qualifying examination to teachers without degrees, was established (Burstall 1933: 263; Lewis 1848: 413). A similar scheme was proposed by Laing to establish professional standards for governesses. The Institute would arrange for examiners to grant certificates of competence bearing the name of the Institute, and in this way provide some guarantee of ability to parents, and some grounds for asking for higher wages for governesses. Various professors from King's College, London, agreed to do the examining, but the standard proved to be so uniformly low that, as F. D. Maurice euphemistically put it, they discovered that 'to do any real good they must go further, they must fit the Governesses for their examination; they must provide an Education for Female Teachers' (Maurice 1848: 7).

As a beginning a series of lectures for governesses by certain King's College professors were arranged, and this attracted the attention of a Miss Murray, one of the Queen's ladies-in-waiting. She had collected a sum of money for the improvement of girls' education, and the lectures, which had been repeated during the day by popular request, seemed to her a possible answer to how this was to be done. She offered the funds she had collected to David Laing to found a college, not just for governesses, but for all women. The house next to the Governesses' Benevolent Institution in Harley Street was rented, the Queen agreed to allow her name to be used, and Queen's College opened in May 1848 (Kamm 1965: 173).

Though Miss Murray and David Laing were instrumental in the founding of this institution, the person who decided the form it should take and who became its first principal and its public apologist was F. D. Maurice. Maurice had at this time a high reputation as a theologian, and was soon to make his name in another sphere as one of the chief propagandists of the Christian Socialist movement. At this date, 1848, he was chaplain of Lincoln's Inn, but was soon to join the academic staff of King's College, London. He had grown up as the only boy in a family of forceful, argumentative girls. His interest in girls' education was shown as early as 1826 when, while still at Cambridge, he wrote what his biographer calls a 'ferocious attack upon the system of young ladies' education'. When their father lost his money, one of his sisters set up a school, and it was through her enthusiasm and interest that Maurice was drawn into the Governesses' Benevolent Institution (Maurice 1884 vol. 1: 66, 455–6).

The college, funded from two different sources, had to serve two functions: the training of governesses and the education of girls. Maurice argued plausibly (though perhaps, in the circumstances, somewhat disingenuously) for the identity of these two aims in a public address in 1848: the education of both must be the same because 'those who had no dream of entering upon such a work this year, might be forced by some reverse of fortune to think of it next year', and also because 'every lady is and must be a teacher – of some person or other, of children, sisters, the poor'. The main aim was not to instruct governesses in pedagogy, but in 'a real, grounded knowledge of that which is to be taught'. It was not wise to 'leave the impression upon our teacher's mind that we are chiefly concerned to put her in possession of a craft which she is to cultivate as if she were the member of a certain guild, and not as if she had interests in common with the rest of her sex' (Maurice 1848: 8–9). Another advantage of seeking a wider entrance was that the college

116

course could be offered free of charge to working governesses in the evenings, a policy which was carried out with much success (Grylls 1948: 17).

Maurice, when he planned the college, seems to have been guided by the philosophy of education developed by female writers during the preceding fifty years. Thus he did not take the boys' educational system as a model. Indeed, he saw the needs of boys and girls as essentially different (Maurice 1848: 10). The teaching was to be done by men, and Maurice, with his academic contacts, was able to produce lecturers of a very high calibre: the author Charles Kingsley was one, and most of the rest were on the staff of King's College. This system had, according to Maurice, two virtues. First, it did not interfere with home influences: the pupils would still receive 'all that is most precious in their experience and discipline, all their highest wisdom, at home'. Second, it was to reverse the emphasis on mindless repetition of facts which most of the education critics saw as a damning characteristic of girls' education. It was to be a college. 'The teachers of a School may aim merely to impart information; the teachers of a College must lead their pupils to the apprehension of principles.' (Maurice 1848: 10–11).

Propriety was upheld at the lectures by a group of lady visitors, one of whom sat in at each lecture. The list of ladies was impressive, among them Lady Stanley of Alderley, a name to be linked with most future educational ventures; Mrs Marcet, the well-known writer on political economy; Mrs Kay-Shuttleworth, wife of the civil servant who pioneered teacher training; and Lady Canning, wife of a distinguished politician. The lecturers undertook to examine their students and issue certificates of proficiency, and the college prospered. After three years it separated from the Governesses' Benevolent Institution, received a royal charter and became an independent establishment (Grylls 1948: 16).

Maurice's initial plan for the college was soon modified. The college took girls from twelve years old upwards, and it was found necessary to supplement the lectures, especially with the younger girls, with lessons by lady tutors, chosen from among the successful older students (Kamm 1965: 176-7). Maurice's early vision of the college as a place for purely intellectual education, leaving moral and emotional guidance to the home, was not fulfilled. In spite of its being a day school, a strong school spirit seems to have been encouraged by the lady tutors. One of these, Sophia Jex-Blake, who was later to lead a campaign for medical education for women, wrote to a pupil in 1861:

> I do not think it would be easy to over-estimate the importance of a high pure tone among the leading girls at such a place as Queen's – perhaps such as you and L. hardly know what a power lies in your hands, for the very life of the College, – and mayn't we look higher than that, and say our Master's work?
>
> (Todd 1918: 100, quoted)

Education at Queen's seems to have settled early into a form which was to set the pattern for girls' schools in the future, a form stressing high academic standards, hard work, and a 'pure tone'.

## The ladies' colleges

Almost from the beginning Queen's College had a rival, another ladies' college where the aims were not quite the same and the development took a different direction. This was Bedford College whose history was most thoroughly investigated by Margaret J. Tuke in the 1930s. The moving spirit here was Elizabeth Reid, a widow of considerable wealth, with intellectual interests and radical opinions (Tuke 1939: 8–9). In 1848, apparently unaware of what was going on at the Governesses' Benevolent Institute, she arranged a series of drawing-room lectures for ladies by professors from University College, London, and early in 1849 began to plan the establishment of a college (ibid.: 22–9). This college differed from Queen's in a number of ways. First, it was not intended to train governesses. Second, Elizabeth Reid wished women to have a much greater say in its running than was ever envisaged by Maurice and Laing. The lady visitors, a title copied from Queen's, had a ladies' committee of their own and representatives on the general committee which was to run the college (ibid.: 29–31). Third, Elizabeth Reid was a Unitarian, and so rather than looking to the Anglican King's College for lecturers, she looked to University College which was nondenominational. Her main helper in organizing the college was F. W. Newman, and he was so well known for his unorthodox views that the Principal of King's refused permission for any of his staff to lecture there, and Maurice refused to co-operate with Newman (ibid.: 64).

The college opened in October 1849, Elizabeth Reid having placed £1,500 in the hands of three trustees, in a rented house in Bedford Square, under the name of The Ladies' College, Bedford Square. To its founder's great disappointment fewer than a hundred women enrolled, compared with two hundred at Queen's at the same date. Of these, forty-two took only one course, and only twenty-six two or more courses. The ladies were in general not well prepared for study and gradually the more eminent lecturers dropped out. In 1853, in an attempt to provide better-prepared students, a day school for girls aged nine to fifteen was opened under a woman who had trained at Queen's, and by 1856 it had sixty pupils paying about £20 a year each, and was the most flourishing part of the institution (Tuke 1939: 83–5). However, when Elizabeth Reid died in 1866 she left a trust fund of £16,400 to the college and this was ultimately used by the women trustees to transform it into a university college preparing women for the degrees offered by London University.

Although Bedford College stayed truer to its original ideals, it remained a follower rather than an innovator in the higher education movement. It was

Queen's that had the long-term influence, for it was there that the model for the girls' secondary schools of the 1870s was developed. An article in the Women's Movement journal, the *Englishwoman's Review*, called 'Three Decades of Progress', listed it as the first achievement of the Woman's Movement (EWR 1878: 337). The full flowering of this influence was still twenty years in the future, but within ten years two ex-pupils of Queen's – Frances Mary Buss and Dorothea Beale – were offering this kind of education to girls geographically out of reach of Queen's. The term 'college' was used in both cases to indicate that a new kind of education was being offered.

Frances Buss (a professional teacher from the age of fourteen) was an early pupil of the college, attending the evening classes for governesses six nights a week in 1849. In 1850, at the age of twenty-three, she set up a private school on Queen's College lines and called it the North London Collegiate School. (Queen's was in Central London.) It too made use of male lecturers, though they were not as distinguished as those at Queen's, her father and brother being two, and the Rev. David Laing another. In 1870 the school ceased to be Frances Buss's private property. She handed it over to a trust, and it thus became a public school, though she continued as headmistress (Burstall 1938: 37–9; Kamm 1958: 18–21, 41–50).

Another early attempt to follow the Queen's College example was Cheltenham Ladies College. It was founded in Cheltenham, a major educational centre at that date, in 1854 by the local HM Inspector of Schools, the Principal and Vice-Principal of the twelve-year-old Cheltenham Boys' College, and three others. It was a proprietary school – that is, its initial capital was raised by selling one hundred £10 shares which gave their owners some say in the running of the school – and the first girls' school to be established in this way. The first principals, Mrs. and Miss Procter, faced a number of difficulties and in 1858 the gossip and criticism in the town led them to resign (Clarke 1953: 22–38). The new appointment was Dorothea Beale, who had been a student, a tutor and lady principal at Queen's. She had left Queen's after becoming dissatisfied with the limited authority allowed to the women tutors, and with the failure to set up an entrance standard. Under her, Cheltenham Ladies College flourished (Kamm 1958: 51–64; Percival 1939: 130).

A number of other schools on the 'college' model were established during this period, but these four schools were the ones representing the new direction in girls' education to the public mind.[4] In 1872, for example, the Registrar of London University made reference to 'the few good public institutions at present in existence, as, for instance, the Ladies College at Cheltenham, the Harley Street and Bedford Square Colleges and the North London Collegiate School' (EWR 1872: 274).

The two newer schools catered for rather different segments of the population. Cheltenham Ladies College was resolved by its founders to be 'for the daughters and young children of Noblemen and Gentlemen'. Tradesmen's children were excluded and a breakdown of fathers' occupations made by Dorothea Beale in 1865 revealed that 27 per cent were daughters of private gentlemen 28 per cent of army and navy officers, 20 per cent of clergymen, 18 per cent of civil servants, doctors and lawyers, and 7 per cent of bankers, merchants, manufacturers and surveyors (Beale 1865: 275; Clarke 1953: 26). Frances Buss's school, on the other hand, served a much less affluent group, her school being open to the daughters of 'Professional Gentlemen of limited means, clerks in public and private offices and persons engaged in Trade and other pursuits', and in the 1860s the girls' fathers included as well as lawyers, doctors and clergymen, a zinc worker, a fish salesman, a linen draper, a cheese factor, and a pianoforte tuner (Kamm 1958: 47).

The chief features of the 'college system' of girls' education as it had developed by the 1860s were defined by Dorothea Beale to the Social Science Congress in 1865. A college was a day school for girls with its internal administration 'strictly under female management', though with highly qualified male lecturers; the governing council of the school had no pecuniary interest in it; any girls living away from home lived in boarding houses run by ladies who were not members of the teaching staff (Beale 1865: 277–8). Frances Buss's school shared another aim with Queen's College which Cheltenham Ladies College, given its particular clientele, was not at this stage prepared to consider. It was devoted to training girls for employment, presumably during these early years, as governesses (Burstall 1938: 47). This was, as Chapter 10 will argue, to have long term implications for the general employment of middle-class women.

Thus it is apparent that Queen's College had succeeded in one of its aims: it had provided an institutional base for girls' education which focussed on the rational component stressed by the female educational writers. However, offering such an education had not been the only aim of Queen's College. The other intention of its founders had been to raise the professional status of governesses. Yet not only had Queen's College turned itself into a school, it had spawned others. The *Athenaeum* pointed out as early as 1849:

> Now, do the promoters of these various – and intrinsically excellent – schemes not see that there is a contradiction between them? Do they not see that the Queen's College fits the governess for the business of education – and the Ladies' Colleges take away her pupils? The development of the very institution which took charge of this long-suffering class as a profession, ends by taking the profession out of their hands.
>
> (*Athenaeum* 1849: 436)

Though some governesses, armed with Queen's College certificates, may have found their way into the employment of families where such qualifications were valued, the general status and situation of governesses does not seem to have improved. One woman who had been concerned for over twenty years with the question of women's employment wrote in 1884 that the number of applicants for pensions to the Governesses' Benevolent Institution was still very high. She put their troubles down to the fact that 'the excellent day-schools which have been established in London and other great towns have almost put an end to the occupation of the daily governess, and have greatly diminished the demand for resident governesses' (Boucherett 1884: 105).

The writer in the *Athenaeum* in 1849 expressed a second fear, still being echoed ten years later (Parkes 1859b: 223), that men would oust women from girls' education, but this did not happen. As more women trained in the ladies'-college tradition became available as teachers, the male lecturers, so much more expensive and so much less flexible, tended to become, except at Queen's College itself, a once or twice weekly treat for the more advanced pupils, while the daily work was supervised by female form mistresses. Maurice's insistence that girls should receive 'all that is most precious in their experience and discipline, all their highest wisdom, at home', had the consequence of defining the ladies' college primarily as a day school, with schools which took boarders arranging that non-teachers should offer this facility away from the main school building (Beale 1865: 277–8).

Frances Buss insisted that the general care and supervision that had been part of the work of the governess and private schoolmistress was not the business of the college teacher: 'The *schoolmistress should be free to devote her best energies to the school*, unshackled by the care of the children out of school. Being less jaded and careworn, she would have greater sympathy with her pupils.' If girls boarded in houses for twenty to forty, quite separate from the school, they would receive 'all the good of a large day-school, with some of the advantages of a loving home' (Buss 1871: 11–12). Thus Maurice's concern with leaving the moral care of girls to the home had the unintended consequence of constructing the female high school teacher as a free wage labourer, with fixed hours of work, and paid a salary which was intended to cover the cost of her living expenses.

These women, though never highly paid, achieved an independence, a dignity and a sense of professionalism far beyond that of the governess (Pederson 1977). Therefore, though Queen's College did not manage to raise the status of the governess, it quite unintentionally transformed that of an even more lowly branch of teaching, the undermistress at the girls' school. Though the certifying of governesses did not fulfil the high hopes of its initiators, the unpremeditated step of appointing lady tutors at Queen's, an *ad hoc* measure intended only to cope with the temporary difficulty of under-prepared students, had far-reaching consequences. Professionalism in teaching developed not among the governesses, but in the teachers in the new sort of girls' school, and it was for this type of school that Queen's College, again without any prior intention, was both the starting point and the inspiration.

The impact of the religious heterodoxy on girls' education in the period before 1870 contributed only marginally to solving the problem of over-stocking in teaching and dressmaking. It did, however, lay the foundation for and determine the form of significant changes in the future. In particular, it established conditions that made it possible to bring the conditions of women teaching middle-class adolescents closer to those of men. First, female teachers outside the state-funded elementary school system began to be incorporated into the movement for training and accreditation that was taking place in the male profession. Not only did they have access to the new art and music schools, the idea of certificates for governesses had its gentil-ity and femininity endorsed by the prestige of Queen's College with its royal patron. Without this endorsement, the initiatives of the College of Preceptors might have made accreditation seem unfeminine, while its emphasis in the preparation of elementary school teachers could have made training seem working class. Secondly, the well-publicised founding of at least a few public schools for girls during the period of the great expansion of such schools for boys, ensured that it never became part of middle-class 'knowledge' that education in a large public school was incompatible with feminine modesty, and so for boys only.

Thus when the big expansion of girls' schools occurred in the 1870s, the acceptability of such schools had already been established, as well as that their teachers should ideally be trained and certificated. The foundation for a new form of teaching had been laid, that shared with the elementary school teacher the security of work as a free wage labourer for a public institution, and yet retained the lady-like status of the governess.

# 7

# TRANSFORMING NURSING

## Female philanthropy
## and the middle class nurse

Between 1851 and 1891 there was a substantial change in both the numbers and the age group of the women in nursing, a change not unlike that in elementary school teaching in the 1830s: the occupation was converted from one filled largely by elderly widows without training to one for young, educated, unmarried women. In 1851 25,775 nurses and midwives were recorded in the census, 0.5 per cent of all women over twenty years old. In 1891 the number had more than doubled, having risen to 53,057, 0.6 per cent of women over twenty. The number aged under thirty-five had changed even more rising from 2,312 in 1851 to 15,650 in 1891, with those in this age group rising from 8 per cent of all nurses to 30 per cent. Table 7.1 sets out the increase in numbers of women in this younger age group, while Figure 7.1 shows the change in age distribution.

As can be seen, the turning point came in the 1880s, and this coincided with a large increase in the provision of hospital accommodation. The number of hospitals (excluding workhouse infirmaries) rose from 346 in 1871 to 691 in 1881, and 1012 in 1891, while the number of hospital beds rose from 6,658 in 1861 to 27,322 in 1891 (Maggs 1983: 7).

## Explanations

It has been usual to attribute the increase in the number of nurses and the change in age, to a crying need to reform the hospitals of the period. In the latter part of the century, discussions of nursing were full of descriptions of the parlous state of hospital nursing before the Nightingale revolution, and the change in the status of nursing was seen as a direct outcome of this situation. As with the changes in girls education, historians have tended to repeat the original analysis (Abel-Smith 1960: 5–10; Nutting and Dock 1907: 176–81; Seymer 1957: 67–71), though more recently there has been

*Table 7.1*: Numbers of nurses and midwives aged under 35 returned by the census, 1851–1911

|  | 1851 | 1861 | 1871 | 1881 | 1891 | 1901 | 1911 |
|---|---|---|---|---|---|---|---|
| *Nurses* | 2,231 | 1,691 | 2,418 | —* | —** | 25,737 | 34,019 |
| *Midwives* | 81 | 59 | 130 | 105 | — | 302 | 1 976 |
| *Total* | 2,312 | 1,750 | 2,548 |  | 15,650 | 26,039 | 35,995 |

\* No separate return for Nurses
\*\* Nurses and Midwives returned together

a tendency to note that the real increases did not follow the Nightingale inter-vention of the 1860s, but came with the expansion and reform of the hospital system in the 1880s (Maggs 1983: 6–11). Monica Baly wrote in 1980:

> Although the nineteenth century nursing reforms are rightly associated with Miss Nightingale, the circumstances produced the leader and the time was ripe. Towards the end of the century a number of factors came together to give the concept of 'trained nursing' an impetus undreamt of by mid-century reformers.
>
> (Baly 1980: 131)

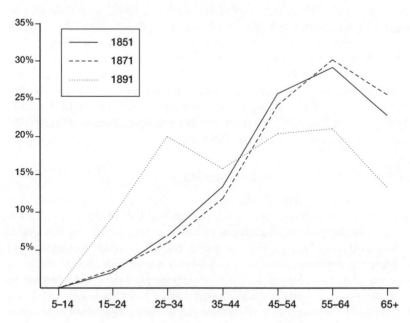

*Figure 7.1* Percentage of nurses and midwives in various age groups as shown in the censuses of 1851, 1871 and 1891.

124

Changes in medical knowledge and practice had by the 1880s, it is argued, created a need for nurses capable of understanding and carrying out the doctors' 'orders' and reporting on the patient's condition in terms which were part of the medical discourse (Abel-Smith 1964: 66; Baly 1980: 131; Summers 1988: 15–16).

Nevertheless, these historians have not assumed that these structural changes made the resulting age and class of nurses inevitable. Baly has invoked the 'redundant women' explanation to suggest that the emergence of this particular workforce was contingent, arguing that 'the change in the population profile' after 1870, late marriage, a falling birthrate and male emigration, created a large group of spinsters seeking work away from home (Baly 1980: 132), while Brian Abel-Smith has laid the emphasis on the 'going mad for want of something to do' motivation, long attributed to Florence Nightingale: 'The movement for nursing reform arose out of the recognition of the importance of bedside care, which was the result of wider medical knowledge and more intensive treatments. But it took the form it did because nursing was able to provide an outlet for the social conscience and frustrated energies of the Victorian spinster.' (Abel-Smith 1964: 66) This chapter will examine in more detail the contingencies which led to the 'pull' from the hospitals for trained nurses in the 1880s being increasingly satisfied by young, unmarried, middle-class women.

Hospital nursing as it developed in the second half of the century was, like elementary school-teaching and work as a shop assistant, a labour intensive area where the employment of young middle-class women had the inestimable benefit of providing a cheap, educated, docile workforce, and where retirement at marriage obviated the need to create a 'synthetic turnover' to keep wages down and reduced discontent at the lack of promotion opportunities. However, it was not, at mid-century, one which conformed to the definitions of gentility and femininity which the parents of young middle-class women (upper or lower) demanded of an occupation for their daughters. Thus it was not one where employers' 'knowledge' of the available workforce led them automatically to regard these women as the group to which to turn. As Monica Baly has pointed out, there had been an earlier expansion in the hospitals at the beginning of the century as the hospitals were transformed from charitable institutions where the sick and dying were given shelter, to places where future medical practitioners learned their trade. This had not, however, led to the creation of trained, professional nurses. She writes:

> But with 200 students watching an operation and jostling for a place on the wards, what need of nurses? Medical students put on bandages, made poultices and made the beds and in fact spent much of their time in nursing. No one had yet asked the question, 'What is the proper task of a nurse?' . . . [J]obs were done, as they had been done down the ages, by the person on hand to do them. In this situation it was hardly necessary to recruit, or indeed train, nurses.
>
> (Baly 1980: 60)

All the medical aspects of nursing were carried out by men, either students, or the doctors' 'dressers'. Women were employed in hospitals for the purely housewifely tasks of cooking and cleaning, and, if necessary, feeding and cleaning up the patients, and these nurses came from the social stratum that provided charwomen (Abel-Smith 1960: 5–10). The main innovation as far as women was concerned was the introduction of 'sisters'. Baly writes:

> As more patients were admitted for treatment rather than custodial care, the doctors began to look for more trustworthy people to supervise nurses, and some hospitals recruited 'sisters' who were not promoted nurses but persons chosen from a higher status in society, perhaps widows in reduced circumstances or housekeepers from aristocratic families, and the records show instances of sisters teaching the medical students from their observation and experience.
>
> (Baly 1980: 61)

Yet when the next big expansion of hospitals came, in the 1880s, the hospitals routinely recruited young unmarried women to perform the tasks previously undertaken by dressers, students and charwomen. What had changed? Why did the new hospitals and workhouse infirmaries recruit young women, and why were the women and their parents happy for them to be employed in this way? The answer proposed here is that there was a very real change in 'knowledge' of hospital nursing in the 1860s, and that this change was brought about by the perception (rather than the reality) of what Florence Nightingale achieved in the Crimea, that as a result of her expedition, hospital nursing became a 'borderland' (in this case between the classes rather than the sexes) that middle-class women were seeking to enter and transform. It is further argued that their right to enter this 'borderland' was justified within the discursive framework provided by the religious heterodoxy, and made possible by the efforts that had already been made, informed by its logic, to improve the quality of home nursing available to the middle class. Thus when, in the 1880s, hospitals were seeking to expand their staff, and doctors were seeking a new kind of nursing support, it had already become accepted that young women could work in hospitals without jeopardizing their gentility or their femininity, and hospital authorities, their 'knowledge' also modified by this process, turned willingly to this source of cheap, dedicated, docile labour.

## The nursing sisterhoods

Since the 1860s most accounts of what hospital nursing was like before the watershed of Florence Nightingale's Crimean expedition refer at some point to Dickens's portrayal of Sairey Gamp in *Martin Chuzzlewit* (1844). However this was not a picture of a hospital nurse but of one of the multitude of women who were available for hire to nurse the sick in their own homes. Furthermore, as was the case with the girls' schools, the picture of hospital nursing that has passed into the historiography of the profession tends to be that provided by the apologists for the new system. As Monica Baly says:

> Before any firm conclusions are reached about the quality of the nursing *within the light of its own time*, a good deal more detailed research is needed, and this might well, to paraphrase Edward Thompson, rescue pre-Nightingale nursing 'from the enormous condescension of history'.
>
> (Baly 1980: 61)

In fact, I have found only one criticism of hospital nursing that dates from before the Crimean war in the printed literature, and none in the archives of the nursing sisterhoods.[1]

The middle-class entry into the field of nursing training and service came as part of the wider movement of such women into philanthropy. Visiting the poor had always involved a particular obligation to the sick and dying, and nursing the sick was seen as providing an opportunity for religious influence that ought not to be wasted, since the right word at the right time could lead a dying soul to salvation (Stanley 1854: 1–3; Summers 1990: 127). Furthermore, many district visitors had had experience in nursing within their own families, and some gave practical help with feeding, lifting and dressing wounds, as well as providing advice, linen and invalid delicacies (Trimmer 1787: 99–103). It was not, however, the experiences of district visitors that began the movement for training nurses, but the increasing involvement of women with establishing and administering subscription charities. The movement was initially a 'mission' aimed at helping their own class rather than the poor.

In June 1840 an organisation was established called the Protestant Sisters of Charity, a name changed within a year to the Institution of Nursing Sisters. Mention of this organisation turns up in most standard histories of nursing as an organisation founded by Elizabeth Fry after she paid a visit to the famous deaconesses institute at Kaiserswerth in Prussia. All these accounts are, however, based on a brief narrative in the *Memoir* of their mother written by Elizabeth Fry's daughters, and on a few scathing remarks made by contemporaries who were part of the post-1856 nursing movement (Nutting and Dock 1907: 73–6). Substantial records of this organization did, however, survive, unconsulted, and have recently been catalogued by the Wellcome Institute and made available to scholars. These make it clear that the Institution was an agency for providing women whose characters could be vouched for to nurse in the homes of those who could afford to pay £10 a quarter to the Institution for their services.[2]

The 'sisters' were employed by the Institution. They were interviewed by a Committee member, sent to one of the London hospitals to gain a couple of months' experience of a range of cases, and then employed at a salary beginning at £20 a year and rising to £23. When they were not out on a case (where they were expected to live in the house of their patient) they could stay at the Nurses' Home. The clothes they were to wear while at work or staying at the Home were provided by the Institution (QNIA/W.1/6). After twelve years' service, if they retired because of age or illness (but not for marriage), they were entitled to receive an income from the Institution's superannuation fund. The main administrative work of receiving applications, sending out the nurses, and receiving the sealed reports on their work from the families of their patients was done by a salaried Superintendent who lived permanently at the Home. The income of the Institution rose from about £400 in 1841 to £4,000 in 1860 by which time the number of nurses employed had risen to more than 80 (QNIA/W.2/1, W.2/4; Howson 1862: 130).

Little information exists on the age and background of these nurses, except for the year 1848 when the current secretary recorded details of applicants in the Minutes (QNIA/W.2/3). The ages of the twenty women interviewed ranged from thirty to forty-eight (which was considered almost too old). Six had already been working as nurses in London Hospitals. Of those whose marital status was recorded, eight were single, six were widows, and one was a married woman with a 'deranged' husband and no children. The information on social background is even scantier. The fathers of three of the single women (aged thirty-four, thirty-three and thirty) were recorded as a Baptist minister, a tailor and a draper, while another sister (aged forty-one) was described as the widow of a tradesman, which suggests that they were attracting mature women of lower-middle-class background.

The Committee was composed of well-to-do upper-middle-class women who were prepared to give up an afternoon a fortnight to the work, with further service in interviewing prospective employees, chasing up their references, and acting on the sub-committees that dealt with the superintendent of the Home, the hospitals and the dress of the sisters. The committee began with a number of Gurneys and Frys (some single, some married) among its members, and one (Mrs Samuel Gurney) was still there in 1860, as was another original member, Miss N. Wilson. By this date, however, the leading figure was Lady Inglis, presumably the wife of the MP for Oxford University. None of these women had any intention of nursing the sick themselves, nor do they seem to have regarded themselves as 'training' the nurses. The expertise they offered was that of estimating 'character' (a skill no doubt honed through years of appointing and managing domestic servants (Summers 1988: 22)) and of running a large charitable organisation efficiently. While they seem to have had some failures in the first – appointing nurses who wore crinolines, drank in public houses, were rude to the relatives of their patients, wanted to have friends visit them at the Home – in the second they were eminently successful, since the Institution continued to operate without any hint of mismanagement or scandal until 1921 (QNIA/SA/QNI/V.9).

There were, however, other ventures into nursing where the 'ladies' were more directly involved with both nurses and patients. These efforts, also, were part of the general female involvement in philanthropy, and were the outcome of a belief that there were huge areas of the country which their mission to the poor did not reach. In 1848, the High Anglican leader Pusey wrote:

> It is a misery of our modern towns that rich and poor are locally separate, and the rich think that there is no poverty to relieve because they do not see it; and they do not see it because they do not look for it; they go from their villas to their counting houses along fair streets, and think nothing of the misery that lurks behind.
>
> (Allchin 1958: 118 quoted)

The problems this caused became a theme continued for many years by other commentators (Howson 1860: 349; Kaye 1857: 302; Phillips 1861: 139–40). The solution proposed by Pusey, and already in operation when he wrote these words, was the establishment of Anglican orders of nuns. By living together ladies could live amongst these poor, and carry out the kind of work performed by women in country parishes where rich and poor lived closer together. The proposal to extend 'woman's mission' in this way drew the support of a number of high church laymen, W. E. Gladstone, Lord John Manners and T. D. Acland among others. These laymen took an interest primarily because they envisaged the nuns doing useful work among the poor, but the High Church clergy who first raised the idea in the *British Critic* were drawn to the idea for additional reasons. They were increasingly convinced of the spiritual importance of celibacy and of the life vowed wholly to the church, and they also saw such a life as an answer to the problem of single women looking for a purpose in life (Liddon 1893 vol. 3: 13, 3–5). Pusey began putting the case for sisterhoods in these terms in 1839:

> I think them desirable (1) in themselves as belonging to and fostering a high tone in the Church, (2) as giving a holy employment to many who yearn for something, (3) as directing zeal, which will otherwise often go off in some irregular way, or go over to Rome. The romanists are making great use of them to entice over our people; and I fear we may lose those whom one can least spare; but this is secondary. I think the other two primary, and that they are calculated to draw a blessing upon the Church in which they are found, as the Fathers always speak of the virgins.
>
> (Liddon 1893 vol. 3: 6)

The first Anglican sisterhood was established in 1845, and by 1854 there were four others (Hill 1973: 143; Trench 1884). Their charitable enterprises were diverse: the Sisters of Mercy at Devonport (founded 1848) had by 1852 established ten institutions ranging in scope from a soup kitchen, through ragged schools and retirement and orphan homes, to industrial schools with associated lodgings, costing altogether about £100 a week to run (Exeter 1852: 12–17), while the Clewer Sisterhood (founded 1849) was concerned almost exclusively with offering prostitutes a chance to change their way of life (Mumm 1996). Nursing does not seem to have played a major part in their activities, being integrated with their visiting of the poor. The Devonport Sisters did, however, gain great credit during the cholera epidemics of 1849 and 1853 for their work in setting up special wards for sufferers (Williams 1965: 44–55, 248–53), and the All Saints Sisterhood (founded 1851) established a home for incurable women and children in Mortimer Street in London (Holloway 1959: 146).

Though the numbers of ladies who joined these sisterhoods was very small (in 1852 the Devonport community consisted only of the Superior, five professed sisters and five novices), they attracted considerable public attention and quite virulent attacks from the more evangelical wing of the Church of England. Strong exception was taken to the 'popish' stress on celibacy and life-long vows, and to the fact that the 'obedience' demanded by these vows seemed to be to the Superior rather than to some patriarchal figure like a chaplain or a parish clergyman. Increasing reference was made to the practices of the famous Deaconess order at Kaiserswerth as offering a more 'protestant' alternative (Hill 1973: 181–3; Howson 1860: 360–3).

In 1848 a plan was devised among a group of doctors and clergy to establish an institution which would offer some of the benefits of the sisterhood free from the 'Romish' elements that marked the earlier foundations, and which would not require vows from the sisters, but would enable them to perform valuable charitable work of the kind it was increasingly believed only ladies could perform. The plan was to provide a residential base from which ladies (to be called 'Sisters') could visit the poor, and nurses could be sent out to private families, as was done by the Institution of Nursing Sisters, these nurses being available when not out on a case to nurse in the homes of the poor visited by the Sisters. The name decided on was the Training Institution for Nurses, for Hospitals, Families and the Poor and substantial records of the organisation survive and have been housed since the 1960s in the London Metropolitan Archives.

Minutes of the original meetings that preceded the actual foundation exist, and show that this was a prolonged process, with many leading philanthropists (including F. D. Maurice) attending from time to time. Even before the formal meeting in June 1848 which established the institution, a salaried clergyman, who later became the Master, had been appointed to keep the minutes. On 14 August 1848 the Council asked Miss Elizabeth Frere, whose widowed father had emerged as a leading figure on the Council, to act as the first Lady Superintendent, and a house in Fitzroy Square was taken as the Home on 24 January 1849.[3] Thereafter the nature of the institution was very much coloured by her views of what was suitable and workable. Her letters to the Council show that she consulted with both the Institution of Nursing Sisters and Whitelands Training College on their experiences, but St John's House, named after the parish in which it was situated, was very much her own creation, and the creation of the Lady Superintendents who followed her.

The administration was divided between a Lady Superintendent and a Master. The Master, a clergymen, was decisively, and with the full concurrence of the Lady Superintendent, given a patriarchal role in the establishment. There seems to have been an early suggestion that the Lady Superintendent should be directly responsible to the Council, but Elizabeth Frere rejected this firmly before the institution opened in a letter dated 1 February 1849:

As far as I can judge by my own feelings and by what I know of those of others it seems to me very unlikely that any lady will be found with a sense of the arduous and responsible nature of the duties attaching to the direction of our Institution, such as would fit her to take a lead in its affairs, who would be willing to take the office if deprived of the assistance to be derived from the constant supervision of the Master, the opportunity of referring difficult cases to him and having the weight of his authority always, in support of her own. Some such guide & counsellor every woman placed in such a position would require whatever her gifts & capabilities might be; and if no such coadjutor is supplied her, she will be obliged to find one for herself.

It would seem essential to good order that where two are jointly placed in authority over others, one should be head and principal. And when one of the two is a man and the other a woman the spirit of St Paul's injunctions that the woman should *not teach* – should *not usurp authority* – should *be in silence* – would seem to require that she should hold the second, rather than the first place, especially when, as in the present case, the religious education & training of the community is the main object for which it has been formed and on this account a clergyman has the superintendence of it.

Whatever honor may be shewn to her still it will be 'as to the weaker vessel' & I think it ought so to be, and that if she is wise she will not consent to accept *supreme* authority.

(HI/ST/SJ/A19/1)

The 1850 rules (revised after considerable prompting from the Lady

131

Superintendent who followed Miss Frere) stated that the Master's 'authority shall be supreme in all matters of discipline, and he shall have power to suspend from the exercise of their respective functions any probationer, Nurse, or Sister, until the Council shall have decided upon the case' and that the Lady Superintendent 'is to defer to the Master in all matters of discipline' (HI/ST/SJ/A10/1-9). In practice, judging by the detailed diaries, minutes and reports that have survived, the Master's main activities were holding twice daily services in the House, acting as buffer between the Lady Superintendent and the all-male Council, serving as secretary to the Council, and keeping records of the finances of the institution.

The Lady Superintendent's role was to oversee and have day-to-day contact with the sisters, probationers and nurses, and with the families where the nurses were employed. It was also her function to act as mistress of the house, supervising the servants, and determining the spending on food and washing. The Sisters were to be ladies of means, paying £50 a year board, and spending their time helping the Lady Superintendent in administering the nursing agency and in visiting the poor of the parish. There was no suggestion that they should undertake any nursing themselves except among the poor, where they could call on the nurses staying at the House between cases to do the main work. There was to be constant contact between the 'ladies' and the nurses, with all members in the House eating and attending prayers together, and it seems to have been expected that these were 'privileges' which would attract the kind of religious women they felt would make suitable nurses.

The Council's original intention had been to ask probationers to pay for their training, but Elizabeth Frere's experience suggested a different plan which she outlined in her Report of May 21, 1849:

> But this subject deserves consideration on other & more important grounds, since it is from the class of probationers that the most essential advantages contemplated in our undertaking are to be derived; and I would beg leave with great deference to state my opinion that if the Council should think proper to waive the fee now required by our Rules, we are not only more likely thereby to encourage candidates to come forward, but also to obtain persons of a better class and to ensure to ourselves more freedoms in making choices of those best suited for our purpose & also shall be less liable to after-trouble in the management of young persons thus placed by their friends unreservedly & confidently in our hands; those who have made a payment will be always considering whether they are receiving a proper equivalent. No one has at present been proposed as a Probationer on the terms stated in the Rules, and all with whom I have consulted say that those who might be willing either have not the means of paying, or having those means, prefer putting their

children to some already known and tried employment as dressmaker, schoolmistress, etc. etc.

(HI/ST/SJ/A19/1)

The system she devised during her months as Lady Superintendent proved workable, and stayed in force until the House changed the focus of its work in 1856. Probationers, the 1850 rules stated, 'must be twenty-five years of age, or upwards, and of habits or attainments such as may justify an expectation of their becoming qualified Nurses after a probation of about six months'. They were required to produce certificates showing that they were baptised members of the Church of England. The nursing training they received was similar to that given by the Institution of Nursing Sisters, spending time in the wards of one of the teaching hospitals, but this was supplemented by the spiritual benefits it was felt they would gain by six months spent living with the Sisters and in daily contact with the Master.

The nurses at St John's House earned less than those at the Institution of Nursing Sisters, beginning at £10.10s, and rising annually until £20 was reached in the fifth year. They did, however, receive an additional 5s. for each month spent out on a case. The House began with a group of nurses who were regarded as experienced enough to go out on cases immediately, but by the end of a few years was relying almost entirely on women who had come to them as probationers. The target of having twenty nurses and six probationers at any one time seems to have been generally met.

If the plan for attracting nurses went relatively smoothly, things were not so easy with the ladies. Elizabeth Frere saw her main occupation as acting as mistress and hostess in her father's house, and expected to hand on the position to one of the ladies who joined the House. This she accomplished in August 1849 when Mrs Elspeth Morrice, who had joined as a Sister in May 1849, took her place. Details about Mrs Morrice are scanty. In the 1851 census she is listed as a widow, aged sixty-five, and born in Scotland. She must have been a woman of some means, because in March 1852, for example, she contributed £45 towards the cost of the removal to a new location, and in November of the same year, when it was discovered that the Master had misappropriated some of the funds, offered the Council an interest-free loan of £100 (HI/ST/SJ/A2/1).

The number of Sisters remained disappointingly small. Between 1849 and 1853 only four women took the step of actually becoming resident Sisters, and of these only two stayed for any length of time. Both of these women and the Lady Superintendent were ill and absent on a number of occasions, and their places had to be filled temporarily by non-resident Associates of the House. In July 1853 Mr Frere announced that he was withdrawing his subscription because the Lady Superintendent was discouraging the admission of Sisters. A committee investigated this accusation, and came to the conclusion that it had no basis, and that the main disincentive was the high charges (£50 p.a.) made, with the lack of a strict rule like a convent a possibly subsidiary factor.

Nevertheless Elspeth Morrice resigned in the next month, having served four years as Lady Superintendent. Her place was taken, not by a lady who could afford to pay £50 a year, but by Miss Mary Jones who had joined the House as a paid housekeeper and whom the Council had at first refused to recognize as a Sister. Her initial appointment was temporary, but on 14 November 1853 the Council unanimously elected her Lady Superintendent, and in the following February passed this resolution: 'That the council beg leave to express their sense of the value of the services of *Miss Jones* to the Institution; request her acceptance of a *gratuity* of £20.' The House was thus headed by two paid officers, a Lady Superintendent and a Master, at the period when Florence Nightingale's Crimean expedition caused a shift in public interest from home to hospital nursing and a consequent reassessment of its own aims by St John's House.

## The Nightingale effect

The 'truth' about Florence Nightingale's life and contribution to the development of hospital nursing has been a matter for challenge and debate for most of this century. The material in Cook's circumspect 1913 biography which preserved the legend of her selfless dedication to the reform of hospital nursing was quickly reinterpreted by Lytton Strachey to present her as another hypocritical, domineering, manipulative Victorian. The 'heroic' portrait was, however, revived in the years that followed, most notably in Cecil Woodham-Smith's 1950 biography, only to be challenged again in the 1980s. It is now generally accepted that Florence Nightingale's interpretation of events was often, in F. B. Smith's words, 'outright mendacity and calculated pleading' (Smith 1982: 175), and that the picture of her work that had, up to that time, been based largely on her correspondence, must be checked against other records. Accounts of her achievements based on such records have now been produced by F. B. Smith, Monica Baly and Anne Summers, and a more balanced picture of her place in nursing history has emerged.

While it is generally accepted that her intervention had a profound and irreversible impact on hospital administration, particularly in the army, it seems that nurse training was not a major concern of hers, and she was drawn into it as much by public expectations as her own wish (Baly 1988: 7–13; Smith 1982: 156). F. B. Smith has further argued that the form finally taken by nursing owed as much to the practices of St John's House as to methods she had pioneered, and that her published views were largely based on experiences recounted to her by the women regarded as her disciples (Smith 1982: 155). It will be argued here, however, that these women would not have seen hospital nursing as their field of endeavour without her example, and that the form they gave it was based on their interpretation of what she had achieved at Scutari. As Monica Baly writes: 'In history what people think is happening is often as important as what actually happened' (Baly 1987: 44).

The events of Florence Nightingale's life are well known, and it is not these but the conventional reading of her character and achievement that has been challenged by recent historians. The picture that has emerged is of a difficult, intense, religious girl who grew up into an ambitious, dissatisfied woman alternately charming, manipulating and rejecting her family and friends. She was, as has long been recognized, an extreme example of the woman (in this case upper class rather than upper middle class) who felt herself trapped and tortured by the prevailing definitions of femininity, gentility and woman's duty to her family. It would seem that she sought solace in the two borderlands opened by the religious heterodoxy, philanthropy and intellectual interests, and that in both cases her work had a single focus: ill-health.

She engaged, from girlhood on, in sporadic practical nursing among the village poor, and on the other read avidly the increasing flood of government publications on the subject of public health – this was the period of the sanitary reform movement associated with names like Edwin Chadwick and Southwood Smith – in the process developing some skill at interpreting and manipulating statistics (M.M.H. 1858; Woodham-Smith 1950: 61, 74). She also made time during her visits abroad with her family to visit the local institutions for caring for the sick, and finally, in 1851, spent some weeks at Kaiserswerth. Here, it appears from her later comments, she realized that there was a difference between the vision of nursing as a spiritual mission propagated there, and her increasing scientific concern with the origins, prevention and cure of disease (Baly 1980: 117; Smith 1982: 21). In 1853 she made up her mind to move away from her family and take a 'post' in some managerial capacity in a hospital, and was invited by the ladies' committee (headed by Lady Canning and including the Lady Inglis who chaired the Committee of the Institution of Nursing Sisters) of an Institution for the Care of Sick Gentlewomen in Distressed Circumstances in Harley Street, London, to manage the reorganized hospital (Smith 1982: 11; Woodham-Smith 1950: 110, 119).

Her work was not, F. B. Smith's researches have revealed, the triumph usually claimed. She managed to charm and manipulate the ladies' committee, but could not build up an effective staff, and there was considerable turnover of nurses, servants, and even the tradesmen patronized. The hospital's expenses increased under her, and yet it was seldom more than one-third full (Smith 1982: 11–17). In August 1854 she gave notice, claiming she had done all that was possible and began to look around for other work (ibid.: 15-16). By October 1854, her next step was settled. In the summer the French and British armies attacked the Russians at Sebastopol, and by the autumn the papers carried accounts of the poor conditions provided for the wounded, with the *Times* asking why there were no British Sisters of Charity to do the nursing. Florence Nightingale was one of a number of men and women who approached the army authorities volunteering to take out parties of nurses. Her friendship with the Secretary of War, Sidney Herbert, and his wife resulted in her being given control of the expedition (ibid.: 25–33).

It was newspaper publicity that led to her appointment, and further newspaper publicity created the picture of her achievements that reached the public. Once arrived in the East she became a 'heroine' in the terms sanctioned by the Angel in the House myth. She and her nurses were credited with having almost magically transformed the hospital system, saved thousands of lives, and acquired the total devotion of the men they nursed. The Nightingale legend was written up in the press and spread by word of mouth (Poovey 1988: 164–5; Smith 1982: 50–2; Woodham-Smith 1950: 234–5). Yet the legend diverged considerably from the picture since gained by historians from the surviving records. Though she took with her thirty-eight nurses, including groups from St John's House and the Devonport Sisterhood and from the Roman Catholic orphanage at Norwood and convent at Bermondsey, her success did not depend on the quality of nursing provided by this 'angel band'. As F. B. Smith has stressed, her major work was the reform of the administration of the hospitals, while 'the greater part of the nursing was done, as it always had been done, by male medical orderlies. She commandeered about 300 more of the them than the army allowed, most of them near able-bodied'. (Smith 1982: 49–52, 43). Furthermore, as Anne Summers' work reveals, 'the bulk of female nursing work of the Crimean War was . . . done outside Florence Nightingale's superintendence, and without reference to her ideas of professional practice'. At the hospitals at Koulali and Balaklava other 'ladies' were developing their own ways of organising hospital nursing (Summers 1983: 44, 42–50).

Nevertheless the influence of the legend on the future development of nursing was profound. The public subscribed £44,000 to a fund to be devoted to the training of nurses, and this was eventually used to set up a Training School for Nurses at St Thomas's Hospital in June 1860 (Seymer 1960: 1-3; Smith 1982: 156–8). Well before this school opened, however, the legend was creating both a 'pull' from hospitals for a new kind of nurse, and a 'push' which transformed an increasing number of young, middle-class women into potential recruits.

## The move to the hospitals

The Crimean expedition and the Nightingale legend that emerged changed 'knowledge' about nursing irreversibly. Florence Nightingale's social position gave her the symbolic capital to invest any work she did with an aura of gentility, and the interpretation of her efforts as those of a 'heroine' guaranteed the femininity of the work. The effect can be seen most strikingly in the records of St John's House. The House had contributed six nurses to the Nightingale party but the impact on the institution was much greater. The women left in October 1854, and by October 1855 the membership of the House had increased substantially: from three to six resident sisters, and nineteen to twenty-six nurses, with eleven associate sisters, while thirteen ladies had 'prepared themselves at St John's House for service in the East'.

The change in 'knowledge' also affected the kind of women who applied to become probationers. This can be seen in Table 7.2 based on the baptism certificates pasted into the Admissions Register of St John's House (HI/ST/SJ/CI/1-3). Many of these certificates are missing, returned to the nurses when they left, but those that remain show that in 1856 and 1857 the House began attracting recruits of a new kind: the young unmarried daughters of farmers and tradesmen, the type who more usually entered dressmaking or teaching.

As can be seen, the women joining in the period from 1850 to 1855 were usually over thirty, frequently widowed and, where younger, daughters of labourers. In 1856 the age began to drop and the fathers' status to rise, and in 1857 most recruits were only just over twenty-five (the lowest age of admission) and firmly positioned in the lower middle class, being the daughters of carpenters, butchers, shoemakers, farmers and the like.

In 1856, however, the kind of nursing being done by St John's House changed radically. The hospital, seen previously only as a place where nurses could gain a range of experience, had become the main site for the work of the House, and for the first time the 'ladies' were involving themselves with the work of their nurses. The connection with the Crimean expedition appears to have galvanized the Master (who accompanied the nurses from St John's House to meet Florence Nightingale in Paris and almost resigned because he was not allowed to go on with them to Scutari) into pressing to have the House involved in hospital nursing (HI/ST/SJ/A18/1). In January 1855 he pointed out that the title page of the rules claimed that the nurses were being trained to work in hospitals and:

> the speakers at the Public meeting, on July 13 1848 at which the House was founded, were unanimous in declaring Hospitals to be one of the objects of their Solicitude. Yet (with the exception of Westminster Hospital during the cholera last autumn), no Hospital or Infirmary has yet directly (if it have indirectly) benefited by means of St John's House.

He went on to argue:

> The occasion is most favourable. The general attention of the Kingdom has been called to the subject of Nurses for the Sick, & hereby to St John's House. A very large number of ladies, & others,

*Table* 7.2: Date of baptism and fathers' occupation of probationers at St John's House 1850–1858

| | |
|---|---|
| *1850 (15 admitted)* | 1828 |
|   1823 labourer | 1816 weaver |
|   1826 Clerk in the Royal Arsenal | 1824 grocer |
|   1826 Messenger | 1824 C.E. Plater |
|   1807 | |
|   1806 | *1856 (34 admitted)* |
|   1806 (married 1833) | 1830 clerk |
| | 1818 sergeant |
| *1851 (9 admitted)* | 1816 farmer |
|   1822 Lighterman | 1819 chairman (married a mason in |
|   1826 |     1842. Father then a mason) |
|   1822 Labourer | 1831 brewer |
|   1810 | 1851 (aged 20) shoe-maker |
|   1810 | 1821 cooper |
|   1818 Tailor | 1832 farmer |
|   1829 engraver of Quebec | 1833 confectioner |
|   1812 mother, widow, no father | 1820 Royal Regt |
|   1827 carpenter |     Horseguards |
| | 1811 |
| *1852 (6 admitted)* | 1829 mason |
|   1820 | 1813 carpenter |
| | 1828 butcher |
| *1853 (12 admitted)* | 1830 harness-maker |
|   1818 Tailor | 1831 lawyer's clerk |
|   1829 engraver of Quebec (late | 1822 Labourer |
|     baptism?) | 1827 turner |
|   1812 mother, widow, no father | 1823 shoemaker |
|   1827 carpenter | |
| | *1857 (30 admitted)* |
| *1854 (17 admitted)* | 1833 servant |
|   1815 wool sorter | 1828 'Own man to his Grace the |
|   1823 farmer |     Lord Primate.' |
|   1821 blacksmith | 1837 stone laizer |
|   1824 smith | 1828 shoemaker |
|   1819 inn-keeper | 1832 carpenter |
|     (married a grocer, the son of | 1829 lockfiler |
|     an innkeeper in 1849) | 1825 |
|   1813 labourer | 1833 Publican |
|   1820 carpenter | 1826 woodman |
|   1828 | 1833 |
|   1809 | 1833 stonemason |
|   1808 | 1832 butcher |
| | 1831 farmer |
| *1855 (15 admitted)* | 1818 farmer |
|   1820 surgeon | 1834 |
|   1828 labourer widow | |
|   1831 labourer | |
|   1825 gatekeeper | |
|     (married a widowed | |
|     gentleman in 1851) | |

*Source:* Baptismal Certificates pasted into Admissions Register (HI/ST/SJ/CI/1-3)

have signified a desire to devote themselves to the work; & tho' their first impulse was towards the Hospitals at Scutari, yet very many of them are without doubt equally anxious to work in England. The number of Probationers, too, who apply has been so large that we cannot admit them, the House being full.

(HI/ST/SJ/A18/1: 31-1-1855)

He then reported that he had received a request from the Physician at the Salisbury Court Infirmary to take over the nursing there.

This proposal seems to have caused a reaction by the three members of the Council concerned with King's College Hospital. According to the historians of the hospital, on March 8, 1855, one of these members, Dr Todd, who was also a driving force within the hospital, 'calmly announced' to the sub-committee discussing the staffing for the new hospital that he had begun negotiations with St. John's House to undertake responsibility for the nursing. The sub-committee accepted his proposal, and after prolonged negotiations Mary Jones and her sisters and nurses took charge on March 31, 1856 (Cartwright *et al.* 1991: 23–5). The 'ladies' now took over the direct supervision of the nurses and a legend soon arose of the wonderful transformation they achieved (Haward 1879: 494–5).[5] The *Times* reported:

In every ward there was the constant presence of its Sister, who not only brought about a condition of exquisite cleanliness, neatness, and order, but who silently checked undue familiarity between patients, nurses, and students, whose cultivated taste produced all arrangements that could gratify the eyes of the sick, whose high moral tone and spirit of self-sacrifice communicated itself in some degree to every person subject to her authority, and whose skill and knowledge, as well as her social position, secured the prompt and cheerful obedience of her subordinates.

(*Times* 14 February 1874: 6)

A version of how hospital nursing should be conducted had thus emerged which had little to do with Florence Nightingale's practice, though it had a good deal in common with the practices implemented by her rival Mary Stanley at Koulali, and incorporated into the army Rules and Regulations in December 1856. There, according to Anne Summers' account, the ladies and nurses wore a different dress, the nurses were only allowed in the wards under the supervision of one of the ladies, and the ladies assumed the right to regulate the nurses' activities on and off duty, just as they did those of their domestic servants (Summers 1983: 45–7). At St John's House two classes of trainees were now admitted, probationers and lady pupils. The probationers undertook a year's training and then became paid nurses either at the hospital or as part of the private nursing force. The lady pupils could become sisters, who were described as 'ladies of education and refinement, who have been fully trained as nurses, who give their services gratuitously, and who bear the cost of their own maintenance' (*Times* 14 February 1874: 6).

Initiatives were soon taken by other groups to have hospital nursing managed by 'ladies'. S. W. F. Holloway has shown how Miss Harriet Brownlow Byron, the Mother Superior and founder in 1851 of the Society of All Saints's Sisters of the Poor (usually referred to as All Saints, Margaret St.) emulated St John's House and took over the nursing of University College Hospital. 'From 1859 to 1862,' he writes, 'Miss Brownlow Byron pursued an unremitting policy of infiltration.' By 1862 the sisterhood had taken over the entire nursing of the hospital on much the same plan as pursued by St John's House at King's College Hospital. In spite of considerable opposition at certain times, the sisterhood remained in charge until 1899 (Holloway 1959). Both St John's House and All Saints professed to be supplying trained nurses, but other institutions were fired by the example of the Nightingale School to set up their own nurse training on a similar pattern. In 1861 the Liverpool businessman and philanthropist William Rathbone opened a training institution at his own expense for the Liverpool Royal Infirmary employing as Lady Superintendent Mary Merryweather, a Quaker lady who had, since the late 1840s, been employed to run evening classes for the operatives at Courtaulds silk factory in Essex (GW 1866: 748–50). By 1863 other training schools under 'Lady Superintendents' had been established at Bath and Bristol (Boucherett 1863: 152).

The entry of these lady superintendents into the field led to an increased stress on the importance of 'training'. Whereas in the older hospitals there was no expectation that a matron would have experience as a sister, or a sister as a nurse, the new training institutions began to set up such a progression. In 1865 the Nightingale School began responding to calls to supply 'ladies' trained there as matrons for other institutions. In that year Agnes Jones went to Liverpool to set up the first training school in a workhouse infirmary, in 1868 Lucy Osburn took a party of nurses to Sydney, in 1869 the Fund established a second training school at the Highgate Infirmary and supplied a matron and seven nurses to the military hospital at Netley. By 1879 thirty-four hospitals throughout the country had Nightingale-trained matrons (Seymer 1960: 49, 53–55, 83). It gradually became possible in practice to extend the expectation that nurses should be trained, which was a recurring theme in the periodical literature (*Saturday Review* 24 November 1855: 62; HW 1855: 461; Martineau 1865: 423–4; Parkes 1860 281: 815), to the ladies who were seen as the most appropriate sisters and matrons.

This was not a development foreseen when the conditions for nurses at the Nightingale School (replicated by Mary Merryweather at Liverpool Royal Infirmary) were first drawn up. It was expected that the women who applied would be from the borderline between the working class and the lower middle class, Florence Nightingale writing that 'the candidates who are best qualified for the ordinary duties of the hospital nurse appear to be daughters of small farmers who have been used to household work . . . and well-edu-cated domestic servants' (Abel-Smith 1960:21–2). Attention was, neverthe-less, paid to ensuring that nothing was done to compromise their femininity, and there was no attempt to treat them as free wage labour. In return for the hard work they did on the wards, they were given their board, uniform and £10 a year. The training lasted for a year and they were then expected to work for the institution as nurses for three years. There was strict supervision both on and off duty. They lived at the Nurses Home, where separate sleeping cubicles and a comfortably furnished sitting-room and dining-room were provided to replicate a domestic atmosphere with the matron as 'mother' (Baly 1988: 221; Woodham-Smith 1950: 346–8).

Gentility was added to femininity when upper-middle-class women, inspired by religious fervour and Florence Nightingale's example (Moore 1988: xiv–xv; Seymer 1960: 38–9), pressed to be admitted to the school. By 1867 the school had moved to a system closer to that of St John's House with its probationers and lady pupils. The school began to admit 'specials', women who paid from £30 to £50 a year board during their training, were relieved from some of the heavier cleaning part of the probationer's tasks, were on duty for only eight to ten hours a day compared with the standard twelve to fourteen, and were bound to serve only one year after their training (Baly 1987: 39–41; Nightingale 1868: 364; Wilson and Wilson 1893: 105). Most of those who moved on to become ward sisters and matrons had begun as spe-cials, but Florence Nightingale nevertheless insisted that the training for both sorts of probationers should be the same thus, as Monica Baly has pointed out, 'giving nursing the tradition of a one portal of entry' (Baly 1980: 124; Baly 1987: 40; Seymer 1960: 37–8). The existence of these ladies no doubt did much to encourage lower-middle-class women to train as nurses, and some of them may even have entered as specials, the amount asked for board being not much higher than the premium demanded for dressmaking. Certainly by the early 1900s nurses were claiming the status due to members of a profession: hospital-trained nurses who moved to private practice expected to eat with the family not the servants, thus demonstrating their membership of the same status group as their employers through the 'commensality' that Weber (1968: 306) saw as denoting it.

Nevertheless the hospitals managed to get considerable work out of the specials. Published advice stressed that ladies training as nurses must expect to do hard physical work and face unpleasant sights. The author of an 1877 article entitled 'A few hints to young candidates for the nursing profession' (WG 1877: 123) warned against 'couleur de rose' expectations. Nurses were required to do many things 'which are far from agreeable, especially to refined and cultivated women; hence they must possess considerable self-control and a hearty determination to accept all the duties of their undertak-ing with patience and good temper'. They would be expected also to 'have some knowledge of domestic duties, such as sweeping, scouring, bed-making &c.; and, not least, that they should know the rudiments of cooking'. These apparently domestic tasks were eventually, as Christopher Maggs has shown, renamed 'ward work' and given a professional gloss by being associated with scientific concepts like 'hygiene' and 'diet', and thus associated with the 'intellectual qualities' that, it was increasingly stressed, were needed to cope with the scientific subjects in their curriculum (Maggs 1983: 26–8; Strachan 1995: 27–8).The message was pressed home that being a probationer was a preparation for a profession, not a dilettante way of filling up the time between school and marriage.

Consequently specials were highly popular with hospitals, as they not only provided free nursing, but actually added to the hospital's income (Abel-Smith 1960: 30; Baly 1988: 221). Indeed the whole probationer system worked extremely well for the hospitals, providing exactly the kind of 'turnover' necessary to keep down the costs of labour-intensive work: a large group of young, strong, reasonably well-educated women who did most of the work on the wards for very low wages or for nothing, most of whom left after three or four years, making it possible for those who remained to advance to the much smaller number of relatively better-paid highly skilled or supervisory positions . Moreover, with nursing, marriage was not the only reason why women might leave. The 'hospital nurse' was in considerable demand for private nursing, and when district nursing services were established, could obtain work which provided a regular income and yet allowed her to be independent of a hospital hierarchy (Abel-Smith 1960: 56–9; Maggs 1983: 153–5).

The legacy of 'woman's mission' was manipulated by the hospitals to their own benefit. Glenda Strachan has shown how the definition of the 'true woman' that was embedded in the Nightingale legend, when transferred to paid hospital nursing, produced a workforce that could be paid a minimum wage and yet expected to give the maximum of service, because any demand for better conditions was seen as incompatible with the professional ideal (Strachan 1995). Although it was accepted by the 1880s that most women, even most ladies, who became nurses were working to support themselves (Maggs 1983: 13–15; Strachan 1995: 26–7), the hospitals invoked the gentility and the expectation of a vocation that the entry of ladies had given the occupation, to demand a dedication expected in no other profession (Strachan 1995: 26–31). A matron trained at Edinburgh Royal Infirmary told a Royal Commission in Australia:

> Any one who contemplates the profession of nursing ought to be thoroughly healthy, young (not too young), well educated, of medium height and of an even and sweet temper. The candidate must be prepared to take her life in her hand as it were, and for the coming two or three years as the case may be make herself and her

personal interests second to those of her patients and the hospital in which she is being trained.

(Strachan 1995: 26, quoted)

Consequently, the religious stress on obedience 'to those placed in authority over me' which the religious heterodoxy had not challenged was perpetuated by hospital authorities, with nurses expected to accept implicitly and without question all orders, while Florence Nightingale's insistence on absolute obedience to doctors' commands was reinforced by the desire for and acceptance of male authority incorporated into the tradition at St John's House (Baly 1988: 221; Maggs 1983: 118–25; Strachan 1995: 28–30).[6] Furthermore, the patriarchal conditions introduced by nursing pioneers to establish the femininity of the work persisted in nursing long after they had ceased to be customary in teaching and dressmaking. For the next hundred years nurses were expected to live at the hospital and, even in their free time, to gain permission before leaving the building. They were not free wage labourers, but were paid in part by having board, lodging and dress provided by the employer.

## Outcomes and implications

The foregoing discussion suggests that though the expansion of hospital nursing in the latter part of the century was the result of changes in social expectations and medical practice, the form it took was shaped, at least in part, by the beliefs and practices of the half dozen or so 'ladies' who joined the early nursing sisterhoods, and that the strategies used by the hospitals to create a viable nursing service were built on this foundation. These practices, in turn, derived their credibility and acceptability from the religious heterodoxy. The numbers of women taking the first initiatives may have been small, but their example was followed because all their actions were compatible with femininity and gentility as defined by a well-established heterodoxy to which many men and women with substantial symbolic capital subscribed. The work of Florence Nightingale allowed hospital nursing to a acquire an aura of femininity and gentility, but it was the meaning attributed to that work by others that had, ultimately, the most powerful impact. Since Florence Nightingale, a woman, was engaged in demanding that the principles of the sanitary reform movement be applied to hospitals, those women interested in nursing for religious reasons took her as a model and claimed the innovations in hygiene she was demanding as part of their brief. Furthermore, it involved no outrage in common 'knowledge' to hand over the creation of cleanliness and domestic order to women.

The borderland of hospital nursing was thus attractive to many religious, philanthropically inclined young women. The prestige of Florence Nightingale and the practices of the nursing sisterhoods and training schools were able to transform it into an occupational area where upper-middle-class young women in search of 'something to do' and lower-middle-class ones who needed to earn some sort of living could follow their religious ideals without jeopardising their social status. A new profession for women had been created.

Yet, as Mary Poovey points out, although the nursing pioneers' tactic of :

> proudly claim[ing] a supportive, subordinate relationship to its male counterpart . . . helped enhance the reputation of an activity overwhelmingly dominated by women, because it helped neutralize the specter of female sexuality contemporaries associated with independent women . . . this representation of nursing helped preserve the domestic ideal it seemed to undermine.
>
> (Poovey 1988: 167)

Nursing, though newer as an acceptable female profession than teaching and the practice of the arts, offered conditions that were more firmly rooted in the past and conformed far more self-consciously to the patriarchal conditions defined as appropriate by the domestic ideology. Whereas in the ladies' colleges and girls' high schools the focus was on protecting the femininity of the pupils and the conditions of teachers were increasingly flexible, depending on their needs and those of the particular school, with nursing the fact that the women worked under doctors and with male patients and students made their 'protection' far more of an issue.

Given the time at which nursing changed, and the particular 'contradiction inherent in the domestic ideal' on which the religious heterodoxy enabled the pioneers to capitalise (Poovey 1988: 166), the outcome is not surprising. It was not until a new discourse was found, a heterodoxy that moved beyond redefining 'women's mission' and challenged the doxa of separate spheres more directly, that new female occupations were found that could offer the same free wage labour conditions to middle-class women that were available to their brothers.

In Part 4 of this book it will be argued that this discourse, which I have called the liberal heterodoxy, was developed by the group of women seen as the founders of what is usually called the nineteenth century Women's Movement, that it had the effect of converting the religious heterodoxy into a set of beliefs that modern historians often characterise as 'conservative', and that it provided the insights that allowed the Women's Movement to open a number of new occupations and professions to women, and to extend university education to them.

# Part IV

# THE WOMEN'S MOVEMENT

# 8

# REDEFINING
# 'WOMEN'S SPHERE'

## Confronting the domestic ideology

Harold Perkin has argued that in the mid-nineteenth century there were three main strands of thought, or 'ideals', competing for the position of the orthodoxy of the age, each congruent with the economic needs of one section of the population, though not held exclusively or universally by those within the group. He has called them the aristocratic, the entrepreneurial, and the working-class ideals (Perkin 1969: 218–52).

The aristocratic ideal was a legitimation of the right of the landed classes not only to control a highly disproportionate share of the wealth of the country, but to exercise, in their roles as magistrates and landlords, patriarchal discipline over their employees and tenants and those who lived in their neighbourhood. This wealth and power was increasingly justified by laying great stress on the obligations these privileges carried with them, in particular, the obligation of the powerful to do unpaid work for the community and to care for the welfare of those they controlled (ibid.: 237–52). The religious revivals of the period, both the evangelical movement at the turn of the century and the High Church movement a few decades later, endorsed this view of the social order, and their founders and supporters built their philanthropic enterprises on these paternalistic imperatives.

The religious heterodoxy had been developed within this broader discursive framework. The framework had also, with its stress on a hierarchic society and patriarchal control, provided the underpinning for central aspects of the domestic ideology like the notions of separate spheres and women as 'relative creatures'. It was not therefore, a framework in which it was easy to visualize paid work in a free wage labour market as the solution to the problems of boredom and economic insecurity of which middle-class women were increasingly aware. So, though the religious heterodoxy made it possible for a minority of such women to undertake work as authors, artists and nurses, it could offer no solution to the broader problems of economic vulnerability and the overstocking in teaching and dressmaking. This had to wait until another heterodoxy developed that could expose 'the contradictions inherent in the domestic ideal' (Poovey 1988: 179) by reference to some other acceptable discourse. This was made possible, this chapter will argue, by the increasing respectability of the entrepreneurial ideal.

The entrepreneurial ideal had its intellectual roots in the doctrines of the social contract developed by theorists from Locke to Rousseau, and thus provided the basis for the demands made by merchants and manufacturers to share the political rights of the landed classes. However it included as well an acceptance of the analysis of the workings of the economy found in the writings of the classical political economists, and thus provided a justification for the *laissez faire* principles which best suited this group, and also legitimized their increasingly non-paternalist and non-patriarchal relationship with their workforce. Out of this grew an individualistic ethic of self-help and self-dependence. People were not to look to patronage or privilege or help from others in life, but to their own sturdy efforts in a free market, and it was their right and their obligation to monitor and control the workings of the state through a representative system of government (Perkin 1969: 221–30).

The emphasis on individualism within the entrepreneurial ideal meant that the emergence of free wage labour and the accompanying decline in patriarchal control over adult men, whether by fathers, employers, or landed gentry, was applauded and justified, and linked with the increasing extension of political power to individuals. Under pressure from the concepts of merit and the career open to the talents incorporated within the entrepreneurial ideal, entry into the professions, the public service and the armed forces was increasingly determined by examinations, and education was beginning to play as significant a role as family patronage in determining a young man's career, while the range of occupations available to middle-class men was wider than ever before. Thus personal choice of occupation was increasingly possible and work was increasingly seen as a means of self-actualization rather than of fulfilling family obligations. A young man's temperament and talents, even his own wishes, were taken into account in deciding his education and his future profession to an extent and in a manner unknown in previous generations (Perkin 1989: 83–91; Tosh 1996: 54).

This increased difference between the opportunities for men and women to achieve self-actualisation and independence from patriarchal control through income-earning work did not at first present itself to women as the major contradiction within the entrepreneurial ideal. They were first struck by the implications for them of the claims to individual political representation, the 'Rights of Man'. These political claims had already been used to justify extreme political action in the American and French revolutions when the economic doctrines were being developed. In addition, this was a discourse which incorporated older beliefs about fairness and justice, and so appealed strongly not just to the emerging commercial elite who could use it as a basis for demanding access to political power for themselves, but to idealistic people who wanted to reform their society and create a better world. It was therefore a discourse in terms of which any sort of political discrimination on the grounds of class, sex or race could be attacked, while its invocation was likely to draw the disinterested support of those called by Karl Mannheim 'socially unattached intellectuals' and by Harold Perkin 'social cranks' (Mannheim 1936: 137–42; Perkin 1969: 220–1, 256–7).

## Women's rights

Even before the full flowering of the ideas of the rights of man there were women who expressed resentment at male privilege and patriarchal control. In the very early eighteenth century certain upper-class women – 'Eugenia', Mary Astell, and Lady Chudleigh – began to question the validity of husbands' dominance over their wives. Mary Astell also put the case for women to have an education more like men's (Rogers 1982: 71–118; Stenton 1977: 207–8, 220–3). In 1792, however, Mary Wollstonecraft followed up Thomas Paine's defence of the French Revolution, *The Rights of Man* (1791), with a book pointing out that these arguments applied equally to women. Women were, she asserted in *A Vindication of the Rights of Women*, not something created for men but persons in their own right, with identical rights and duties. The apparent differences in temperament and abilities between the sexes were culturally created (Wollstonecraft 1792: 60, 27–8, 48). Women were just as likely to be made more virtuous by work, even paid work, as men (ibid.: 63–4, 154, 162). She attacked particularly the claim that women exercise power through the men bound to them sexually, calling such power 'illegitimate' and 'arbitrary', that is, like the power of kings, not of democrats (ibid.: 25–6).

The book was received with approval, even by quite conventional women – a large part of the text was merely a more forceful statement of the blue-stocking moral position – going into three editions in four years. In 1798, however, Mary Wollstonecroft's husband, Godwin, published a frank memoir showing how very far from conventionally moral her life had been, and approving references to the book abruptly ceased, except in the more extreme radical press (McGuinn 1978:189–91) where her ideas continued to have a following.

Several books defending women's rights from this radical perspective were published in the years before 1850. In consequence, not only was Rousseau's specific exclusion of women from political rights not integrated into English radical thought, but when James Mill tried to use similar arguments he was met with a vigorous rebuttal (Rowbotham 1975: 39–41). Furthermore, as Kathryn Gleadle (1995: 71–139) has shown, radical thinkers, men quite as significantly as women, identified specific problems and formulated specific political demands on behalf of women: for the suffrage, and for reform of the marriage and divorce laws, though they did not build on Mary Wollstonecraft's identification of paid work as a significant area.

The term 'women's rights' continued to be known and used beyond radical circles. There was little discussion of such topics in the serious upper-middle-class press, but passing references, assuming that the audience will know what the phrase implies, make it clear that the topic must often have come up in private conversation (Adams 1849: 368; *Fraser's* 1833: 600; Kaye 1855: 540). Moreover, in spite of a general editorial lack of interest, one of the leading women journalists of the 1830s and 1840s, Harriet Martineau (1802–1876) was associated with these ideas, advocating them quite openly in an article in the *Westminster Review* in 1838 and in her book *Society in America* in 1839, while in the early 1850s the popular poet Eliza Cook (1818–1889), wrote essays denouncing the disabilities and injustices suffered by women in her periodical *Eliza Cook's Journal* (Todd 1991: 162). In the mid-1850s, however, the 'rights of women' ceased to be a set of ideas which people mulled over and sometimes discussed; they became a basis for formal, organized political action.

## The birth of the Women's Movement

In the 1850s and 1860s one of those periods of heightened intellectual excitement seems to have occurred when old ideas are questioned and new theories of the meaning of life, the proper social organization, and so on, are fervently advocated. In Britain the energies of political liberals and radicals which in the late 1840s had been concentrated on the repeal of the Corn Laws were released to move over a wider field, while the general rise in prosperity in the 1850s eased the immediate pressure on philanthropists to deal with cases of acute distress, and allowed them more time for taking a general and more theoretical view of the problems of their society (Clark 1962: 32, 136–8; Halévy 1951: 250–61). In this climate, the ideas that had once belonged simply to a radical fringe began to enter mainstream debate on political and social issues and were taken seriously by politicians and philanthropists in the upper middle class.

The 'modern spirit' according to Matthew Arnold filled people with 'a sense that this system is not of their own creation, that it by no means corresponds exactly with the wants of their actual life, that, for them, it is customary, not rational' (Fawcett 1878: 853 quoted). This was the spirit in which members of the Women's Movement chose to look at the world in which they found themselves. For them the prescriptions of the domestic ideology were 'custom', while the new individualist philosophies were an inspiration and an urge to action. They therefore assessed the 'customs' of their age in regard to women in the light of these new insights and found in them much that needed to be altered.

The organized movement grew out of the friendship of a group of young women from well-to-do, politically radical backgrounds, who looked at the world in this way. The leading figures were Barbara Leigh Smith and Bessie

Rayner Parkes. Barbara Leigh Smith (1827–1891), a cousin of Florence Nightingale, grew up in a family where both political activity and personal independence were seen by her father, the radical MP Benjamin Smith, as perfectly acceptable for his daughter. At twenty-one she was given an independent income of £300 a year while still apparently allowed the full use of the family home as a residence and as a place for entertaining her own friends. Bessie Rayner Parkes (1829–1925) also came from a radical Unitarian family. Her great-grandfather was Joseph Priestley the chemist and her father was a radical lawyer, a manager of the Liberal Party, and a founder of the Reform Club. The two women had artistic ambitions, Barbara to be a painter, Bessie to be a poet, but family background had also led to their taking an interest in public causes, and for Barbara at least, the Anti-Corn-Law agitation had been of passionate concern throughout her teens.

Furthermore, as Kathryn Gleadle has pointed out, they grew up in those radical unitarian circles where the rights of women had been a matter of debate for decades, and came to adulthood just as they were brought into new prominence by the American Seneca Falls Conference in 1848, and its repercussions in the English press in articles like Harriet Taylor's in the *Westminster Review* in 1851 (Blackburn 1902: 48; Gleadle 1995: 177–83; Johnston 1997: 219; Rendall 1989: 137–55) As early as 1848 Bessie Rayner Parkes had begun to question the Angel in the House myth in print, attacking the view that women were 'angels by nature', and 'in the ordinary cant of the day, are supposed to have a mission' (Rendall 1989: 150 quoted).

The cause first taken up by Barbara Leigh Smith and Bessie Rayner Parkes was already part of the radical unitarian program: reform of the marriage laws, in particular the common law as it was applied to married women's property.[1] Their most innovative contribution, however, was to extend the concept of women's rights to include the emerging right enjoyed by middle-class men to work which provided self-actualization and independence from patriarchal control. They achieved this by moving beyond pointing out the contradictions between women's position and morality as defined by the political philosophers, and engaging with another strand within the entrepreneurial ideal. They made it their task to look at the contradictions revealed when the doctrine of separate spheres was measured against the morality that had been built on the ideas of the political economists.

## Anna Jameson and the gospel of work

Their concern with work seems to have been aroused by the literary journalist and art critic, Anna Jameson. In the early 1850s, aged almost sixty, she met Barbara Leigh Smith and Bessie Rayner Parkes through Adelaide Procter, the daughter of long-term and close friends, and found herself regarded as mentor by a circle of idealistic young women. 'This group of girls', writes her biographer, 'was encouraged by Anna to make her stopping place their headquarters . . . She was their patroness and she called them her "adopted nieces".' (Johnston 1997: 219, 224; Thomas 1967: 209) She supported them actively in the married women's property campaign, allowing her name to figure prominently in the petition (Burton 1949: 59; Johnston 1997: 225–7). She also drew to their attention a problem that had figured in her writings for the last ten years: the contradiction between the expectation that women should be dependent on men, and the actual fact that many of them had to earn their own livings. Her earliest writings on the topic (for example her article titled 'Condition of the Women and the Female Children' in the *Athenaeum* in 1843 which drew attention to the harsh conditions imposed on dressmakers) reveal, as the passages from it quoted in Chapter 3 show, an awareness of the contradiction combined with an unwillingness to reject the idea of 'women's mission'. By the mid-1850s she seems to have found a way out her dilemma.

As Judith Johnston (1997: 222) has pointed out, Anna Jameson was not a professed supporter of women's rights, which she saw as implying primarily a demand for political equality. She was, however, deeply committed to the religious heterodoxy's stress on the *moral* equality of men and women, and was prepared to expose and exploit the contradictions between the domestic ideal and wider interpretations of morality in the interests of women. The double standard of sexual morality was a matter of longstanding indignation with her, but in her last years she became increasingly determined to expose another double standard where there was just as wide a disparity between the ethic provided for men by their society and that considered suitable for women: the attitude to work. A crusade against this double standard occupied the last years of her life, but while she advocated forcing the male sexual ethic to fall into line with the female one, on work she took the opposite view. There was to be no defensible double standard of morality over work either: what religion demanded of men it must also demand of women.

One of the most pervasive ideals running through the writings of the intellectuals, poets and clergy of the period was the belief in the necessity and nobility of work. Walter Houghton has shown in *The Victorian Frame of Mind* how, in the early part of the nineteenth century, the aristocratic leisured way of life which had been justified by the theory of *noblesse oblige* (the theory that the aristocracy used their leisure and wealth to do unpaid service for the community) came increasingly under attack, while the work ethic of the business community with its emphasis on the secular vocation and the identity of hard work and morality was pressed on the whole community as a superior ideal. With the evangelical revival of the 1790s these ideas were transported from the non-conformist sects into the mainstream of nineteenth-century religious thought and were accepted even by High Church Anglicans. The gospel of work was embraced even more fervently by those who found orthodox religion unsatisfactory. Carlyle argued passionately for it, and it can be found advocated in the writings of Clough, Ruskin, and Leslie Stephen (Houghton

1957: 242–62). Houghton sums up: 'Puritanism, business, and doubt met together to write the gospel of work' (ibid.: 254).

The gospel of work as advocated in the mid-nineteenth century was totally androcentric in its conception – the men who argued for it never thought how it might apply to women – yet it was expressed in morally universal terms. Women who had heard and read these moralisings applied them to themselves and yet found no way provided by their society for putting them into practice. It was another version, in new ideological dress, of the conflict described in Chapter 5 between the evangelical injunction to serve humanity and the definition of women's sphere as the home. It was this conflict Anna Jameson set out to resolve, even though it required the complete rejection of one basic premise of the doctrine of separate spheres: that women had no place in the extension of the public sphere created by industrialism, the sphere of work.

The year 1855 was characterized by a huge wave of popular enthusiasm for women's charitable work, prompted by the reports of Florence Nightingale and her nurses in the Crimea. The members of the new Women's Movement were as deeply affected as anyone, Anna Jameson among them, and thus the campaign for a single work ethic for men and women was opened, and the destruction of the doctrine of separate spheres begun, in a haze of Nightingale worship. In 1855 and 1856 Anna Jameson gave two drawing room lectures in a private house arguing that far more women should devote themselves to public service (Johnston 1997: 219–22; Thomas 1967: 206). The first was called 'Sisters of Charity, Catholic and Protestant, At Home and Abroad', and the second 'The Communion of Labour: A Second Lecture on the Social Employment of Women'. The main purpose of these lectures was to argue that English ladies should be playing the same part as French nuns in running schools, hospitals, asylums. In the process, as well as putting the case for a married women's property act, and arguing strongly against the double standard of sexual morality (Jameson 1856: 7–18), she produced a new theoretical argument to support the actions of those women seeking 'something to do', an argument which began the theoretical demolition of the doctrine of separate spheres.

Anna Jameson seems to have internalized pretty thoroughly some aspects of the Angel in the House myth, while rejecting others that could not be logically reconciled with her experience and her moral beliefs. She still held to the position that men's and women's natures were different, and that they therefore had different roles to play. However she would not accept the tenet of the Angel in the House myth that women's role was simply to 'influence' men. She followed Mary Wollstonecraft in rejecting influence as a legitimate exercise of power. Both sexes, she believed, were called on to work, and it was in a joint work that men and women should play out their separate roles:

> Is it not possible that in the apportioning of the work we may have
> too far sundered what in God's creation never can be sundered

without pain and mischief, the masculine and feminine influences?
– lost the true balance between the element of power and the
element of love?

(Jameson 1856: 22–3)

Such joint efforts, she argued would raise, not lower, the moral nature of
women:

> I have the deepest conviction, founded not merely on my own
> experience and observation, but on the testimony of some of the
> wisest and best men among us, that to enlarge the working sphere
> of woman to the measure of her faculties, to give her a more practical
> and authorised share in all social arrangements which have for their
> object the amelioration of evil and suffering, is to elevate her in the
> social scale; and that whatever renders womanhood respected and
> respectable in the estimation of the people tends to humanise and
> refine the people.

(Jameson 1856: 24)

Anna Jameson's point of attack seems to have been particularly well
chosen, for in these two lectures she did little more than give a theoretical
defence of the activities of women inspired by the religious heterodoxy, something which had not yet been done. She retained enough of the Angel in the
House theory – the complementary nature of the male and female character
– still to speak the language of those for whom 'woman's mission' was an
integral part of their habituses, and yet at the same time struck at the very
root of the practical inactivity which the theory seemed to imply, and which
indeed it was probably invented to justify. Furthermore she linked the gospel
of work with the high-minded strand of the aristocratic ideal – belief in the
duty of self-sacrifice and service to the poor – to which the religious fervour
of the period gave a significant place. Her 'communion of labour' argument
was to remain pertinent for many years and be used many times, as the
Women's Movement gained momentum, to defend the right of women to
work outside the home (Beale, Soulsby, and Dove 1898: 5–6; Butler 1868:
23–5; Contemporary 1870: 526; Cornwallis 1857: 50; Craik 1887, 372;
Haddon 1871: 461; Hinton 1870: 455; Milne 1857: 122–6; Smith 1857:
47; Twining 1887: 660).

Philanthropic work was the easiest area on which to bring the work ethic
to bear, since it was a borderland where women had been accepted in practice for some time, even if the theory to support it had not been very adequate. However the gospel of work proved to have a wider application.
Though for men it was, if not quite doxa, a widely accepted orthodoxy
throughout this period, it was interpreted rather differently by the conflict-
ing and clashing sectional ideologies of the period. For those who held to the

aristocratic ideal, the gospel of work implied primarily service to the community through political and philanthropic activity. For holders of the entrepreneurial ideal, however, the gospel of work was interpreted in terms like 'self dependence', 'self help', and the 'self-made man'. Yet once again the formulation was androcentric: its propounders had never considered whether or not it should apply to women. Anna Jameson's arguments carried the implication for women's rights supporters that they should use the 'self dependence' strand of liberal thought to claim for all women that economic independence from the patriarchal family which the entrepreneurial ideal endorsed for men.

Furthermore she produced arguments, evidence of serious social problems, to support her case, in particular, the sufferings of single women with no man whom they could succour in return for economic support:

> The great *mistake* seems to have been that in all our legislation it is taken for granted that the woman is always protected, always under tutelage, always within the precincts of a home, finding there her work, her interests, her duties and her happiness: but is this true? We know that it is altogether false. There are thousands and thousands of women who have no protection, no home.
>
> (Jameson 1855: 9–10)

'There are 800,000 women over and above the number of men in the country' she told her adopted nieces, 'and how are they all to find husbands, or find work and honest maintenance? The market for governesses is glutted' (Thomas 1967:209).[2]

It was the relevance of her arguments to the entrepreneurial ideal that had the most immediate impact on public opinion. In 1857 a number of books and articles made this need for paid employment the focus of their response to the published lectures. I have shown elsewhere how reviewers related Anna Jameson's emphasis on the importance of work to the multifarious problems discussed together as the 'woman question', and suggested that work was a solution to all of them (Jordan 1994). For example, Caroline Cornwallis (1786–1858), a woman journalist who had already supported the married women's property campaign, argued in the January number of the *Westminster Review* that prostitution was caused by the dependence of women on men, and that a woman turned to it because she knew 'nothing is to be hoped from her exertions, if she belong to the lower orders, but the most precarious existence', and suggested that young women might find employment as nurses or in offices if they had the appropriate training (Cornwallis 1857). In February 1857 another reviewer, J. W. Kaye (1856: 256), who had already raised the question of domestic violence in the *North British Review* and argued that the ultimate cause of the problem was women's economic dependence on men, used the printed Jameson lectures as a pretext for investigating the work available to women and noting the extent to which it could free them from the need to marry for economic support. He concluded that 'What every woman, no less than every man, should have is an ability, after some fashion or other to turn labour into money. She may or may not be compelled to exercise it, but every one ought to possess it. (Kaye 1857: 305).

In the same year Barbara Leigh Smith took up the theme in a book called *Women and Work*, taking as her premise the gospel of work in its most widely accepted form. Everyone, she stated, had a duty to 'do God's work in the world', and yet when girls asked what their work was to be they were told it was to be found in marriage (Smith 1857: 6–8). But this led women to waste their girlhood waiting for a lover who might never come. 'We do not mean to say' she wrote, 'work will take the place of love in life, that is impossible; does it with men? But we ardently desire that women should not make love their profession.' (ibid.: 9) Thus she placed at the centre of her discussion the problems caused by the emptiness and boredom of the life between school-room and marriage. She also, however, pulled to the front of the discussion the point Anna Jameson had been making for so many years, the limited number of occupations available to middle-class women and the consequent overstocking, and outlined what was to become the Women's Movement's solution. Unless fathers were able to give their daughters an independent income, she argued, they must have them trained for an occupation which produced a reasonable income. Only in this way could they avoid forcing them into a marriage not for love but for maintenance, or leaving them no option, on their father's or husband's deaths, but to follow the overstocked trades of governess or dressmaker (ibid.: 10–11).

It appears that at about this time Barbara Leigh Smith and Bessie Rayner Parkes came to the conclusion that they should follow Anna Jameson's lead and focus on women's exclusion from the world of work and its economic consequences, rather than trying to redress the legal and political discrimination which a more conventional women's rights analysis identified as the most glaring contradictions in their society. In January 1858 Bessie Rayner Parkes wrote to Barbara Leigh Smith that she believed there was no 'abstract public for divorce and the suffrage' and that in her journalism she aimed to change public opinion slowly rather 'than to smash my head & your money against a brick wall' (Rendall 1989: 163 quoted). Thus in the movement they founded the initial focus was on women's work, and its first task was to extend women's rights to include the new rights that growing industrialism had brought to middle-class men: economic independence of fathers and self-actualization through work. There were consequently two problems to solve, one ideological and one structural. They must convince middle-class girls and their parents that all girls not possessed of independent means ought to work before marriage, and they must alter the occupational structure of the society so that work which pro-vided a competence was available to all middle-class women.

## Langham Place

Their first step was to establish a base from which to begin influencing public opinion. In 1857, with the help of Isa Craig and Matilda Hays, new recruits to their circle, Bessie Rayner Parkes took on the editorship of an Edinburgh-based paper, the *Waverley* and moved it to London. In February 1858 it folded, and she became editor of the *English Woman's Journal*, a new monthly funded by Barbara Leigh Smith (Nestor 1982; Rendall 1987; Rendall 1989: 158–9). The need for women to work and for more occupations to be open to them were the major themes stressed in the *English Woman's Journal* (Nestor 1982: 98; Rendall 1987: 121–5). The arguments first developed in 1857 were repeated over and over again in articles with titles like 'The profession of the teacher' (March 1858), 'Female education in the middle classes' (June 1858), 'Going a-governessing' (August 1858), 'On the adoption of professional life by women' (September 1858), 'Domestic life' (October 1858), 'Why boys are cleverer than girls.' (October 1858), 'Colleges for girls' (February 1859), while the letter columns were full of suggestions for alternative occupations.

The offices of the *English Woman's Journal* at 14a Princes Street became a meeting place for women interested in the issues it raised, and these facilities were extended. One of the rooms in the building became a reading room, and when the Society for Promoting the Employment of Women was founded in July 1859, this became its address. In December 1859 a building was leased at 19 Langham Place, a luncheon room was added to the reading room and for a guinea subscription women had the right to use the room, read the papers, have lunch and leave their parcels. The whole complex was called The Ladies' Institute, Langham Place and the group meeting there began to be referred to as Langham Place group or circle (EWJ November 1859: 288; Davies 1970: 214; Blackburn 1902: 248–50).

This institute was the closest the Women's Movement as a whole came to a formal organization. Most of its campaigns, though inspired and linked by members of the Langham Place circle, looked for their formal organization and patronage to a far more widely known and prestigious organization, the National Association for the Promotion of Social Science. This society, founded in 1857, held annual Congresses which brought together in one town reformers of various casts in various areas. Its leaders were those most notable in the areas of philanthropy and political reform – Lord John Russell, Lord Shaftesbury, Lord Brougham – and its conferences gave an opportunity for many lesser figures who had an idea to air, or an interesting local experiment in philanthropy to report, to find a sympathetic audience. The meetings were reported in the press, and the association published many of the speeches in its own *Transactions*. In the years in which it flourished it seems to have served the purpose of publicising innovative ideas and practices, and it also provided a platform from which the Women's Movement could address the nation.

In the Association's early years the Women's Movement supporters used the congresses to ensure that the expansion of women's work and, a few years later, of educational provision for them, became part of the progressive agenda. They seem, from the first, to have had a sympathetic reception. On the one hand, unattached intellectuals from the radical wing of politics seem to have had little difficulty in adding these issues to their established 'women's rights' agendas. On the other hand the conditions of dressmakers and governesses had long been among the recognised concerns of philanthropists, and notable figures like F. D. Maurice and Lord Shaftesbury already numbered these among the causes they supported. Both groups were used to working with women, and made a place for them in the association from the beginning. Isa Craig became one of its assistant secretaries, and not only were women allowed to attend its Congresses, they were welcomed on the platform, having their papers read at first by men, but later, as the confidence of the movement grew, by the women themselves (Stephen 1927:74–6; Strachey 1928: 93–4). Speaking at the 1862 Congress, Bessie Rayner Parkes paid this tribute to the male leaders:

> From the first semi-private meeting at Lord Brougham's house, to which he referred in his address last Thursday, and at which Mrs Jameson, Mrs Austin and Mrs Howitt were present, down to the prest time; Lord Brougham and Mr. George Hastings, and all the numerous gentlemen who have been brought in contact with the question, of whom I would specially name Lord Shaftesbury as President of our Society, have shown the utmost desire to give women fair play, and not only fair play, for they have so managed the meetings and discussions as to enable them to be carried on with perfect ease and propriety by all ladies desirous of taking part in any of the sections. I believe I may truly affirm that never before in the world's history have women met with such equal courtesy and true deference as that which has been shown them here.
>
> (Parkes 1862: 340–1)

The Social Science Association developed a procedure whereby groups with specific aims could be formed 'in connection with' it. A paper would be read at a Social Science Congress, a discussion would follow, and then a resolution would be passed setting up a new society or committee. These societies adopted the structure used for less innovative charitable activities (Prochaska 1988: 36). An impressive set of peers, MPs and well-known philanthropists would agree to act as president, vice-presidents and committee members, while the real work would be done by a managing committee composed of people prepared to dedicate time and emotion to the enterprise.

The three organizations which worked for the first objective of the Women's Movement, making more work available to women and convincing their parents that girls should be trained for work, were organized in this manner: the Society for Promoting the Employment of Women (1859) with Jessie Boucherett as its moving spirit, the Committee for Obtaining the Admission of Women to University Examinations (1862) with Emily Davies as Secretary, and the National Union for the Education of Girls of All Classes above the Elementary (1871), directed by Maria Grey (Blackburn 1902: 50, 251; Kamm 1971: 42; Stephen 1927: 84).

## Debates about women

The practical initiatives of these committees will be described in Chapters 9 and 10. The change in 'knowledge' which made the practical changes possible has, however, to be seen in the context of the wider debate about the purpose and position of women which was generally known as the 'woman question'. The task which the Women's Movement undertook was to demonstrate that the domestic ideology was at the heart of most of the problems, and to attack its premises by pointing out the contradictions between its prescriptions and the facts of social life.

The attack was began by the Langham Place circle in the late 1850s. Two basic points were continually reiterated by these women in the *English Woman's Journal* and at the Social Science Congresses: young women must be made financially self-dependent and they must enter occupations other than the traditional teaching and dressmaking. This ran counter to two of the principles identified by June Purvis ( 1991: 2–3) as basic to the domestic ideology: that women were 'relative creatures' their lives governed by the needs of their male relatives and that women's sphere was the home. But Women's Movement members, as women's rights supporters, were ideologically opposed to the patriarchalism underpinned by these views, and so for them these injunctions were not principles but simply customs, and, given the problems they created, not very rational ones. Such customs could therefore be attacked by invoking principles which were central to the entrepreneurial ideal: the gospel of work and the ideal of self-dependence.

The Langham Place campaign had a mixed reception, depending, it would seem, on the extent to which the domestic ideology had become part of the respondent's habitus. There was an immediate positive response from several leading women writers. In 1858 Dinah Mulock Craik (1826–1887), the author of the widely read novel *John Halifax, Gentleman* who had for many years supported herself and her family with her writing, devoted a chapter of her book *A Woman's Thoughts about Women* to 'Self-Dependence', and argued the case along the lines laid down in 1857. In 1859 the journalist and women's rights advocate Harriet Martineau (1802–1876), now retired to the Lake District, used the 1857 books as the basis for a long article in *The Edinburgh Review* on 'Women's Industry'. It also brought a new and vocal supporter to the movement, Frances Power Cobbe (1822–1904), a woman who had already made a name for herself as a writer on philosophic and religious topics, and who had come to London to supplement the £200 a year her father had left her by working as a journalist. Between 1861 and 1863 she wrote six major articles on women for *Fraser's Magazine* and *Macmillan's Magazine*, and throughout the 1860s and 1870s her pen was available to the Women's Movement (Todd 1991: 150, 452–6, 489).

However, there were others who were deeply disturbed. There was little rejection at first of the argument that something must be done for the women crowding into overstocked occupations, and some writers were even prepared to concede that 'enlarging the field of labour for all who require it' might be an answer (*Fraser's* 1860: 364; Greenwell 1862: 70–1; *Saturday Review* 1857: 238), though Margaret Oliphant (1858: 142–4) argued in *Blackwood's Edinburgh Magazine* that there were plenty of men also facing the problem of having been trained for an overstocked occupation .

Nevertheless, the suggestion that the principle of self-dependence should be applied to all women could be met with outright rejection without looking callous, and writers invoked the Angel in the House myth to defend the preservation of women's 'relative' status. 'Establishing the principle would be a social evil,' said a writer in *Fraser's Magazine*, arguing that women's dependence on men was a primary social need. 'It is valuable to women as giving them leisure to fit themselves for their true vocation as educators of the young, and the guardians of all that is refined and pure in social morals' (*Fraser's* 1860: 369, 370). A writer in *Blackwood's* was even more outraged: 'To make women wholly independent, which is the real object of the recent agitation, implies an inversion of the laws of nature, which is simply impossible and absurd' (Aytoun 1862: 201). A number of female journalists, Margaret Oliphant, L. F. M. Phillips and Dora Greenwell, expressed similar fears (Greenwell 1862: 71; Oliphant 1860: 712; Phillips 1861: 100–6).

When, in the 1860s, the Society for Promoting the Employment of Women began to make known the sort of work it considered suitable for women, even more concern was aroused, for the patriarchal conditions seen as essential to preserve a girl's femininity seemed threatened. Economic dependence was the instrument by which the patriarchal father controlled his daughters. This was why, as was argued in Chapter 4, the definitions of appropriate women's work stressed the domestic setting and moral supervision, and why – though the reason was never made explicit – most of the payment for work was in board and lodging rather than money. However the sorts of work the Society for Promoting the Employment of Women was suggesting would involve a girl's living at home and earning enough to pay her father for her board. Middle-class girls would therefore have the power to defy their parents, and even move out and live in lodgings as had the factory girls, accounts of whose independence had so shocked the Social Science Congresses.

In 1862 W. R. Greg, a major literary journalist and a liberal who tended to attack liberalism from within, set himself the task of finding a solution to the problem of unsupported women which would not undermine the patriarchal control of women. He set out his views in the article already referred to in Chapter 4, 'Why are Women Redundant?' in the *National Review*. Greg saw the basis of the problem in the large number of unmarried women, and believed that there was a tendency 'to call the malady by a wrong name, and to seek in a wrong direction for the cure' (Greg 1868: 341). Nature, he argued, laid down the rule that most women should be supported by husbands, but not all, since she allowed between two per cent and five per cent more women than men to reach adulthood. This percentage showed the size of the group of natural spinsters: those women temperamentally unsuited to marriage. Moreover work for these women had been beneficently determined: domestic service (ibid.:342, 344, 363–4). However in English society in the 1850s, instead of only 3 per cent of women being unmarried, more than 30 per cent of those between twenty and forty were single. The reasons for this Greg argued, were first, that male emigration was much greater than female, and second, that the luxury and profligacy of men made them unwilling to marry: luxury prompted them to postpone marriage and prostitution made it no hardship (ibid.: 348–50, 364–7).

The answer to the whole problem, as he saw it, was mass female emigration. If all those who could not find occupation as domestic servants were to leave the country they would find marriage partners in the colonies and the supply of prostitutes would be controlled (ibid.: 377-8). This would attack the problem at its roots; the cause would be eradicated. If, however, the Women's Movement suggestion was followed and single life made more tolerable for women, this unnatural state of things would be prolonged. Such a policy would run the risk of turning women away from marriage, just as luxury and profligacy were deflecting men. 'To surround single life for them' he argued, 'with so smooth an entrance, and such a pleasant, ornamented, comfortable path' as the Women's Movement sought to do, would lead to women regarding marriage 'not as their most honourable function and especial calling, but merely as one of many ways open to them, competing on equal terms with other ways for their cold and philosophic choice' (ibid.: 368–70).

Greg's article apparently aroused considerable interest, being much read, quoted and argued about. No one questioned his basic, and erroneous, assumption that the problems of female employment were caused by an increase in the numbers of unmarried women. The members of the Women's Movement, his main opponents, after all, themselves believed this to be the case. He was opposed, rather, on the grounds that his prescription for the female condition was inconsistent with certain generally accepted principles of what female nature should be.

The vision of thousands of women sailing off in pursuit of husbands jarred with current ideas of female decorum and maidenly modesty, and was quite out of keeping with the idealisation of marriage which had thrown into disrepute the eighteenth century practice of shipping poverty-stricken ladies out to India to find husbands for themselves (Austen 1963: 194). Arthur Houston (1862: 31) wrote ironically of the 'delicacy of sentiment which characterises a scheme for shipping so many loads of female humanity in search of husbands, with whose tempers, habits, or character they are unacquainted'. Ten years later Emily Faithfull (1871: 382) was still protesting that the idea was 'far from pleasant'. Frances Power Cobbe, in her reply to Greg, 'What shall we do with our old maids?', treated the whole proposal as farcical:

> The mildest punishment, we are told, is to be transportation, to which half a million have just been condemned, and for the terror of evil doers, it is decreed that no single woman's work ought to be fairly remunerated, nor her position allowed to be entirely respectable, lest she exercise 'a cold philosophic choice' about matrimony. No false charity to criminals! Transportation or starvation to all old maids!
>
> (Cobbe 1862a: 599)

Greg's other argument, however, that agreeable well-paid work for women would lead them to reject marriage, seems to have been taken far more seriously. Certainly the Women's Movement felt called upon to argue pertinaciously against it. Frances Power Cobbe led the way by trying to show that Greg's idea was incompatible with the other widely held belief that marriage should be for love not money. Only economically independent women, she argued, could afford to realise this ideal:

> Loving marriages are (we cannot doubt) what God has designed, not marriages of interest. When we have made it *less* women's interest to marry, we shall indeed have less and fewer interested marriages, with all their train of miseries and evils. But we shall also have more *loving* ones, more marriages founded on free choice and free affection.
>
> (ibid.: 596)

More than ten years later advocates of more work for women we were still confronting the suggestion that independence might dissuade women from marriage. 'Do men value themselves so lightly' asked Louisa Hubbard, 'that they think the pressure of want needed to force upon women the acceptance of the homes which they offer to them, or to add to the treasure possessed in the love of a husband and child?' (Hubbard 1875: 3).

As a total defence of patriarchalism, Greg's article left much to be desired. His justification for it was no more than that it was 'natural', and he made no attempt to integrate it with any of the powerful, but still androcentrically expressed moral imperatives in the society. Moreover he had, fortunately for the future of women's work, missed an opportunity. He had not defended specifically the proposition that women should not be directly paid a wage which would cover their living expenses. Stressed strongly at this time, it might have redefined the working conditions insisted on by the Society for Promoting the Employment of Women. As it was, the Women's Movement initiatives gradually opened for girls work where the custom was to pay a full living wage, rather than provide keep and pocket money. As more and more middle-class girls rejected both young ladyhood and the obligation to work within the family business, the patriarchal power of the father was gradually eroded. By the early twentieth century girls' relationships with their parents in early adult life were approaching parity with those of their brothers.

However, Greg's stress on the threat to marriage and women's possible rejection of home life for work led the Women's Movement to take a stand which was somewhat at odds with the principle that underlay the Married Women's Property Campaign. They hastened to protest that they were not attacking economic dependence within marriage: their campaign for more work was, they insisted, intended only to help single women. Of course married women were needed in the house to make it comfortable for their husbands and children, and if they were doing this they were entitled to be generously supported by their husbands. This position was taken by many leading Women's Movement members throughout the 1860s: Bessie Rayner Parkes, Frances Power Cobbe, Emily Davies, Emily Faithfull, even John Stuart Mill, all on occasion added this qualification when they claimed the right of women to economic independence (Parkes 1862: 341; Cobbe 1862: 597; Davies 1866: 99; Faithfull 1871: 382; Mill 1869: 264). They were not, in fact, claiming that women must not combine marriage and a career, but their continued expressed support for the full-time housewife did nothing to stop this idea becoming entrenched in the world view of the new working middle-class girl.

The next initiative of the Women's Movement, the claim for self-realisation through education and work, involved a challenge of a different sort and to all aspects of the domestic ideology. Once the education movement got under way, it became obvious to observers that major changes in the socialization of girls were being proposed. Middle-class girls were being encouraged to leave the home for education in the years usually devoted to 'young ladyhood', and to pursue an aim of self-realisation rather than one of being primarily supportive of men. Therefore attempts were made to restate the domestic ideology, and make it seem as attractive as possible to women, by stressing the Angel in the House aspect: the homage, the power, and the glorious role in life, it provided for women.

The most notable attempt in this line was John Ruskin's public address, later reprinted as an essay, 'Of Queen's Gardens'. Ruskin was, in David Sonstroem's words (1977: 285), a believer in 'what might be called radical Toryism, a conception of society as a loving family of disparate but mutually helpful members.' He was, that is, an apologist for, even a formulator of, the aristocratic ideal. However he was not, apparently, a convert to the heterodox view of women based on this ideal. Whereas holders of the religious heterodoxy tended to support the Women's Movement on education and up to a point on work (Yonge 1873: 232–3), Ruskin was, as he made clear at the beginning of his lecture, trying to oppose sense to what he saw as the Women's Movement nonsense:

> There never was a time when wilder words were spoken, or more vain imagination permitted, respecting this question – quite vital to all social happiness . . . We hear of the mission and of the rights of Woman, as if these could ever be separate from the mission and the rights of Man.
>
> (Ruskin 1865: 98)

He began his argument with a restatement of the main points of the Angel in the House myth: that men's and women's natures were different but complementary, that woman's sphere was the home with her only outside duty that of charity, that her duty and her power were those not of action but of influence (ibid.: 110–2, 129, 132–3, 136). The main body of the lecture was, however, devoted to describing the education appropriate to fitting women for their sphere.

Because of women's different nature, education could not change a girl as it did a boy. It could only hinder or encourage her pre-ordained organic development. 'You may chisel a boy into shape, as you would a rock . . .But you cannot hammer a girl into anything. She grows as a flower does' (ibid.: 133). Her education must prepare her for her function of creating a spiritual 'home' about her, and for this she must be made 'enduringly, incorruptibly good, instinctively, infallibly wise – wise, not for self-development, but for self-renunciation, wise, not that she may set herself above her husband, but that she may never fail from his side' (ibid.: 112). Therefore what she learned was to be determined by how far it helped to make her a helpmeet. A girl should study the same subjects as a boy but she must not study them 'thoroughly' as a boy must, 'but only so far as may enable her to sympathise in her husband's pleasures, and in those of his best friends' (ibid.: 119). Ruskin exhorted his audience to bring up their girls according to this plan, and the women to use their power of influence for its true purpose. In this way, he suggested in a final lyrical, and somewhat obscure, passage, they would be fit in the end to meet Christ at the gate of a garden (ibid.: 156–8).

The Women's Movement had, up to this point, tended to treat the life decreed for girls by the domestic ideology as 'custom', and to judge it by its practical results. These, as Langham Place and its supporters argued, caused girls to fritter away their youth waiting for marriage (Milne 1857: 121–2; Smith 1857: 9; EWJ October 1858: 9). Therefore, when the Women's

Movement was faced with this new glorification of the Angel in the House myth, one major strand in the response was to reply that the reality was very different from the ideal. Girls, they argued in the serious reviews, did not spend the period of young ladyhood in preparing for their role as wives but in 'idle selfishness', 'busy idleness', and 'idle dreaming' (Fawcett 1867: 516–7; Holland 1869: 323–31). They could not settle to any course of study because there were so many interruptions and distractions. The home, Emily Shirreff said, was 'quiet enough for doing nothing in' but not a good place for study (Shirreff 1873: 91; Wedgwood 1869: 250–3). They had unlimited leisure and were prevented from doing anything with it. They were, as Emily Davies (1866: 68) put it, 'liberally gifted with the kind of freedom enjoyed by the denizens of a village pound. Within their prescribed sphere, they may wander at will.'

Moreover, it was pointed out, most of the qualities complained of in women were caused by these conditions. The extravagant behaviour of the 'girls of the period', the fast Society girls who used slang, went out fishing and shooting with men and followed them into the smoking room, was the result of a foolish education, idleness, and frustration of the natural abilities (Fawcett 1867: 517; Holland 1869: 324; Mayor 1869: 201). Women were criticised for indulging in 'scandal and slander', but the reason for this was that their lives provided them with no other stimulating topics of conversation (Davies 1866: 121–2).

However by the mid-1860s, Women's Movement members were coming to realize that they were up against a body of belief, not just a set of contemporary practices, and that the belief system as well as the practices must be analysed and attacked. In the late 1860s the conception of women as 'relative creatures' began to be described and ridiculed. Emily Davies wrote: 'The only intelligible principle on which modern writers show anything like unanimity, is that women are intended to supply, and ought to be made, something which men want' (ibid.: 23). Frances Power Cobbe (1869: 21) renamed it the theory of 'Woman as Adjective' and discussed it at some length. Men, she said, believed that 'the final cause of the existence of Woman is the service she can render to Man' (ibid.: 6). She found this particularly striking in the writings of Comte, a translation of whose *A General View of Positivism* with its chapter on women integrating the Angel in the House myth with his general philosophy had been published in English in 1865. She wrote:

> [Comte] has all along been thinking, *not* of what is Woman's own end and aim; how she can attain to Happiness or to Virtue, and what can she then do for her fellow creatures? But simply, like all the rest, he has thought, 'What can Woman best do for *me?*
>
> (Cobbe 1869: 21)

Women, she argued like the bluestockings before her, were created to serve God. They, like men, had immortal souls, and part of their duty on earth was to use their God-given powers to the full:

> It is, to say the least, illogical to suppose that the most stupid of human females has been called into being by the Almighty principally to the end that John or James should have the comfort of a wife; nay, even that Robert or Richard should owe their birth to her as their mother. Believing that the same woman, a million ages hence, will be a glorious spirit before the throne of God, filled with unutterable love, and light, and joy, we cannot satisfactorily trace the beginning of that eternal and seraphic existence to Mr. Smith's want of a wife for a score of years here upon earth; or to the necessity Mr. Jones was under to find somebody to cook his food and repair his clothes. If these ideas be absurd, then it follows that we are not arrogating too much in seeking elsewhere than in the interests of Man the Ultimate *raison d'être* of Woman.
>
> (Cobbe 1869: 22–3)

The fundamental purpose of a woman's life was for her, as it had been for the bluestockings, and as it was for many of her Women's Movement contemporaries (Davies 1866: 35–7; Smith 1857: 6–7), a religious one.

Women's Movement members began to attack quite specifically the belief that women's 'sphere' was restricted to the home, suggesting that it was out of date, irrational, and should be abandoned. A writer in the *Westminster Review* spoke of the 'honest prejudice' which opposed 'all that tends to widen the sphere of woman's interest and usefulness' (Conway 1868: 458). Julia Wedgwood commented that 'the ideal of Woman and Domestic Life' was based on a 'bundle' of arbitrarily joined facts. She wrote:

> To say, then, that 'Home is the proper sphere of woman', that 'No education of women is valuable which does not fit them for domestic life', to use any of the well-worn formulas, in short, is to say that you must bring girls up to hanker after husbands.
>
> (Wedgwood 1869: 26, 264)

Alternatively, Emily Davies (1866: 118–23) argued, women educated for self-realization would be better company for their husbands than under the present system which produced only empty-headed gossips. Marriage under the doctrine of separate spheres was far from a satisfactory relationship. The helpmeet ideal was not fulfilled. Therefore, she suggested:

> May we not welcome, as at least a step in the right direction, a change in our conventional habits, which may extend, though in

ever so small a degree, the region of common thoughts and aims, common hopes and disappointments, common joys and common sorrows?

(Davies 1866: 128–9)

With these attacks, the domestic ideology ceased to be doxa. It had been dragged out of the realm of the 'undiscussed and undisputed' by the Women's Movement advocates, and by the end of the 1860s the heterodoxy by which it was to be opposed had been pretty thoroughly thrashed out.[3] Moreover, in 1869 John Stuart Mill's *The Subjection of Women* was published, and the objections to the domestic ideology – as Kate Millet (1972: 121–39) has shown, Mill discussed and demolished all the major propositions defended by Ruskin – were integrated with the liberal, individualist ideas which were becoming increasingly orthodox among the commercial and professional classes. Ruskin had argued for the domestic ideology as being in accordance with the aristocratic ideal. Mill set out to show that it was incompatible with the entrepreneurial ideal.

Mill's main argument was that altering the position of women was the next step in the liberal path to gaining equality for all. Slavery, absolute monarchy, and martial law had been shown to be wrong. Now it was time that women should be freed from subjection in accordance with the same arguments. The present situation of women was quite out of step with the modern world and its principle of the career open to the talents.

If the principle is true, we ought to act as if we believed it, and not to ordain that to be born a girl instead of a boy, any more than to be born black instead of white, or a commoner instead of a nobleman, shall decide a person's position through all life – shall interdict people from all the more elevated social positions, and from all, except a few, respectable occupations.

(Mill 1869: 235)

He would not accept that there was any 'natural' difference between men and women and so rejected the Angel in the House celebration of woman's 'moral influence' and 'higher nature'. All this meant, he said, was that women were trained in 'exaggerated self-abnegation', and would sacrifice themselves for others in their families. This, rather than influencing men for good, taught these men 'to worship their own will as such a grand thing that it is actually the law for another rational being.' This self-worship was the result of privilege in class and sex. Christianity disapproved of such self will, and yet blindly continued to sanction the institutions which nourished it (ibid.: 258). The family was far from being a school of the virtues: 'the true virtue of human beings is fitness to live together as equals; claiming nothing for themselves but what they as freely concede to everyone else.' For men, the family was rather a place where 'the virtues of despotism, but also its vices, are largely nourished' (ibid.: 260).

With Mill's intervention the 'brick wall' that Bessie Rayner Parkes felt she was confronting in 1858 began to crumble. When he stood for parliament in 1865 he put female suffrage back on the Women's Movement agenda by naming it as part of his political platform, and a number of suffrage societies were founded (Strachey 1928: 102–3). With the publication of his book in 1869, the 'women's rights' agenda of the pre-1850s Unitarian radicals became once more the focus for progressives. In consequence, I shall suggest later, the campaigns for expanding women's work and women's education lost much of their glamour, and the next cohort of unattached intellectuals devoted their energies to these more overtly political campaigns.

During the 1860s and 1870s, however, the focus of the Movement was still on work. The Langham Place circle had created a flourishing heterodoxy which made it possible to argue that all women should be trained for an occupation and practise it while they remained unmarried. Furthermore, the Society for Promoting the Employment of Women managed to persuade some employers to consider young women in previously all-male areas, and their example was copied, while gentility and femininity were redefined in the schools founded by the education movement to make work before marriage acceptable. It is of course possible, even likely, that these developments would ultimately have eventuated without the intervention of the Women's Movement. Nevertheless, as was argued in Chapter 1, the form of such changes is in no sense predetermined. If the agents initiating change had been different the manner and outcomes of the change would have been different also. What actually happened is the subject of the next two chapters.

# 9

# REDEFINING
# 'WOMEN'S WORK'
## Creating a 'pull factor'

On the twentieth anniversary of the founding of the Society for Promoting the Employment of Women in 1879, its Annual Report noted the great increase in the variety of occupations in which women were employed, and claimed:

> There is every reason to believe that the advance has been steady, and that the census of 1881 will show a proportionate increase in numbers. That the Society has been one of the main agents in bringing about this result, in opening new fields of occupation for women, and thereby increasing their usefulness and – as a natural consequence – their happiness is, the Committee believe, indisputable.
>
> (EWR 1879: 295)

Historians of the Women's Movement have, as was pointed out in Chapter 1, tended to reject such claims, and placed little emphasis on its contribution to the expansion of women's work. The economic determinist belief that this expansion was a response to employers' needs has led to the assumption that the focus on work in the *English Woman's Journal* and the activities of the Society for Promoting the Employment of Women did no more than persuade a few hundred individuals to take advantage of new opportunities which were the outcome of economic and industrial change. They have assumed that although the Society may have done good work in encouraging some young women to respond to a new 'pull' from employers in such areas as clerical work and hairdressing, they played no part in creating that pull (Holcombe 1973: 18; Levine 1987: 100).

In this chapter a rather different interpretation of the process is being offered. It is suggested that the members of the society, through their precept and example, created a pull from employers who would not otherwise have considered employing young middle-class women. Elementary school teaching and retail work were not the only areas where the educational requirements were relatively high and the chances of promotion low; employers in clerical work, librarianship, hospital dispensing and hairdressing had similar needs. Yet they were prevented by their androcentric blindness, their 'knowledge' of the appropriate workforce, from discovering for themselves the same solution. When, however, the Society for Promoting the Employment of Women began arguing that there were many previously male occupations where young women would make suitable employees and demonstrated it by arranging employment for a few pioneers, employers in the areas pioneered gradually realised that they could solve many of their problems by employing some of the relatively well-educated, well-spoken and reliable young women who had previously competed for work as dressmakers and governesses.

The women who composed the Langham Place circle saw themselves as unattached intellectuals, committed to combatting 'the misery in the world and its ignorance' (Rendall 1989: 162, quoted) not simply by palliative philanthropic work, but by analyzing the manner in which their society operated and if necessary bringing about structural change. In the radical circles in which Barbara Leigh Smith and Bessie Rayner Parkes grew up the arguments of the classical political economists were widely discussed, and it was in terms of these ideas that they analyzed the society around them and strove to understand the problems facing women. When they looked at these problems in terms of the belief deriving from Adam Smith that unfettered competition was the basis of social prosperity and happiness, the constraints and impediments imposed by the demands of gentility and femininity became apparent (Parkes 1859a: 149–52). Thus their earliest and perhaps greatest contribution to improving the situation of women came through their recognition, not simply that women's economic situation was precarious, nor that the problems of dressmakers and governesses came from the overstocking in these occupations, but that their situation would be improved if they could compete for some of the work at that date restricted to men.

## The Society for Promoting the Employment of Women

That a wider range of occupations should be opened to women was not a solution that sprang readily to mind in the 1850s. Even though suggestions that the cause lay in overstocking had been first made in the 1840s (Greg 1844: 152; Pinchbeck 1930: 313), this possible cause was not addressed by the charitable endeavours proposed in the following decade. The various societies formed to help needlewomen concentrated their efforts on trying to eliminate the middle man between worker and customer (*All the Year Round* 1860: 427–8; Ritchie 1861: 329–30), while the society formed to help governesses, as was recounted in Chapter 6, concentrated its efforts on raising qualifications, a project which, though it might improve conditions for those who qualified, could do nothing to diminish the numbers pressing for work.

Each of these solutions seems to relate back to one of the competing ideologies of the day. The attempts to help needlewomen would appear to have
had their roots in the aristocratic ideal with its conception of a rigidly strat-
ified society where each class had its duties and where relations were softened
and humanised by the doctrine of *noblesse oblige*. If rich and poor, the theory
would seem to have been, could be brought back into proper relations and
the middlemen eliminated, the problems would vanish. The poor would
work directly for them.

The Governesses' Benevolent Institution, on the other hand, dominated as
it was by men who were later to become Christian Socialists, looked to the
sort of solidarity that at one level of society was allowing the professions, by
organizing themselves into chartered bodies, to raise both their status and
income, and at another level was protecting the skills and incomes of tradesmen through the craft unions. Such beliefs in co-operation and solidarity
among workers are seen by Harold Perkin (1969: 232) as important characteristics of what he has called the working-class ideal, and it was these tactics
which the Governesses' Benevolent Institution was employing when its leaders
tried to solve the problem of overstocking in the profession by setting up a cer-
tificate of proficiency which they hoped would become a criterion for entry.

The entrepreneurial ideal, however, made it possible to see the solution as
altering the contemporary definition of women's work. Even in the 1840s
this had appealed to Anna Jameson. Like the classical economists, she saw
society as in a constant state of flux, with changes in one sector needing
changes in another to maintain equilibrium. The problem of overstocking,
she believed, could only be solved by making a wider range of employments
available to women. In 1846 she wrote bitterly that a woman's opportunities
for employment were 'limited by law – or custom, strong as law; or prejudice, stronger than either, – to one or two departments, while, in every other,
the door is shut against her' (Jameson 1846: 230). Yet women were, she felt,
quite capable of doing other work:

> She can write a good hand, and is a quick and ready accountant. She
> might be a clerk, – or a cashier, – or an assistant in a mercantile
> house. Such a thing is common in France, but here in England, who
> would employ her? Who would countenance such an innovation on
> all our English ideas of feminine propriety? I have heard of women
> employed in writing and engrossing for attorneys, but this is
> scarcely an acknowledged means of existence; they are employed
> secretly, and merely because they are paid much less than men.
>
> (Jameson 1846: 236–7)

Other brief suggestions of a similar sort had been made (Adams 1849:
370; *Fraser's* 1844: 580–1; HW 1852: 84–5; HW 1853: 576), but the real
publicity for the idea came only with the organized Women's Movement.

171

Barbara Leigh Smith put the whole case with confidence and aplomb in *Women's Work*:

> There is no way of aiding governesses or needlewomen but by opening more ways of gaining livelihoods for women ... apprentice 10,000 to watchmakers, train 10,000 for teachers of the young; make 10,000 good accountants; put 10,000 more to be nurses under deaconesses trained by Florence Nightingale; put some thousands in the electric telegraph offices over all the country; educate 1000 lecturers for mechanics' institutions; 1000 readers to read the best books to the working people; train up 10,000 to manage washing machines, sewing machines, etc. Then the distressed needle-women would vanish; the decayed gentlewomen and broken down governesses would no longer exist.
>
> (Smith 1857: 16–17)

This was the view which the *English Woman's Journal* put forward, and its early issues had a number of optimistic articles pointing out the advantages of such occupations as telegraph work, wood and steel engraving, life assurance agency, typesetting and medicine (EWJ March 1858: 10; April 1859: 120–1, May 1859: 259–70; May 1860: 145–61).

Though their intention may have been simply to change public opinion, to alert employers to the existence of a suitable workforce and encourage women to make efforts to enter new work, the editors soon found themselves called upon to deal in practical terms with large numbers of distressed individuals. They were, Bessie Rayner Parkes told a Social Science Congress, 'literally deluged' with applicants for employment, with up to twenty women a day coming in person to ask for work which they had no hope of supplying. These women were, she said, 'all of them more or less educated – all of them with some claim to the title of lady' (Parkes 1860: 812–3).

This put pressure on the Langham Place group to move beyond the attempt to change public opinion to actually showing that it was possible to find alternative work for some at least of these women. Most of the women who called at the office were beyond the movement's help, being too set in their ways and too anxious to cling to gentility to consider the kind of radical solutions proposed.[1] Nevertheless, they provided a pool out of which some promising recruits could be chosen to move into new occupations and give a practical demonstration that such things were possible. The initiator of this project was Jessie Boucherett (1825–1905), the daughter of a Lincolnshire landed proprietor, who encountered an early copy of the *English Woman's Journal* and was impressed by the point of view expressed there. In 1859 she was prompted to action by Harriet Martineau's article on 'Female Industry' in the *Edinburgh Review*. One passage in particular clarified her ideas, and showed her the path to take:

The tale is plain enough – from whatever mouth it comes. So far from our countrywomen being all maintained, as a matter of course by us, 'the breadwinners', three millions out of six adult Englishwomen work for subsistence; and two out of the three in independence. With this new condition of affairs, new duties and new views must be accepted.[2]

(Martineau 1859: 336)

By June 1859 she had made contact with the *English Woman's Journal* group and, with the help of the poet Adelaide Procter, had held the initial meeting which established the Society for Promoting the Employment of Women (Boucherett 1864b). By November the Society had gained the official support of the National Association for the Promotion of Social Science and a prestigious list of office bearers recruited from the Association's stars: Lord Shaftesbury as president, as vice-presidents the Bishops of London and Oxford, the Rt. Hon. W. E. Gladstone, and the then Vice-Chancellor, Sir Wood Page, and a committee composed of both men and women which included a number of Langham Place stalwarts (EWJ 1859: 287). Its objects were defined as:

the opening up of new employments for women, and their more extensive admission into such employments as are already open to them. The providing of technical instruction for girls and young women by apprenticeship or other means, in businesses of various kinds suited to their strength and capacity, and the procuring of employment for them, when trained.

(EWR 1879: 291 quoted)

It would appear from this statement that Jessie Boucherett, who was to be the main driving force behind the Society, had taken as her focus just one of the of ideas being mooted by the Women's Movement: the idea that problems of 'overstocking' in teaching and sewing, and of 'surplus women' left unmarried, were to be solved by changing the sexual division of labour and thus making more sorts of work available to them. In spite of her apparently conservative, land-owning background, she was a wholehearted convert to belief in unfettered competition for work. The title of the book she published in 1863, *Hints on Self-Help*, indicates support for the entrepreneurial ideal as expounded by Samuel Smiles, and in this and her other writings her commitment to current political economy is manifest (Boucherett 1863; 1864a; 1869).

Unlike Barbara Leigh Smith and Bessie Rayner Parkes, she was not particularly concerned about the problems of the upper-middle-class girl trapped in the drawing room with nothing to think about but a future marriage. Nor was she concerned with the problems of the same sort of girl whose father had gone bankrupt or died leaving her penniless, and who was now desperately looking for work which would both keep her alive and let her remain a lady.

She believed that it was her 'mission' and that of the Society to broaden the range of occupations for which lower-middle-class women could be trained, and thereby take the pressure off the traditional teaching and sewing. The areas she chose for her operations were the areas that the brothers of such girls might enter, the typical lower-middle-class occupations of clerk and skilled tradesman.

## The Society and the trades

Although no archives have survived of the Society for Promoting the Employment of Women, extracts from its annual reports appeared in the *English Woman's Journal* and the *Englishwoman's Review* for more than fifty years. These allow some estimate to be made of the extent of its activities. What is very clear is that these were limited. The annual income of the Society seldom reached £500 a year, and the number of women for whom positions were found was usually about fifty. However, unlike most philanthropic organizations, its primary aim was not to help individuals in distress, but to use individuals to create a society where that particular form of distress was less likely to occur. It was believed that although 'some time must be allowed to elapse before the idea involved in these model experiments could be expected to be seized by the commercial public' (Parkes 1860: 815) eventually the example set by the Society would be followed. Thus the individuals towards whom the Society directed its slender resources were chosen primarily because of their suitability as pioneers in unusual occupations for women, and the Society was prepared not just to find work for them, but to pay for the training necessary to fit them for that work.

In these early years, the most innovative and successful initiative appeared to be that undertaken by Emily Faithfull, the daughter of an Anglican clergyman who, like Jessie Boucherett, was brought into the Langham Place group by reading the *English Woman's Journal*. In March 1860 she established the Victoria Press as a private commercial venture and undertook to have girls trained as compositors (Stone 1994: 42–8). The Society paid out £50 to have the first five girls apprenticed, and by August 1861 twenty young women were employed (Boucherett 1861: 217). Emily Faithfull gave an account of the founding of her press to a Social Science Congress which spells out the Society's criteria for deciding which occupations were suitable for young women:

> Having ascertained that if women were properly trained, their physical powers would be singularly adapted to fit them for becoming compositors, though there were other parts of the printing trade – such as the lifting of iron chases in which the pages

are imposed, the carrying of the cases of weighty type from the rack to the frame, and the whole of the presswork (that is, the actual striking off of the sheets), entailing, particularly in the latter department, an amount of continuous bodily exertion, far beyond average female strength, – the next step was to open an office on a sufficiently large scale to give the experiment a fair opportunity of success.

(Faithfull 1860: 819)

The long term view of the Society that its object was to modify the sexual division of labour, not help distressed ladies, is obvious in her concluding remarks:

For compositorship it is most desirable that girls should be apprenticed early in life, as they cannot earn enough to support themselves under three or four years, and should, therefore, commence learning the trade while living under their father's roof. Boys are always apprenticed early in life, at the age of fourteen; and if women are to be introduced into the mechanical arts, it must be under the same conditions. I can hardly lay enough stress upon this point; so convinced am I of its truth that I now receive no new hands over eighteen years of age.

(ibid.: 822)

Yet although the press was a considerable success, gaining royal patronage and publishing many of the later books and pamphlets of the Women's Movement and of the National Association for the Promotion of Social Science (Stone 1994: 42–8), it did not initiate the feminization of typesetting as an occupation. There was little attempt made by printing firms beyond the influence of the Employment Society to take female apprentices, and the experiment was considered 'a wild scheme of social reformers and cranks' by the male printers' unions (Cockburn 1983: 25–6). The union members resisted the admission of women, and according to Emily Faithfull, 'the girl apprentices were subjected to all kinds of annoyance. Tricks of a most unmanly nature were resorted to' (Faithfull 1884: 24). The Royal Commission into women's work in the 1890s, however, gave credit to a different union tactic for the 'very small' number of female compositors:

There is no doubt whatever, that this is due to the policy of the London Compositors' Society, which, while declaring itself by no means hostile to the employment of women, will only allow them to be employed in a union shop at the same rate as men.

(P. 1893–4 vol. 37: 93)

It would seem that though Emily Faithfull had shown that women were capable of performing the work of compositors, the advantages they offered were not sufficient to encourage employers to persevere in the face of opposition from their male employees.

Similar union opposition seems to have prevented the feminization of other trades into which the Society sought to introduce women. The Society concentrated primarily on trades which had some connection with art, possibly because art-related crafts had already been established as feminine through the success of women at the School of Design, and because women were already established as wood-engravers for publishers (Martineau 1859: 333). Efforts were made at different times to have women taught glass-painting, glass-engraving, illuminating, gilding, art-engraving, china-painting, plan-tracing and wood-carving, mostly by paying apprenticeship fees (EWR 1876: 223–4; 1879: 293–5). They were, however, as Harriet Martineau (1865: 411) reported, 'hampered and vexed at every step by the jealousy and ill-will of men who are . . . dead set against women doing anything but sewing'.

In one area, however, the Society seems to have gained a foothold for women by encouraging them to act as strike-breakers. From its foundation the Society had seen hairdressing as an occupation which ought to be women's work (Davies 1910: 12). Women had apparently been hairdressers until the mid-eighteenth century, when a fashion for French hairdressers had driven them out of the occupation (Pinchbeck 1930: 291–2). In 1861 the Society began a hairdressing class in London, and in 1865 persuaded a few hairdressers to take female apprentices while in 1868 it helped a former apprentice 'set up in business'. (EWR 1868: 534; 1879: 292). In 1869 a Mr Douglas of Bond Street had a strike among his employees and took the opportunity of employing twelve women in their place (Faithfull 1871: 380). (The Society members, being at this date supporters of the entrepreneurial ideal and so opponents of the idea of combination, had few scruples about arranging strike-breaking.) The next year the Society's Report noted:

> In hairdressing, Mr Truefitt has followed the example of Mr Douglas and now employs women in his establishments both in London and Brighton. The plan has also been adopted by another hairdresser at Brighton. The girls formerly apprenticed by the Society naturally find employment in these shops.
>
> (EWR 1870: 116)

In 1876 the *Englishwoman's Review* reported (225) that a woman had set up her own hairdressing shop in Kensington, and by 1884 Emily Faithfull (1884: 304) could write that 'women are very generally employed in this suitable occupation'.

Nevertheless, as Table 9.1 shows, the census returns suggest that the fem-

*Table 9:1* Number of women returned as employed as hairdressers and wigmakers in the censuses from 1841 to 1911 with percentage of women in the category each year.

| *1841* | *1851* | *1861* | *1871* | *1881* | *1891* | *1901* | *1911* |
|--------|--------|--------|--------|--------|--------|--------|--------|
| 249 | — | 412 | 1,240 | 768 | 1,274 | 1,745 | 4,687 |
| (2.6%) | | (3.7%) | (9.4%) | (5.1%) | (5.0%) | (4.9%) | (9.6%) |

inization of the occupation was not rapid. Although a large rise was recorded in the percentage of women employed between 1861 and 1871, this seems rather early for the influence of the Society to have had such an effect, while no similar increase was again recorded until 1911, which seems rather late to be a response to the Society's example. It would seem that, as with printing, the Society had directed its efforts to an area where employers could see no particular benefit in moving from male to female employees.

In one new occupational area, however, where neither unions nor professional organizations had yet established themselves, the Society achieved a modest success. Hospital dispensing proved to be an area where the particular characteristics of young female employees, once encountered, were appreciated, and the Society succeeded in introducing women into this new and expanding occupation which, without its intervention, would almost certainly have remained dominated by men at least for some decades. As with printing, it was an initiative from a core member of the Langham Place group which provided the first place for women to train in this relatively new occupation, and it seems that here, her example was followed by employers in institutions well beyond her personal influence.

In 1865 Elizabeth Garrett, the first woman to qualify in Britain as a medical practitioner, set up house in London with her old school friend Jane Crow, who had been Secretary to the Society for Promoting the Employment of Women since 1860, and began to build up a medical practice (Boucherett 1864b: 19; Manton 1965: 167–70). In 1866 she set up a Dispensary for Women and Children, employed an experienced male dispenser to make up the medicines, and persuaded him to take on two young women as paying pupils. The first pupil took over as dispenser in 1868 and by 1870 two others had moved on to positions in other dispensaries (Faithfull 1871: 380; EWR 1870: 115–16).

I have described elsewhere how, when it became known in 1872 that there were members on the Council of the Pharmaceutical Society sympathetic to their cause, three of these young women were put forward as pioneers for the entry of women into pharmacy (Jordan 1998). These women all passed the examinations that entitled them to be listed as pharmaceutical chemists, and were, after a struggle among the membership, admitted to the Society. Two of them, Louisa Stammwitz and Isabella Clarke, then set up their own chemist's shops, Isabella Clarke later becoming a pharmacy lecturer to female medical students, while the third, Rose Minshull, continued to work all her life as a hospital dispenser (Buchanan and Neve 1926: 374–375; C&D 1892: 143–6).

These women are three of the very few protégées of the Society for Promoting the Employment of Women whose names have survived. I have found the entries for the families of Rose Minshull and Isabella Clarke (but unfortunately not Louisa Stammwitz) in the 1881 census enumerators' books, and these reveal that they were typical of the group of women who were the concern of Langham Place, in their thirties, living with elderly parents and with unmarried younger sisters. In the 1881 census Rose Minshull was recorded as aged 34, living with a 70-year-old bristle merchant father and a 33-year-old dispenser sister. According to a late undocumented source, Isabella Clarke's father had been a solicitor (Shellard 1996: 2), but by the time of the 1881 census she was aged 38, and living with a widowed mother of 73 and two unmarried sisters (aged 36 and 34), one of whom was a dispenser and the other an artist.

While only a very few women went on to become pharmacists in the decades following the success of these women, evidence from the 1890s suggests that the expansion and reform of the hospital system in the 1880s was accompanied by an expansion of the number of women employed in hospital dispensaries (Maggs 1983: 6–11). In 1895 the Local Government Board reformulated its rules relating to the qualifications of hospital dispensers, and recognized in addition to the qualifications administered by the Pharmaceutical Society, the Assistants' License issued by the Society of Apothecaries (PJ&T 1895: 1178). This qualification had been established in 1815, and for the first seventy years of its existence was obtained by a fluctuating (always under a hundred) number of men. In 1887, at the same time as the Society lifted its twenty-year ban on examining women for its medical licence, a woman presented herself for the Assistant's examination and over the next six years fourteen women were granted this licence. Then a striking feminization occurred: in 1894 fourteen of the seventy-nine new licensees were women, rising to 100 out of 136 in 1900 (Guildhall Library: Ms. 10,987). The Annual Registers of Chemists and Druggists show a similar increase of women during this period: between 1873 and 1891 only sixteen women took the Minor Examination of the Pharmaceutical Society; by 1900 thirty-four more names had been added to the list.

In hospital dispensing, it seems, the Society had found an occupation where, like elementary teaching and retail work, the relatively high educational qualifications and rapid turnover offered by young women suited the employers' needs, and where the introduction of a few pioneers led to a wider feminization.

## Clerical work

The Society's greatest success, however, would seem to be its impact on clerical work, and particularly the fact that its efforts ensured that employer's 'knowledge' had been extended to see women as possible employees before the invention of the typewriter transformed the more routine aspects of this occupation.

In this area, too, the Society encouraged the establishment of a pilot enterprise to show what women could do. In February 1860, Maria Rye (1829–1903), an early supporter of the married women's property campaign and a founder member of the Society, set up a law copying office, where, under the guidance of 'an invalided law-stationer's clerk', women not only learned the business but carried out work for legal firms. By 1868 eight women were regularly employed in the office while a further fifty were called on for casual work (EWR 1868: 534) while as early as 1862 two quite independent agencies had been set up by others (Boucherett 1884: 98; EWR 1868: 534; Diamond 1996: 157–8; EWJ August 1862: 378).

By 1864, however, the hope that 'established law-stationers' would employ the women trained had encountered the same problems as printing and the other crafts, 'viz., the jealousy of men already engaged in the profession'. 'The law-copyists of London,' the *Alexandra Magazine* reported, 'form a sort of close corporation or guild, into which none are admitted without having served a seven years' apprenticeship.' Although women were proving themselves cheaper and more reliable they were not being employed because 'in the way of this consummation arises the grand difficulty, that should a law-stationer engage a female clerk, it is at the risk of all the men in his employ instantly leaving him' (*Alex-Mag* 1864: 305).

Maria Rye's office, in consequence, broadened its field to include other forms of copying, and in 1864 was advertising in the following terms:

> Miss Rye's Law Copying Office, 12, Portugal Street, Lincoln's Inn. Law Papers of all kinds, Specifications, Bills of Quantities, Parish Returns, Ships' Books, Sermons, and Petitions, carefully copied and punctually returned. Deeds engrossed. Envelopes addressed. Miscellaneous MSS. copied in running hand. References and Specimens of work done may be had on application to the Manager, Miss N. E. Frances. N.B. – Only Female Clerks are employed in this Office.
>
> (*Alexandra Magazine* 1864: 4)

Nevertheless, this venture seems to have established the commercial viability of running copying agencies staffed by women. It is noteworthy that the appearance of the typewriter was quickly followed by the establishment of typing agencies run by and employing women (EWR 1884: 290, 479;

1886: 189, 514).

The Society had more success in its efforts to obtain clerical work for young women as bookkeepers. This was not work which could be regarded as unfeminine since it had traditionally been done by the wives and daughters of shopkeepers and merchants (Martineau 1859: 311; Pinchbeck 1930: 295). The only innovation was that it was being done outside the home and for money. Jessie Boucherett's view in the early days was the one put forward by Harriet Martineau in her *Edinburgh Review* article: that it was only their lack of arithmetical skill which kept women out of this obviously suitable work (TNAPSS 1859: 728). In 1860, therefore, the Society began to run evening classes in bookkeeping, and to make efficient use of the rented premises a day school, financed by Jessie Boucherett, was opened which concentrated on the handwriting and arithmetical skills a clerk would be likely to require. In 1870 this school had an average attendance of seventy and it continued until 1875 (EWR 1879: 292).

An account of the Society for Promoting the Employment of Women's efforts in the clerical area was given to the Civil Service Commissioners in November 1874 by its current secretary, Gertrude King. Most of their placements, she told the commissioners, were as bookkeepers in shops. Such work was 'very largely increasing', and it was much easier for women to get such employment than formerly. These positions were mostly filled by 'daughters of the better class of tradespeople'; the 'ladies' the Employment Society tried to help had 'rather a reluctance to go into shops', though some did. The Employment Society had, however, opened two other areas where these ladies could get clerical employment. 'For many years' they had been placing them as bookkeepers in warehouses, and, more recently, as temporary clerks with the Society for the Propagation of the Gospel and with fourteen other charitable societies.

All the women they recommended had been tested for suitability, sitting for an arithmetic examination, writing a letter and taking a dictation test. Over the years they had had very few complaints from employers of any of their protégées and though the charitable societies had never had female clerks before, they continued to employ them once they had tried them. The women they placed were, she said, 'chiefly of the tradesman rank', but there were as well 'ladies of the middle rank who have had homes until perhaps their parents die, and then, at 30 or 35, they are thrown upon the world'. They had placed sixty-eight women in permanent employment during 1873 (PP 1875, Vol 23: 218–9).

One of the Society's greatest successes was its involvement in the decision made by the Post Office to employ female clerks. The census figures suggest that even in 1841, when the expansion following the introduction of the penny post had scarcely begun, the Post Office had had some female employees, but these were presumably elderly female shopkeepers who did the post office business in their villages. By 1861 a new pattern was developing, part of the general movement of young women into retail work. In 1851 126 women aged fifteen to twenty-four were returned in the census as working for the Post Office, 291 in 1861, and 1,063 in 1871. Though some of those recorded in 1871 may have been 'messengers', many of them were probably 'counter women', 'a class of young women who are employed and paid by the letter-receivers . . . and who are not in the direct service of the Crown' (Trollope 1877: 384). It was not, however, until 1870, when the Post Office took over the telegraph service from the railway companies and with it acquired the 201 young women employed in its central office, that any question arose of making women part of the Post Office central establishment (Martindale 1938: 16).

Women's presence in the telegraph service was the result of an initiative by one of the few men who, before the appearance of the Women's Movement, had seen the possibility of using middle-class girls in a new occupation. According to an account given in the *English Woman's Journal*, Lewis Ricardo, the chairman of the International and Electric Telegraph Company, discovered that the daughter of one stationmaster was doing all his telegraph business for him. This led Ricardo in 1853 to introduce a staff of young women as telegraph operators into the central office of the company where their femininity was preserved by the presence of a matron, Mrs Craig, and where they eventually replaced most of the male operators. The women were reported to be 'not only more teachable, more attentive, and quicker-eyed than the men clerks formerly employed, but . . . also . . . more trustworthy, more easily managed, and, we may add, sooner satisfied with lower wages' and the number employed had risen to ninety by 1859 (Rye 1859: 261). In the 1861 census 213 women were returned as employed in telegraphs (8.2 per cent of the total number), but by 1871 the number had only risen to 222 women, now only 7.6 per cent of the total, almost all presumably employed in the Central Office.

The Society for Promoting the Employment of Women had been recommending the Service to young women and finding operators for the service throughout the 1860s. When the transfer to the Post Office occurred, they discovered that, in Jessie Boucherett's words, 'by good fortune, or more correctly speaking, by the mercy of Providence, Mr Scudamore, whose official duty it was to regulate the telegraphs, was favourable to the employment of women' (Boucherett 1884: 94), and the Society was able to list thirteen telegraph clerks among the '63 permanent situations gained through the Society's Register' in its 1870 Annual Report (Martindale 1938: 16; EWR 1870: 117).

The acquisition of the telegraph service marked the beginning of a move by senior civil servants in the Post Office to take advantage of the cheapness and efficiency of female labour which Frank Scudamore praised so highly (see Chapter 1). Within a few years women, as well as operating the telegraph machines, were being employed on simple clerical work in the Telegraph Clearing House and the Returned Letter Office. These women were described as being 'from the class from which assistants behind the counters of shops are recruited' (Manners 1881: 184) and did the work of very low level clerks. In December 1873, however, when the Controller of the Savings Bank asked for some of the 'boy clerks' and 'writers' who currently made up his staff to be replaced with more responsible, but more expensive, 'Third Class Clerks', the Secretary to the Post Office, Sir John Tilly, responded by suggesting that he consider using women (POST 30/275 D [E 3613/1875] File No. I).

The Controller seems to have been appalled at this suggestion. He fought a seven-month rearguard action against the move, producing long and elaborate reports explaining why female clerks would not be suitable, and, finding the Secretary adamant, trying to have writers rather than the requested clerks replaced by women, a tactic which brought the stern rejoinder:

> Mr Thomson's answer is not satisfactory. My memorandum of the 15th Instant does not affect the point in question.
>
> On the 10th of April last Mr Thomson was informed in the clearest possible language that the Postmaster General had decided to appoint Female Clerks instead of increasing the Established Force of male Clerks, and yet on the 16th Instant he says that the Female Staff will take the place of writers.
>
> I must therefore ask Mr Thomson to be so good as to state that he now clearly understands the Postmaster General's intentions and that he will exert himself to carry them into effect.
> JT June 23 1874
>
> (POST 30/275 D [E 36/1875] File No. II)

By July 1874 the plan was fully formed. The planned establishment was to consist of:

> 1 Lady Superintendent at £165 by £15 to £300
> 2 Principal Clerks £110 by £10 to £150
> 10 First Class Clerks £80 by £7.10/- to £100
> 52 Second Class Clerks £40 by £7.10/- to £75.

The records suggest that a role for the Society for Promoting the Employment of Women had been incorporated into the scheme.[3] The Postmaster General, Lord John Manners, favoured appointing the women by what was known technically as 'limited competition', a system in which a group of candidates nominated as under the old patronage system, sat for competitive examinations. When Sir John Tilly pointed out that, because they now favoured open competition, it was 'very difficult to move the Treasury in this direction' ( POST 30/275 D [E 3613/1875] File No. III) the following case was put to the Treasury and accepted:

> Assuming that your Lordships adopt my propositions the question will arise as the best mode of proceeding in order to obtain candidates.

They must be persons who have been somewhat carefully educated and to my mind it is very undesirable to collect a crowd of young ladies by public advertisement and subject the good majority of them to trouble and expense only to end in disappointment. ['I am almost ashamed to repeat what' crossed out] I stated in my letter of the 13th instant that no fewer than 700 female candidates presented themselves on a recent occasion to compete for 5 places ['the value of which was only 14/- a week' crossed out] I think therefore the competition should be limited and that the candidates who must in that case be nominated should be in the proportion of three to each vacancy to be filled.

I should propose, as the most convenient arrangement, to place myself in communication with persons who take a prominent part in obtaining ['suitable' crossed out] employment for educated women and by this means I have little doubt that a sufficiently large number of suitable candidates can be readily collected.

(POST 30/275 D [E 3613/1875] File No. IV)

An appropriate examination with papers in handwriting and orthography, English grammar and composition, arithmetic (including vulgar and decimal fractions), and geography was devised and the first female clerks began work on July 16, 1875. The system of 'limited competition' continued for some years, but when Henry Fawcett, husband of the suffrage leader Millicent Fawcett, became Postmaster General in 1880, it was gradually phased out, and the examinations became open to all women (Manners 1881: 187).

Using the lists of names printed in establishment books of the Post Office, I have been able to identify many of the first female clerks in the 1881 census enumerators' books. This search has revealed a number of demographic differences between the women employed in the mid-1870s and those who entered later, in fact a difference not dissimilar to that found by Frances Widdowson in the young women who entered Whitelands Training College in the 1850s. The first group have the characteristics one would expect from women who appealed to the Society for Promoting the Employment of Women and which the Society was most eager to help. The average age on entry of the thirty-six 1875 entrants I have traced was twenty-two, with the youngest only fifteen and the eldest thirty-four, with four women in the group aged over thirty. Twelve were living with fathers, twelve with widowed mothers, seven were lodgers and four came from orphaned households with a young sister or brother recorded as head. In four cases more than one sister was appointed in 1875, and in six other cases sisters were appointed in the next few years. The fathers' occupations included clerks, clergy, librarians, teachers and a 'retired piano-tuner'.

The second group, those appointed in 1880 and 1881, have less of the appearance of ladies down on their luck than of young women from families where the daughters were expected to go out to work, and who had gained their nomination through the traditional Civil Service patronage channels. The average age of the twelve women I have traced was eighteen, with the youngest sixteen and the eldest twenty-four. All were living with parents and only two of those parents were widowed. The fathers' occupations were, however, similar to the first group, mostly clerical and scholarly but including an architect and a printer.

## Wider influence

As Lee Holcombe (1973: 18) says, 'foreseeing a development is not the same as causing it'. Though the Society was able to demonstrate that women could do the work in a number of occupations not previously undertaken by them, only a small proportion of the occupations involved actually became feminized. This, as was pointed out in Chapter 1, has suggested to historians that the Society did no more than predict certain inevitable trends. To demonstrate, as is claimed here, that its role was crucial in opening a wider range of occupations to middle-class women, it is necessary to demonstrate three things: first, that the numbers of women in an occupation began to increase from the time when the Employment Society began to recommend their employment, second, that there was little structural change in the industry involved which can explain a change in employment policy, and third, that the speeches and writings of employers reveal the influence of Women's Movement propaganda.

The clearest and best-documented case where the influence of the Women's Movement's propaganda can be demonstrated is the introduction of women into librarianship, an area which it had not occurred to the Society for Promoting the Employment of Women to recommend, but where it is recorded that it was Women's Movement discussions which aroused employers to the possibility of hiring young women. In 1879 Alderman Thomas Baker told the Library Association of the United Kingdom how the Manchester Public Free Libraries came to employ young women. For nineteen years after their foundation, he said, the libraries had employed only men and boys, but they had a high turnover of staff, some being dissatisfied with the long hours and others lured away by the prospect of higher wages:

> At this time the subject of woman, her rights, duties and employment – particularly her exclusion from certain trades and professions – was engaging the attention of thoughtful people. Their chairman suggested to the committee that young women should be tried as assistants in libraries. To this they assented: and though it was known that the number of women was greater in proportion to

that of the other sex, it did not occur to them that the situations they had to offer would be so much sought after, and by so superior a class of applicants as made their appearance.

(EWR 1879: 472)

Their first advertisement appeared on 5 September 1871. The library took on three girls to start with and the experiment was so great a success that they now had thirty-one. The women were 'regular in their attendance, attentive to their duties, uniformly courteous to borrowers, and contented with their employment and position, evincing no disposition to leave'. Those who left did so only because of poor health or marriage, and the committee had never had to advertise again, there being applicants waiting for every situation (ibid.; Weibel, Heim and Ellsworth 1979: 35).

This example was followed, albeit slowly. In 1899 the International Congress of Women was told that in rate supported libraries there wer etwenty-eight female librarians, sixteen female branch librarians, and 255 female assistants. Whereas in 1894 only thirty-seven such libraries had female employees, eighty-one had them by 1899, and there were twenty-four other libraries with female employees (Weibel, Heim, and Ellsworth 1979: 4, 35–6). Speakers at the conference felt the work was very suitable for women but that the payment was inadequate, and these views were echoed by M. Mostyn Bird in 1911. She felt that though it was 'an occupation thoroughly suited to women, and for which they are well fitted by nature' the conditions of employment did not make it at that date a 'good opening'. The salaries were low, the examinations 'very stiff', and the competition fierce (Bird 1911: 233–4; Weibel, Heim, and Ellsworth 1979: 35–7).

Librarianship, though the case which demonstrates most clearly the way the Society's influence could operate, is not the one where it had its greatest indirect impact. This occurred in the area in which the increase in middle-class female employment was itself greatest: the employment of women as commercial clerks. An examination of the census figures suggests that the 1860s saw the beginning of a sudden, dramatic, and continuing increase in the number of female commercial clerks. Table 9.2 shows the numbers of commercial clerks returned in each census between 1841 and 1911, the percentage increase in each ten years, the number of female clerks and the percentage they formed of the total number. In the twenty years between 1841 and 1861 the number listed rose by 112 from 162 to 274, that is, by 68 per cent, whereas between 1861 and 1871 it rose by 1,138 or 415 per cent. The rise of 5,477 (324 per cent) between 1871 and 1881 cannot be seen as comparable because there was a change in the definition of the census category (though the overall increase was only 99 per cent) but between 1881 and 1891 the increase in female clerks was 198 per cent compared with an overall increase in clerks of 36 per cent.

This was a faster rate of increase than that occurring in the category of

*Table 9.2:* Number of commercial clerks returned in the censuses from 1841 to 1911 together with the percentage increase in each decade, number of women clerks, and the percentage of women clerks in total number.

| Year | Total no. of commercial clerks | Percentage increase | Women commercial clerks | Percentage of women in total number of clerks |
|------|------|------|------|------|
| 1841 | 48,689 | — | 164 | 0.3% |
| 1851 | 37,529 | -23.0% | — | — |
| 1861 | 55,936 | 49.0% | 274 | 0.5% |
| 1871 | 91,042 | 62.8% | 1,412 | 1.5% |
| 1881 | 181,457 | 99.3% | 5,989 | 3.3% |
| 1891 | 247,229 | 36.2% | 17,859 | 7.2% |
| 1901 | 363,673 | 47.1% | 55,784 | 15.3% |
| 1911 | 477,535 | 31.3% | 117,057 | 24.5% |

female photographers (1861–1871, 313 per cent; 1871–1881, 89 per cent; 1881–1891, 194 per cent) and of female drapers under 25 (1851–1861, 127 per cent; 1861–1871, 67 per cent; 1871–1881, 59 per cent), the two other really fast growing middle-class women's occupations recorded in the census. (The figures for drapers are restricted to those under twenty-five, since the existence of elderly keepers of small drapers' shops depresses the figure for all ages. In the other two categories the under-twenty-five age group also shows a greater rate of increase: commercial clerks rising by 500 per cent, 366 per cent and 231 per cent and photographers by 398 per cent, 131 per cent and 96 per cent.) Something evidently occurred in the 1860s to set off a trend comparable to that in a brand new occupation like photography, or one, like the selling of drapery, where there had been radical reorganization.

Commercial occupations were defined by the census of 1871 as those which only bought and sold but did not effect any change in the commodities dealt in (PP 1873 vol. 71: xliii), therefore commercial clerks recorded in the censuses prior to 1881 would seem to be those employed in the offices of import houses, cotton brokers, corn chandlers, warehouses collecting goods from the various manufacturers and selling them to retailers, and the like while excluding any clerical workers in shops, factories, and, since these were returned separately, banks, insurance companies, shipping firms, and railways.

Lee Holcombe has suggested that the main reason why women began to be employed as clerks in the late nineteenth century was that the growth in size of business enterprises had led to the deskilling of clerical work: 'the expanding scope of industrial and commercial enterprises . . . led naturally to a growth in the size of business offices', to 'a tremendous increase in the amount of clerical work to be done', to 'rationalisation and mechanisation of office work', and to 'considerable specialisation and division of labour within offices' (Holcombe 1973: 142, 144). Yet there does not seem to be much evidence that the size of firms increased appreciably in the 1860s, nor that it was increase in scale which led to the deskilling of clerical work, while the census returns do not support her assumption that women were hired primarily by large firms.

While in the retail trade the number of women shop assistants began to grow in the same decade as the department stores emerged, the entry of women into clerical work does not seem to have coincided with any equivalent structural change. It does not seem to have been in the 1860s that 'independent proprietors and partnership firms gave way before large joint-stock companies, which in turn tended to be replaced by large scale amalgamations, representing huge agglomerations of capital' (Holcombe 1973: 142), but after 1890, when women's place in the office was already well established. According to P. L. Payne, though the first joint stock legislation was passed in 1855, the organizations registered under it even in 1886 were little different from those, the vast majority, which continued to operate as private businesses. It was only in the last years of the century that large scale mergers began, and it was the decade before the First World War which saw the real transformation of Britain's industrial structure (McCord 1991: 442–3; Payne 1974: 19–21, 57). Gregory Anderson (1976: 10) has pointed out that even in the 1870s on average only four people were employed at any one time in the offices of warehouses in Liverpool and Manchester.

Furthermore, the deskilling of clerical work seems to have begun, not with the emergence of large firms in the 1890s, nor with the entry of women in the 1860s, but right at the beginning of the century. According to Sidney Pollard, the apprentice clerk learning the business either as a future entrepreneur or in the expectation of a life spent in loyal service to one employer had ceased to be the typical office worker by 1830. The dual labour market that developed at this time seems to have relied on the use of boys and young men for routine work, with a 'synthetic turnover' created by dismissing most of them after a few years to avoid having to raise their wages (Pollard 1965: 138). This male secondary sector workforce was still very much in evidence in the 1860s. Gregory Anderson writes:

> In Liverpool's cotton brokerage trade apprentices 'passed through a painful spell of drudgery, called a juniorship, which lasted for about twelve months and was nothing less than the respectable work of a common office lad'. . . After about a year the cotton broker's apprentice was placed in charge of a new junior, and after three years he became a senior, at which point he had probably learned all that was required for office work. He should then, perhaps, have been given the opportunity to learn more of the buying and selling side of the business, but 'instead of being transferred to the sales room the unfortunate apprentice was retained in the office for another year

as a junior cashier, a junior book-keeper or any post which could not be supplemented except by a salaried clerk'. In this way, it was felt, many 'ingenious but grasping cotton brokers gained a double advantage from their apprentices', trimming their costs by extending the period of apprenticeship and using apprentices in place of fully qualified clerks. Even worse, only a percentage of apprentices were retained by their brokers at the end of their apprenticeships.

(Anderson 1975: 14–15)

This is not to say there were not large concerns employing huge clerical staffs in the 1860s. However such large concerns, the evidence seems to suggest, had already created a secondary sector labour force similar to that in small offices, entirely composed of males, and relying heavily on the use of boys and apprentices. In the London and North-western Railway in 1874, the Civil Service Commission was told, the salaried staff consisted of 3,534 employees earning less than £100 a year, 892 earning between £100 and £200, 126 earning £200-£300, and 95 earning £300 to £3,000. Of these, 1,770 were clerks and 1,590 apprentice clerks. All of these, except for eight or ten women in Birmingham, were male. The officers of a bank examined by the Commissioners reported that there were two levels of entry there, one for Directors' nominees aged eighteen and another for junior clerks aged sixteen, who at eighteen became 'eligible for appointments as tellers when vacancies occur'. The civil service itself made use of 'boy clerks'. The Civil Service Commissioners found 'that their employment, under proper supervision, is both desirable and economical', and they proposed that 'the Lower Division should embrace a class of boys, a limited number of whom should be promoted to be Clerks after approved good service, those not so promoted being discharged on attaining their nineteenth year of age' (PP 1875 vol 23: 203, 182–3, 15).

These practices do not seem to have dried up the supply of aspirant male clerks. The bank and railway officials interviewed by the Civil Service Commissioners claimed they had no trouble getting clerks, an officer from one bank saying that 'the supply is greater than the demand' and another that his bank was 'overdone with applications', and the railway official said that 'up to about £100 or £120 a year we can command any number of clerks'. The Commissioners, in their report, did not seem to envisage any drying up of the supply of boy clerks (PP 1875 vol 23: 182, 185, 202, 15).

The second deskilling of office work can only be seen as beginning, at the very earliest, with the introduction of the typewriter in the late 1870s: in the United States, its country of origin, there were 154 typists (male and female) in 1870, 5,000 in 1880, but 33,400 by 1890 (Davies 1974: 10). The other features of the second deskilling of clerical work, the adding machine, filing systems, and Taylorite office organization, really belong to the early decades of the twentieth century, by which time women had been employed in clerical work for nearly fifty years (Strom 1992: 197–204).

Such evidence as there is of the size of the firms which first employed women clerks suggests that they went into smaller rather than larger firms. The large firms seem to have lagged behind rather than led the way in the employment of women. In 1891, when women composed 7 per cent of commercial clerks, they were 2 per cent of the clerical force in insurance companies and only 0.4 per cent in banks. In my reading of the Parliamentary Papers and the periodical press of the 1860s and 1870s I have come across mention of only two cases of large firms (neither of the sort classified by the census as commercial, and both in the 1870s rather than the 1860s) taking on young women as clerks: the Prudential Insurance Company in London and the London and North-Western Railway in Birmingham (Jordan 1996; P.P. 1875 vol 23: 203).[4]

There is evidence, however, to suggest that female clerks were going by ones and twos into much smaller offices. In 1874 the Employment Society had been sending female clerks to warehouses 'for many years', and yet the 'large warehouse in Houndsditch' which employed five women would seem to have been their largest customer in the commercial field. The census returns of 1871 suggest that this may well have been the pattern throughout the country. Table 9.3 shows the number of male and female commercial clerks returned in each county in 1841 and 1871 – the 1861 census did not show female commercial clerks separately in the county returns – and Table 9.4 gives the numbers of clerks aged over twenty in the 'Principal Towns' (according to the 1871 definition) throughout England and Wales. (The 28,231 male and 319 female clerks aged under twenty in 1871 were only returned by county.)

It can be seen from these tables that the distribution was scattered rather than concentrated, and that the numbers in most districts were small. While there is no way of knowing how many different firms employed the 440 female clerks aged over twenty in London, or the 160 found distributed between Brighton (where there was an active branch of the Employment Society), Birmingham, Leicester, Liverpool, Manchester and Sheffield, the distribution of the other 156 in Table 9.4 is in groups of ten or fewer, while there were another 337 female clerks aged over twenty apparently working in towns too small to be classified as 'principal'. This table therefore suggests that almost half of these women clerks were employed in small numbers by small firms (most of the towns where women clerks were found had fewer than 200 male clerks), while nothing to the contrary is known about the rest. There is, it would appear, as yet no evidence to suggest that it was the 'large joint-stock companies' which were the early employers of female clerical labour.

What, it might be asked, was the appeal of these women to small scale employers which led to their being in the vanguard of those who hired women? Those merchants who first employed girls in their offices do not seem to have been prone to discussing their experiments in public. If they

Table 9.3  Numbers of male and female commercial clerks in England and Wales returned by county in the censuses of 1841 and 1871

| | 1841 Male | 1841 Female | 1871 Male | 1871 Female |
|---|---|---|---|---|
| London | 5,094 | — | 33,620 | 557 |
| Surrey* | 1,171 | 9 | 1,415 | 44 |
| Kent* | 411 | — | 924 | 38 |
| Sussex | 653 | 2 | 555 | 50 |
| Hampshire | 328 | 2 | 799 | 19 |
| Berkshire | | — | 270 | 10 |
| Middlesex* | 15,720 | 51 | 1,485 | 21 |
| Hertfordshire | 197 | 1 | 226 | 13 |
| Buckinghamshire | 225 | 1 | 68 | 2 |
| Oxfordshire | 218 | 2 | 185 | 6 |
| Northamptonshire | 288 | — | 255 | 9 |
| Huntingdonshire | 86 | — | 46 | 2 |
| Bedfordshire | 96 | — | 91 | 4 |
| Cambridgeshire | 302 | — | 167 | 4 |
| Essex | 457 | 1 | 1,493 | 6 |
| Suffolk | 439 | — | 419 | 6 |
| Norfolk | 811 | 1 | 603 | 22 |
| Wiltshire | 403 | 1 | 204 | 4 |
| Dorsetshire | 265 | — | 135 | 8 |
| Devonshire | 793 | 2 | 688 | 37 |
| Cornwall | 369 | 1 | 180 | 3 |
| Somersetshire | 710 | 2 | 650 | 18 |
| Monmouthshire | 271 | — | 386 | 3 |
| South Wales | 658 | 1 | 1,215 | 18 |
| North Wales | 531 | 3 | 476 | 11 |
| Gloucestershire | 985 | 4 | 1,438 | 20 |
| Herefordshire | 210 | 1 | 93 | 2 |
| Shropshire | 457 | — | 304 | 4 |
| Staffordshire | 1,500 | 9 | 2,174 | 29 |
| Worcestershire | 567 | — | 1,335 | 12 |
| Warwickshire | 1,846 | 5 | 2,916 | 73 |
| Leicestershire | 415 | — | 561 | 26 |
| Rutlandshire | 23 | — | 16 | — |
| Lincolnshire | 616 | 1 | 408 | 16 |
| Nottinghamshire | 470 | 1 | 784 | 10 |
| Derbyshire | 620 | 3 | 644 | 14 |
| Cheshire | 1,135 | 9 | 2,829 | 17 |
| Lancashire | 8,004 | 19 | 19,523 | 161 |
| Yorkshire | | | | |
| – West Riding | 2,773 | 7 | 5,180 | 50 |
| – East Riding | 176 | 1 | 1,170 | 8 |
| – North Riding | 336 | 1 | 193 | 4 |
| City and Ainsty of the City of York | 200 | — | — | |
| Durham | 714 | — | 1,735 | 9 |
| Northumberland | 643 | 1 | 1,402 | 1 |
| Cumberland | 365 | 1 | 288 | 9 |
| Westmorland | 116 | 1 | 82 | 2 |

* Includes London in 1841 census.

Table 9.4 Numbers of male and female commercial clerks in the 'principal towns' of England and Wales as returned in the censuses of 1841 and 1871

| Town | 1841 Male | 1841 Female | 1871 Male | 1871 Female |
|---|---|---|---|---|
| London | 17,299 | 55 | 23,238 | 440 |
| Canterbury | 63 | — | 24 | 2 |
| Chatham and Rochester | 66 | — | 105 | — |
| Dover | 54 | — | 33 | 3 |
| Maidstone | 58 | — | 42 | 2 |
| Brighton | 105 | 2 | 147 | 20 |
| Chichester | 27 | — | 7 | 1 |
| Portsmouth | 112 | 2 | 128 | 2 |
| Southampton | 86 | — | 211 | 5 |
| Winchester | 22 | — | 21 | 1 |
| Reading | 68 | — | 76 | 1 |
| Oxford | 77 | 1 | 71 | 1 |
| Northampton | 44 | — | 58 | 4 |
| Bedford | 24 | — | 15 | — |
| Cambridge | 115 | — | 43 | 2 |
| Wisbech | — | — | 11 | — |
| Colchester | 53 | — | 30 | — |
| Bury St. Edumunds | 35 | — | 15 | — |
| Ipswich | 67 | — | 119 | 3 |
| Kings Lynn | 61 | — | 37 | — |
| Norwich | 218 | — | 196 | 9 |
| Yarmouth | 53 | — | 39 | 5 |
| Chester | 119 | — | 148 | 3 |
| Macclesfield | 51 | 2 | 38 | 1 |
| Stockport | 68 | — | 123 | — |
| Barrow-in-Furness | — | — | 45 | — |
| Blackburn | 82 | — | 184 | — |
| Salisbury | 43 | — | 11 | 5 |
| Dorchester | 20 | — | 6 | 1 |
| Poole | 12 | — | 10 | — |
| Exeter | 70 | — | 67 | 6 |
| Plymouth/Dvnpt | 234 | — | 163 | 10 |
| Truro | — | — | 15 | — |
| Bath | 110 | — | 54 | 8 |
| Bridgewater | 15 | — | 31 | 1 |
| Bristol | 300 | 2 | 647 | 8 |
| Gloucester | 54 | — | 50 | 2 |
| Hereford | 42 | — | 33 | 1 |
| Shrewsbury | 91 | 1 | 69 | — |
| Stafford | 18 | — | 28 | 1 |
| Wolverhampton | 178 | 1 | 204 | 1 |
| Dudley | 90 | — | 83 | — |
| Worcester | 111 | — | 108 | 3 |
| Birmingham | 1,174 | 4 | 1,651 | 41 |
| Coventry | 59 | — | 46 | 3 |
| Leicester | 129 | — | 276 | 17 |
| Boston | 29 | — | 22 | — |
| Lincoln | 63 | — | 45 | 2 |
| Newark | — | — | 20 | — |
| Nottingham | 143 | — | 297 | 5 |
| Derby | 187 | — | 90 | 1 |
| Durham | 45 | — | 12 | — |
| Gateshead | 58 | — | 148 | — |
| South Shields | 44 | — | 55 | 1 |
| Sunderland | 15 | — | 200 | 1 |
| Newcastle-on-Tyne | 192 | — | 615 | 10 |
| Bolton | 160 | 1 | 157 | 1 |
| Lancaster | 66 | — | 42 | — |
| Liverpool | 2,799 | 5 | 5,151 | 29 |
| Manchester | 1,683 | 6 | 3,594 | 39 |
| Oldham | 88 | — | 269 | 2 |
| Preston | 157 | — | 128 | 1 |
| Bradford | 84 | — | 439 | 2 |
| Halifax | 188 | — | 144 | 1 |
| Huddersfield | 99 | — | 195 | 3 |
| Leeds | 574 | 2 | 692 | 6 |
| Sheffield | 484 | 4 | 647 | 14 |
| Wakefield | 77 | — | 64 | — |
| Hull | — | — | 599 | 6 |
| York | 148 | — | 77 | — |
| Middlesbrough | — | — | 129 | — |
| Tynemouth | 44 | — | 84 | — |
| Carlisle | 92 | — | 74 | 6 |
| Whitehaven | 33 | — | 13 | 1 |
| Kendal | 30 | 1 | 28 | 1 |
| Newport | — | — | 94 | — |
| Cardiff | 27 | — | 187 | 9 |
| Merthyr-Tydfil | 60 | — | 42 | — |
| Swansea | 34 | 1 | 148 | 1 |
| Pembroke | 11 | — | 8 | — |
| Carnarvon | 17 | — | 15 | — |

had made any public pronouncements, it is likely they would have been reported in one of the Women's Movement journals, the *English Woman's Journal* or the *Englishwoman's Review*, and there are no such pronouncements recorded there. Nevertheless if the benefits listed by Frank Scudamore as belonging to telegraph operators, cheapness, docility, good education, tolerance of sedentary work, and a short working life, appealed to a large employer like the Post Office, they must presumably have brought as great or even greater benefits to small employers. In the first place, in these private businesses the money saved on a clerk's wages was likely to be so much more in the employer's pocket. When Scrooge raised Bob Cratchit's wages he lost in income exactly what the clerk gained.

It has been suggested that office managers (whose incomes are not tied directly to profits) tended to resist feminization of their offices because of what G. S. Becker called a 'taste for discrimination' against women, a preference for the atmosphere and an enjoyment of the 'non-economic utilities' of an all-male office (Cohn 1981: 33, 35–7). Among proprietor employers these tastes would presumably have been counter-balanced by the absolute addition to their own incomes that a cheaper clerk would ensure. Thus the first benefit of female labour – its cheapness – would have had an obvious appeal for them.

A small number of merchants had apparently seen these advantages by 1841, but, as Table 9.3 shows, they were widely scattered throughout the country, and their example seems not to have been copied by their neighbours. Lancashire, with nineteen female commercial clerks, had the largest number outside London while many counties returned only one. Nor was their lead followed during the ensuing twenty years, for during this period the number of female commercial clerks rose only from 162 to 274. During the 1860s, however, many more employers seem to have come to the same realization, though taking on girl clerks still seems to have been a matter of individual initiative rather than spreading local practice, since even in 1871, out of a total of 1,466 female commercial clerks, only London with 577 and Lancashire with 161 had more than 100.

Such a widely scattered, apparently idiosyncratic pattern of change suggests a series of individual responses to some nationwide prompting, and, since economic conditions do not seem to have changed radically in this decade, the prompting which suggests itself is the Society for Promoting the Employment of Women's propaganda campaign. It was members of this society who during this decade were arguing that employers need not be bound by the customary and the usual, that just because women had not so far been seen in certain occupations they should not forever be excluded from them. Moreover they suggested motives for making changes which went beyond simple self-interest: they appealed to public spirit as well. The Women's Movement continually stressed the plight of the 'surplus women', and appealed to employers to do something about it. Surely the most likely explanation for the big increase in the number of female commercial clerks during the 1860s is that certain men all over the country made the double discovery that it they abandoned their customary 'knowledge' of the proper sort of clerk, they could both save themselves money and regard themselves as progressive, public-spirited businessmen.

This double motivation seems to have been behind the initiatives taken by the high-ranking Post Office officials who extended the employment of women within their establishment. The Postmaster General's report of 1873 used rhetoric borrowed from the Women's Movement's campaign when it spoke of 'removing those artificial barriers which have hitherto shut out women from lucrative employment' (Martindale 1938: 20, quoted), and Lord John Manners's wife gave evidence of similar influence when she wrote that these moves were the result of a belief 'that in the existing constitution of society, ladies are practically excluded from many occupations which women of the middle class and of lower social station enter as a matter of course' (Manners 1881: 185).

The lower level clerks in the civil service who resented the introduction of women saw their superiors as driven by a commitment to Women's Movement ideas. The introduction of women into the savings bank was seen as 'the agreeable fad of a few influential people', and the *Civil Service Review* called it a gain for 'the asserters of Women's Rights' (Martindale 1938: 25, quoted; EWR 1876: 564, quoted). The fact that the secretary of the Society for Promoting the Employment of Women was called to give evidence to the Civil Service Commission suggests that the Post Office employment of women was seen as connected to their campaign.

There can be little doubt that the importance of the Society's work lay far more in the propaganda campaign which spread its ideas than in the actual efforts, important though they may have been for individuals, to find work for particular women.

## Diffusion of the practice

By 1880 female clerks had become a visible, and up to a point an accepted, part of the office. After this date, there was not, I would suggest, any necessary connection between the Women's Movement and the further feminization of clerical work. By that date the initial work had been done; women had been tried in offices and found satisfactory. Employers' 'knowledge' had been changed and the androcentric view of office work broken down.

Moreover, typewriters had appeared on the scene and the firms that sold them often provided female typists with the machines (Martindale 1938: 67). Business schools offering typing courses sprang up and were patronized primarily by women, and in the early 1900s girls' high schools began offering secretarial training (Burstall 1907: 202). The further feminization of office work was no more tied to Women's Movement ideas than the feminization of the retail trade. It became for employers simply a question of balancing the 'non-economic utilities' of an all-male office against the savings it was now known female labour would produce.

In spite of the fact that women were now accepted in many offices, the 'taste for discrimination' seems to have remained strong among lower managers and staff. It was not only in the Post Office that a fiat from the very highest level was needed to overcome employee resistance. In 1876 the Great Western Railway board had suggested introducing female clerks, but the difficulties raised by the various managers caused the suggestion to be dropped. It was not until 1906 that one director was so impressed by the use of girl clerks in the American railways that he insisted on the practice being copied in his own company (Cohn 1985: 93–6; EWR 1877: 81). It was also possible for men in some environments to resist the ascription of the typewriter women. In the Great Western Railway, before 1906, all typing was done by male clerks who were taught by the company after appointment, though girl typists employed by other organizations were not usually hired unless already trained. Even in the Post Office, though women typists were employed elsewhere, in the all-male engineering offices typing was taught to male clerks 'on the job' (Cohn 1981: 173, 174, 259).

Table 9.5 shows the degree of feminization in the various clerical areas by 1911. It can be seen that the extent varied from sector to sector. Commercial offices and the Post Office had taken eagerly to the hiring of women; the resistance of lawyers and the rest of the civil service was only beginning to break down. Insurance offices had found some place for women, banks and railway companies had largely neglected them. The reasons are surely to be found in the internal histories of each organization and group of organizations, and contact with Women's Movement ideas probably had little to do, after 1880, with the way the decision went.

Nevertheless, the separation of men's and women's work operated just as strongly within the organizations which employed women as in those that continued to reject them. A dual labour market developed which was far more rigidly segmented than that in the pre-1860s office. At that period, even though many of the apprentices and 'boy clerks' had been dismissed when they reached their twenties, there were opportunities for a proportion of them to rise to positions of seniority and responsibility. A career ladder did exist. When women came into the office this channel for rising was denied them (Hogarth 1897: 932). Indeed, as I have argued elsewhere in discussing the admission of women to the Prudential Assurance Company, the motive for importing women could be a desire to preserve a male career ladder in the face of changed conditions (Jordan 1996). Keith Grint has identified two strategies used by unions when faced with female competition: preserving male pay levels by enforcing rigid segmentation with low pay for women which then subsidizes male jobs, or protecting male jobs by demands for equal pay for women to decrease management's incentive to replace men with women (Grint 1988: 95–100).

*Table 9.5*: Total numbers of clerical workers in certain occupations returned in the Census of 1911 with number of women and percentage of women in the total number

| Occupational Area | Total Number | Number of Women | Percentage of Women |
|---|---|---|---|
| Post Office -telegraphists | 10,338 | 6,093 | 58.9% |
| Post Office officers and clerks | 50,210 | 20,337 | 40.5% |
| Other civil service officers and clerks | 33,037 | 1,697 | 5.1% |
| Law clerks | 36,265 | 2,159 | 6.0% |
| Commercial or business clerks | 477,535 | 117,057 | 24.5% |
| Bank officials and clerks | 40,379 | 476 | 1.2% |
| Insurance officials and clerks | 45,897 | 4,011 | 8.7% |
| Railway officials and clerks | 85,922 | 1,120 | 1.3% |

The second of these was used, as was seen above, by unions to keep women out of printing. The first seems to be the strategy employed when faced with women in the white-collar area. During the second, Taylorite, rationalization of office work, certain areas of it, shorthand, typing, filing, acting as receptionist, were demarcated as female, and the skills involved were devalued and discounted. It was made almost impossible to move from such work to the lower level management positions still available to men who entered as clerks. A rapid turnover and disincentives to ambition were enforced through marriage bars (Anderson 1988: 13). Thus though the Women's Movement was responsible for breaking through the androcentric blindness of employers, it did not establish gender equality in the office. It achieved no more than the replacement of an exploited male secondary sector workforce with a far more rigidly segmented female one, a replacement which served the employers' interests well.

However, although women were only considered in situations where it suited the employers' interests, it seems clear that feminization as a solution would not have occurred, at least at the date when it did, to the employers of clerks, hospital dispensers and librarians (and possibly hairdressers, though the evidence here is less conclusive) without the propaganda and activities of the Society for Promoting the Employment of Women. It was this propaganda which broke through their androcentric blindness and altered their 'knowledge' of what was men's and women's work.

## A change of focus

All these initiatives were, however, concentrated in the 1860s and 1870s, and by the middle of the 1870s the innovative phase of the Society for Promoting the Employment of Women seems to have been over. Though the Society continued in existence into the twentieth century, it was concerned primarily with acting as a loan society to help women in need undertake training or establish themselves in business. Its focus became primarily philanthropic, its leading figures no longer acting as unattached intellectuals intent on changing their society.

From the mid-1870s the unattached intellectuals concerned with women's work seem to have turned their attention to a far more disadvantaged group, working-class women. In the early 1870s Jessie Boucherett became heavily involved in the Vigilance Association, a group formed to watch parliamentary legislation as it was applied to women's work, in particular restrictive legislation which might result in their being replaced by men (EWR 1873: 249–58; 1874: 48, 278, 308; 1875: 32; 1876: 25, 558). Furthermore, the working-class ideal which added a demand for economic justice to the demand for political freedom, was in the 1870s gaining in middle-class support.

An active new entrant into the Women's Movement drew many of its members, especially those concerned with women's work, further in the collectivist direction. In 1874 Emma Paterson, a dynamic woman with a lower-middle-class background who had acted as secretary to the Women's Suffrage Association, aroused the interest of Women's Movement members in trade unionism which she had studied on a recent visit to America. In July 1874 she founded the Women's Trade Union League and drew a number of Women's Movement members in as supporters (Drake 1920: 10–11; Paterson 1875: 1–12). From this date on approving references to trade unionism for women began to appear in the *Englishwoman's Review* (EWR 1874: 281–4; 1875: 494–6, 504–11; 1876: 28–9, 62–4, 133–5).

In the 1880s the focus of those anxious to bring about social change in the area of women's work moved away from the need to find new openings for women to the need to improve pay and conditions, and a number of articles on women's work in the serious periodical press laid great stress on unionism (Bremner 1888; Routledge and Dilke 1891). The writers of these articles believed that in the ultimate aims of unionism – shorter hours, regulated wages, limitation of apprentices in overcrowded trades – lay the only solution to women's industrial problems. They devoted themselves year after year to a heartbreaking attempt to have women's unions accepted by the movement, and so were desperate to modify the currently held union view that women were, like immigrant workers, strike breakers and undercutters of wages (Drake 1984: 46–52). They accepted the principle of equal pay for equal work, and thus, as Grint (1988: 19) notes, effectively debarred young women from entering the skilled trades by withdrawing the only incentive they could offer to employers who preferred an all-male environment.

With this change in focus and tactics, the opening of new areas to middle class women stopped happening. Though there was a large increase in the numbers of middle-class women employed in the period 1891 to 1911, no new occupations opened. All the innovation took place in the period 1860 to 1880, the period when the Society for Promoting the

Employment of Women was actively looking for new openings and arguing its case in the press.

This comes out very clearly when one compares the books on women's work written in the different decades. In the late 1850s Dinah Craik, in *A Woman's Thoughts about Women*, saw only teaching, dressmaking, and retail work as open to women in this rank of life. By the 1860s Jessie Boucherett's *Hints on Self-Help* was suggesting hopefully the addition of clerical work, nursing, and photography, while in the 1870s Louisa Hubbard's *Year Book of Women's Work* described the same occupations, with the addition of pharmacy and hairdressing, as definitely open to women. In the 1890s Amy Bulley and Margaret Whitley's *Women's Work*, though written with even more confidence, did not describe any additional occupations, and there were no changes, except for the addition of librarians (first employed, as was mentioned above, in the 1870s) in M. Mostyn Bird's *Woman at Work* published in 1911. When the Society for Promoting the Employment of Women stopped working actively to open new occupations to women, no further occupations became available to them.

# 10

# REDEFINING 'LADIES' WORK'

## Creating a 'push factor'

In the early days of Langham Place, Barbara Leigh Smith and Bessie Rayner Parkes had established two aims for the Women's Movement. First, it must widen the range of work available to middle-class women, so that 'overstocking' in teaching and dressmaking would cease to be a problem, and single women would be able to earn a living wage. Second, it had to persuade upper middle-class parents that their daughters must be made self-dependent, trained for an occupation so that they might support themselves if their fathers or husbands died or failed in business, and so that they would not need to marry 'for a situation'.

The Society for Promoting the Employment of Women had concentrated on the first aim, making the provision of suitable work for lower middle-class girls its focus. However the sort of work the Society concentrated on was not really what Bessie Rayner Parkes, for example, had envisaged as fulfilling the needs of ladies. Such 'semi-mechanical occupations' did not, she felt, supply the 'needs of educated women, – of women who have been born and bred ladies'. She could not see the young lady with intellectual leanings finding content in trotting off each day to work a telegraph machine or dress another woman's hair, and nor did the wages such activities brought in provide for a standard of living suited to the usual habits of ladies (Parkes 1860: 813–14). They and their parents needed to be persuaded that they, like their brothers, should be educated for an honourable and lucrative career.

It will be argued in what follows that this aim was pursued by the Education branch of the Women's Movement. Two large groups of women existed who were in effect in the market for education, the leisured ladies wanting 'something to do', and the very large pool of teenage girls whose parents wanted an education for them that would guarantee their gentility and femininity. The Women's Movement members undertook to provide this education, using their own symbolic capital as unimpeachable gentlewomen and that of their noble and royal patrons to guarantee its respectability , and yet ensuring that the new institutions spread the message that it was not just education for leisure but for work, and that young women should undertake paid employment at least before marriage.

## Emily Davies

The chief strategist in this campaign was Emily Davies (1830–1921), and although many accounts of her life and work exist, it seems unavoidable to look once again at her career with the specific purpose of noting her contribution to the conversion of upper-middle-class women to the ideal of self-dependence. She was a clergyman's daughter who spent the first thirty years of her life acting out that role along more or less conventional lines in her father's parish in Gateshead. Her views seem to have been very largely developed as a result of her own situation in life, and the restraints this placed on her inner drives. Though she developed a 'feeling of resentment at the subjection of women', it was not the result of any contact with the Women's Rights theories which inspired Barbara Leigh Smith and Bessie Rayner Parkes, and it is possible she did not encounter these ideas until she made contact with members of the Langham Place circle (Caine 1992: 60–4; Stephen 1927: 29–31). Yet of all the early Women's Movement members she seems to have had the least commitment to the domestic ideology, and the strongest determination to destroy all vestiges of patriarchalism in the economic and intellectual spheres.

Growing up in a clever argumentative family of boys and girls, she appears to have felt that there was little difference between the males and the females. She held to the Mary Wollstonecraft view that masculine and feminine qualities were culturally created, rather then believing like Anna Jameson and Frances Power Cobbe that there were basic, unalterable differences (Cobbe 1863: 224–7; Davies 1866: 169–70; Jameson 1856: 15–16; Wollstonecraft 1792: 25–30). She was scathing about such assumptions as 'the wonderful unconscious instinct, by which women are supposed to leap to right conclusions, no one knows how', and believed that 'there is between the sexes a deep and broad basis of likeness' (Davies 1866: 75, 169–70).

Her protest was primarily an intellectual one. She was no bohemian, and the pressures to behave in a restrained and ladylike manner did not bother her.[1] She had no sympathy with the extravagances of the 'girl of the period', and was later to squash without a qualm any attempts by Girton students to deviate from the conventional (Delamont 1978a: 146–7; Stephen 1927: 225, 240–1). She did, however, feel very strongly the cramping pressure of the young lady's life, and her criticisms of home life were almost as trenchant as Florence Nightingale's. She summed up the problem for a Social Science Congress thus:

> Dulness is not healthy, and the lives of ladies are, it must be confessed, exceedingly dull . . . Busy people, and especially busy

men, have a very faint and feeble conception of what dulness is . . . And they think dulness is calm. If they had ever tried what it is to be a young lady, they would know better.

(Davies 1910: 69–70)

She was also apparently as moved as Barbara Leigh Smith and Bessie Rayner Parkes to apply the gospel of work to herself. 'The case of the modern girl', she wrote, 'is peculiarly hard in this, that she has fallen upon an age in which idleness is accounted disgraceful. The social atmosphere rings with exhortations to act, act in the living present', and yet in her own life she finds that 'so long as she is quiet and amiable, and does not get out of health, nobody wants her to do anything' (Davies 1866: 50, 55).

In her twenties she began to make contact with women who felt similarly. In 1854 she first met her life-long friend Elizabeth Garrett, the future medical pioneer, and having met Barbara Leigh Smith's sister by chance in Algeria, visited Langham Place when she stayed with her brother John Llewellyn Davies (who was an associate of F. D. Maurice and later Principal of Queen's College) in London. As a result of contacts made there, she established a branch of the Employment Society in Durham in 1860 (Caine 1992: 68–71; Davies 1910: 28; Stephen 1927: 26–8, 52–6).

She did not, however, find in the society's recommendations the answer to what she saw as the needs of women like herself. The occupations it was opening did not fulfil her notions of what was due to upper-middle-class women either in the status they bore or in the opportunities they offered to the exercise of the talents (Davies 1910: 37). What she wanted for women, she made quite clear in the book she published in 1866, *The Higher Education of Women*, was what was available to men. She did not believe that men and women were different in kind, 'distinct races, handing down their respective characteristics from generation to generation' (Davies 1866: 165–80), and therefore she believed that the education and occupations appropriate to one sex were equally appropriate to the other. It mattered far more to her that girls' education should open the career paths available to boys than that it should serve broader educational ideals (Caine 1992: 87–8). It was not, however, as a theorist that Emily Davies made her real mark, nor did she see this as her main role. Her 'vocation' was, she wrote, 'to work at public affairs, not at a definite profession' (Stephen 1927: 114). She consequently devoted most of her life to the narrow and elitist aim of gaining for upper-middle-class women the educational and vocational opportunities available to their brothers.

Emily Davies was a consummate politician and so her statements are often no guide to her real beliefs and intentions (Strachey 1928: 132). Nevertheless it seems likely, looking at her whole career, that her reasoning on girls' education went something like this: if women were to be able to pursue the standard upper-middle-class careers of physician, barrister, upper division civil servant and (for those with independent incomes) politician, they must be admitted to university education, and to fit them for university education they must pursue the same secondary curriculum as boys.

Moreover, she seems to have decided to use as her instrument the women's public education movement that had begun with the founding of Queen's and Bedford Colleges in the late 1840s, and push it in the direction she desired. She was so skilful in her choice of points of attack and methods of procedure that while at the beginning of the 1860s girls' education had been seen as wholly private, and the responsibility solely of their parents, though boys' education was a matter of national concern, by the end of the century the curriculum in both boys' and girls' secondary schools was dictated by the need to prepare for common public examinations, government grants were available on the same terms to both boys' and girls' schools, and university degree courses were open to women in all universities, although Oxford and Cambridge still refused to grant full degree status. Margaret Bryant (1979: 76, 106) has argued that the development of girls' education was part of a wider movement for reassessing and upgrading secondary schooling. This is undoubtedly the case, but it was Emily Davies who ensured that this was so.

## Gaining official recognition

In 1862, following the death of her father, Emily Davies settled with her mother in London. Her friend Elizabeth Garrett was beginning her struggle to gain a medical education, and Langham Place was supporting her attempt to matriculate at London University. Emily Davies became honorary secretary of the campaign to have women admitted (Davies 1970: 247). The issue was raised at the Annual Congress of the Social Science Association when Frances Power Cobbe read a paper entitled 'The Education of Women, and How it would be Affected by University Examinations'. Cobbe's main argument, couched in terms designed to appeal to holders of the entrepreneurial ideal, was that there should be 'Free Trade in knowledge established between the sexes'. She brought up the standard Women's Movement argument that girls were 'frittering away the prime of their days in the busy idleness of trivial accomplishments', and were then often left penniless to fend for themselves. She argued that allowing them to undertake the men's course of study would provide a standard for measuring their efficiency and an incentive to thorough, accurate work. It would give a universal standard for teachers and its benefits would thus be felt throughout the entire female education system (Cobbe 1863: 219, 233–5).

In the discussion that followed, it emerged that most speakers were against women attempting the same courses and examinations as men (TNAPSS 1860: 340–2), but the meeting did adopt unanimously an amended resolution:

That this meeting is of opinion that means ought to be provided for testing and attesting the education of women of the middle and higher classes, and requests the Council of the Association to take such measures as they may deem expedient for the attainment of this object.

(TNAPSS 1862: 342)

Emily Davies seized on this as a starting point. It was admitted that an external standard was needed, and she was determined that that external standard must be the same as the one currently applied to boys. By October 1862 she had organized a special meeting of the Social Science Association which set up a Committee for Obtaining the Admission of Women to University Examinations with the standard complement of Social Science luminaries, and herself as its secretary (Davies 1970: 260; Stephen 1927: 82–4).

During the 1850s, examinations as a means of testing the quality of education and of selecting candidates for positions had become very much the fashion. A group of men interested in raising the standard in the endowed grammar schools had sought to do this by persuading the universities to provide an external examination. The first of these 'local examinations' – local, because they were held at centres throughout the country – was established by Oxford in 1857, and Cambridge followed in 1858 (Stephen 1927: 83). Emily Davies' committee's earliest success came not with matriculation examinations, but with these more junior tests.

Opening these examinations to girls was congruent with Emily Davies' broad aim of integrating boys' and girls' education. If the external standard were the same, it followed that the internal instruction in the schools must follow a similar pattern. Furthermore she was already in contact with the headmistress of the North London Collegiate School, Frances Buss, whom she found deeply in sympathy with her views (Davies 1970: 210a). Davies knew she could rely on her, and on the heads of other schools claiming to offer an education of the Queen's College type, to enter pupils for these examinations.

As secretary of the committee she was soon writing off to both Oxford and Cambridge Local Examination Boards. It soon became apparent that neither the Oxford Board, nor any of its local centres, would consider allowing the girls to sit for its examinations, but in her negotiations with Cambridge Emily Davies devised a tactic she was to use again in gaining university education for women. The London Local Committee of the Cambridge Board was persuaded to give the girls informal access to papers and have them privately marked by the official examiners. The first set of girls sat for these examinations in 1863. No difficulties arose, and by 1865 girls were officially accepted as candidates not just for the Cambridge Locals, but for the Durham and Edinburgh Universities' local examinations as well. In 1870 Oxford followed suit. (Kamm 1965:185–97; Stephen 1927: 84–91)

This move had far-reaching consequences for the way girls' secondary education was to develop. First, the examinations gave practical proof that girls and boys had roughly similar intellectual abilities. Even in the first examinations, though girls did badly in mathematics, their literary subjects were praised (PP 1867–8 vol. 28: 554–5). By the 1870s the equality was more striking. In 1874, for example, according to the analysis of the results by *The Englishwoman's Review*, though boys did better in mathematics, girls gained higher average marks in grammar, Old Testament, catechism, French, German, and Latin (EWR 1875: 264). Girls were also doing well enough to qualify for prizes and exhibitions.[2]

Second, a standard by which, for example, governesses could be judged had been established, one approved by people like Charlotte Yonge (1877: 84) whose interest in girls' education was supported by the religious heterodoxy. Girls working at home with a governess now had an outside syllabus to direct and test their studies, and schools with pretensions to offering an intellectual training had an external standard to meet.

Above all, the standard was not one for girls alone, but for both sexes. Girls' and boys' secondary educational curricula were being brought into conformity with one another. Examinations in 'feminine' subjects like music and modern languages were being taken by boys, 'masculine' ones in classics and mathematics by girls. As Margaret Bryant points out, there was, thereafter, a two-way influence between girls' and boys' schools, the girls' schools leading the way in some areas like teacher training, the broader curriculum, and the specially planned physical education programme (Bryant 1979: 109, 111).

Having set in train this integration of the curriculum, Emily Davies turned her attention to breaking down the concept of 'separate spheres' in the official view of education. In 1863 the Taunton Commission had been set up to look into 'middle class education', and, though the intention had been to look at boys' schools, so androcentric was the official view of education that there was nothing in the wording of the guidelines which specifically excluded girls. Emily Davies saw this as another opportunity, and began to campaign, successfully, for the Commission to include middle-class girls' education in its inquiry (Kamm 1965: 199–200; Stephen 1927: 130–2).

She did as much as she could to see that witnesses whose evidence might influence the findings in the direction she wanted were called (Stephen 1927: 132–9; Strachey 1928: 136–7), and once again the results had far-reaching consequences. Though the Commissioners did not integrate their report on girls' schools with the rest of their remarks, they made two points which meant a great deal for her campaign. First, they agreed that girls' education was in dire need of reform, and second, they reported (though incidentally, not as a major feature) that where boys and girls were taught together they were able to cope with the same subjects, and without any 'noticeable difference of attainments in the two sexes' (PP 1867–8, vol. 28: 553). The findings of the Commission were widely commented on in the serious press, and a whole rash of articles appeared stressing points which Emily Davies felt important: the very low standards in most private schools and the need for external examinations.

One of the Commission's aims had been to examine the way in which endowments – some dating from the sixteenth century – were being administered and to make recommendations which would make them better suited to the needs of nineteenth-century schools. It had for some time been one of the complaints of the Women's Movement that old endowments providing for the education of both boys and girls were being used exclusively for boys' education (TNAPSS 1860: 432–4; Beale 1865: 287; Maurice 1860: 235). In their report, the Commissioners expressed concern at the fact that 'the endowments for the secondary education of girls bear but an infinitesimal proportion to the similar endowments for boys'. They recommended specifically that part of the very large fund of Christ's Hospital should immediately be directed to girls' education and that 'the full participation of girls in Endowments should be broadly laid down' in the guidelines for the proposed Endowed Schools Commission which was to examine and re-allocate each endowment individually (PP 1867–8 vol. 28: 564–8).

The Endowed Schools Act of 1869 followed these recommendations, and the Commission it set up, and the Charity Commission which later took over its work, implemented the recommendations, though perhaps not as generously as most supporters of girls' education would have liked. At any rate, though the Taunton Commission had listed only fourteen endowed girls' secondary schools, by 1897 there were eighty-six (PP 1867–8, vol. 28: 565; Bryant 1979: 101).

The Commission, because of Emily Davies' efforts, had linked together for official consideration the secondary education of boys and girls, and the link was never again broken. When the Bryce Commission was set up in 1895 not only were girls' schools included in the inquiry, but three women commissioners were appointed. When government grants to secondary schools began, girls' schools received them on more or less equal terms. In the period 1904–5, 292 boys', 99 girls', and 184 co-educational schools received grants. By 1921–2, these numbers had risen to 462, 450, and 331 (Bryant 1979: 108). The development of girls' secondary education was certainly part of a wider movement, but without Emily Davies' intervention at two crucial points, the integration with boys' education would certainly have come much later, if at all.

## Opening university degrees

Emily Davies' real interest, however, was in 'higher education', in persuading universities to open their degrees as well as their local examinations to women. At the same time as working for the integration of boys' and girls' secondary education she had been using the Committee for Obtaining the Admission of Women to University Examinations to press for women's access to the London University Matriculation examination. Here, however, she found herself in conflict with the deeply ingrained belief in 'separate spheres' for men and women and continually confronted with the Angel in the House arguments used to justify it. The Social Science discussion in 1862 had revealed something of the depth of this feeling. One speaker believed that what was needed was a 'special university to take up the education of women alone'; another that women should not do the men's courses but 'that the examinations and the whole course ought to be such as was adapted to the wants of women', being unwilling to accept that 'the same training and discipline should be applied to men and to women' (TNAPSS 1862: 340–2).

The same feeling flourished within London University. Though it refused to open its matriculation examination to women, it offered, in 1866, to establish separate examinations for women, of a higher standard than the Cambridge Locals, but different in emphasis from the matriculation. Emily Davies wrote caustically thanking 'Convocation for their kind intentions in offering us a serpent when we asked for a fish', and was met with the argument from one member of the Senate who was known to be 'strongly in favour of some general educational standard in the University for women' that 'you are so eager to be reckoned equal, that you will not hear of difference, even tho' difference involve as much superiority as inferiority'. The examinations were established in 1868 and Emily Davies' Committee passed a resolution that 'women above the age of 18 be advised to avail themselves provisionally of this examination' (Stephen 1927: 103–5).

In 1869 the Committee was disbanded, but by this time Emily Davies had already embarked on a far more ambitious scheme to open university education to women by establishing a separate women's college where women could work for the Cambridge degrees. She had by this time attracted a group of prestigious supporters and was able to dispense with the patronage of the Social Science Association and the need to argue her case in a less than sympathetic forum. Her most significant backer was Barbara Leigh Smith (now Madame Bodichon) and she gained two other notable supporters in Emily Shirreff (1814–1897) and Lady Stanley of Alderley (1807–1895). Lady Stanley had been an early lady visitor at Queen's College and Emily Shirreff had written on women's education in the 1850s. Both, like Frances Buss, seem to have been completely converted to Emily Davies' views and prepared to defend them to the hilt (Stephen 1927: 162–3, 227–8).

After discreet inquiries Emily Davies had come to believe that Cambridge, which had proved so helpful in the local examinations, might be persuaded to open its degree examinations informally to women, and she approached Queen's and Bedford Colleges to see if they would be interested in preparing students for them. The result was discouraging, and she therefore came to the conclusion that the best solution would be to start a separate college training women for this purpose alone (Stephen 1927: 146–7). From 1866 to 1869 she worked furiously for this scheme and in October 1869 the institution which was later to become Girton College was opened in a house in Hitchin. The women admitted were to be taught by Cambridge dons, were to follow the course set down for Cambridge undergraduates in the time usually allotted, and were to sit for the same examinations. There was, as yet, no official recognition of the scheme by the university, but it was hoped that the procedure which had opened the Cambridge Locals would once again prove successful. Once the women had demonstrated that they could do the same work as the men it would be possible to argue from a much stronger position. The first women sat for the Previous Examination in December 1870 (Stephen 1927: 149–79, 202–38; Strachey 1928: 157).

At the same time as Emily Davies was pursuing her specialist goals, the earlier movement based on the bluestocking legacy, given legitimacy by the religious heterodoxy, and headed in a new direction by Queen's and Bedford Colleges in the 1850s, was gathering momentum. In his history of the adult education movement J. F. C. Harrison has shown that the expansion of the railway system in the 1850s made it possible for academics from Oxford and Cambridge to add to their incomes by making overnight trips to provincial centres to give lectures. The first intention was to contribute to working-class male education by lecturing to mechanics' institutes, but it was soon found that there was also a lucrative market for lectures to ladies. Queen's and Bedford Colleges had been offering this service to adult women in London since their foundation, and in the 1860s Ladies' Educational Associations began to be formed in other major towns (Harrison 1961: 220–2).

In 1867 Josephine Butler (1828–1906), the future leader of the campaign against the Contagious Diseases Acts, and Anne Clough (1820–1892), the sister of the poet who ran her own school in the Lake District, persuaded the Ladies' Educational Associations of Liverpool, Manchester, Sheffield and Leeds to combine to form the North of England Council for Promoting the Higher Education of Women. The council arranged to have courses of lectures, with accompanying reading lists and essays to be marked by the lecturer, repeated in each town, and in 1869 arranged for Cambridge University to extend its local examination system by adding a special Women's Examination. This council began cooperating with working men's clubs, notably the Crewe Mechanics' Institute and the Equitable Pioneers' Cooperative Society in Rochdale, and, in response to joint requests, Cambridge University took responsibility for the programme in 1873 by setting up a Syndicate for Local Lectures, and men were admitted to the Women's Examinations which became the Higher Locals (Harrison 1961: 222–7; Strachey 1928: 151–3). Even before this, in 1871, local lectures for ladies were established in Cambridge and Anne Clough was invited to take charge of a house where women from elsewhere could stay while attending the lectures and preparing for the Women's Examinations (Clough 1903: 147–56).

Emily Davies feared that these moves might jeopardize her plan for integrating women's higher education with that of men. 'It makes me very unhappy,' she wrote, 'to see Ladies' Lectures, Ladies' Educational Associations, etc., spreading. It is an evil principle becoming organized, and gaining strength which comes from organisation' (Stephen 1927: 194).

Sara Delamont has divided the campaigners for women's education in Britain and America into two groups: 'the uncompromising – who were determined that women should do what men did, warts and all – and the separatists – who favoured modified courses for wome.' (Delamont 1978a: 154). There can be no doubt that Emily Davies belonged unequivocally to the 'uncompromising' camp and that she had convinced the other Girton patrons that her approach was the right one. Emily Shirreff, for example, wrote:

> Whether or not the Cambridge course is the best that might be laid down, it is a deservedly honoured one, and its standard is recognised; and a recognised standard . . . was beyond all things what women needed . . . Till women in their turn become authorities, their obvious policy is to abide by established authorities.
>
> (Shirreff 1873: 90)

The speakers at the Social Science meeting and the members of London University quoted above were obviously 'separatists', and even Dorothea Beale of Cheltenham Ladies' College took this line. But the rival Cambridge group were by no means as separatist as Emily Davies feared. For Anne Clough the Women's Education Movement was not, as it was for Emily Davies, primarily a way of transforming women's position in society, but a way of allowing individual women to develop their potential for self-realization and service to the full (Clough 1903: 252–9; Strachey 1928: 163). Both she and her backers were quite prepared for women who had had sufficient preparation to study the same courses and sit for the same examinations as men.

It was not long before the Cambridge house, which was to become Newnham College, was following the example of Girton and having its students study the standard Cambridge courses for men and sit for the examinations, though there was never the same insistence as at Girton that the length of time taken for the course must be the same as that laid down for men. As better-prepared girls began to come from the new public schools, places at Newnham were restricted to those studying the standard university courses (Clough 1903: 173–7; McWilliams-Tullberg 1977: 129–30).

Furthermore, male unattached intellectuals were increasingly won over to the cause. In 1866 Emily Davies wrote to Barbara Bodichon:

> Mr Charles is getting up our case for the London University in a most businesslike manner. He is a very able man, a barrister, & is likely I believe to take a high stand in his profession. What possesses him to

take up our cause, nobody knows. His goodness is quite spontaneous & unaccounted for.

(Bodichon 1970)

When the question of women and universities was first mooted in 1863, the Earl of Shaftesbury had commented:

We may indeed yet come to it, for Heaven only knows what may come to pass. I have seen so many changes, so many reversals of opinion, so many things accepted, which, when first mentioned almost filled people with horror, that hardly anything would now surprise me.

(EWJ August 1863: 423)

The women's education campaign achieved the change in 'knowledge' he envisaged, and support for women's higher education was added to the 'progressive' creed.

Men holding such progressive views had a presence on the staff and governing bodies of many universities and colleges, and were now prepared to press the claims of women. Nevertheless, just as the progressives on the Council of the Pharmaceutical Society had needed the Society for Promoting the Employment of Women to provide them with pretexts and recruits (Jordan 1998), the progressives in the universities needed similar outside groups to inspire and encourage them. This function, Carol Dyhouse has shown, was performed by the Ladies' Educational Associations:

The Ladies' Educational Associations . . . played an important part in facilitating women's access to the universities. They had powerful patrons and supporters of both sexes. The president of the Glasgow Association was Princess Louise, marchioness of Lorne, and the executive committee of the Edinburgh Association in 1878 was headed by the Duchess of Argyll. Some of the office holders and many of the subscribers to these associations were the wives and daughters of wealthy local citizens, or widows and unmarried daughters with considerable wealth at their disposal, who were in a position to make significant educational endowments. . . . Supporters and subscribers also included a large number of professors' wives and daughters. . . . The support of university professors and teachers sympathetic to the cause of women's education was crucial in fostering academic links, and in ensuring that the educational work of the associations was of an appropriate standard. This meant that when the universities opened their degree examinations to women, there were women whose previous attendance at classes enabled them to qualify almost immediately, without much further study. In Edinburgh, for instance, the 'first eight ladies' who graduated in arts in 1893 had all been students of the Edinburgh Association for the Higher Education of Women, and in Glasgow, the medical classes at Queen Margaret College had been carefully arranged so that in 1892 attendance at these classes qualified students to proceed immediately to university examinations. Marion Gilchrist, a student at Queen Margaret College, became the first woman to obtain a Scottish medical degree in 1894.

(Dyhouse 1995: 17)

For all these initiatives Girton and Newnham provided 'uncompromising' models. Though full Cambridge degrees were denied women until 1948, the danger Emily Davies had fought to avert was avoided. No separate universities for women were founded. (This did not necessarily imply a 'separatist' approach; American colleges for women like Vassar and Bryn Mawr were firmly committed to the uncompromising line (Delamont 1978a: 155–6).) In 1878 London University degrees became available to women and Bedford College began to transform itself into an institution preparing women for degrees, while Royal Holloway College, plans for which had already been made in 1875 as an independent women's university, began instead, when it opened in 1886, to prepare women for the London Degrees. In 1879 two women's colleges were founded at Oxford, and Trinity College, Dublin, admitted women to its degrees. When the various colleges in provincial cities banded together to form the federal Victoria University in 1880, its charter allowed for women taking its degrees, thus solving the problem of the women who had been prosecuting a campaign not unlike the Cambridge one within Manchester's Owens College (Fiddes 1941: 1–14; Kamm 1965: 261–7; Tuke 1939: 127–9). By 1900, 16 per cent of the university student population was female and this had risen to 24 per cent by 1920 (Dyhouse 1995: 17).

Emily Davies' contribution, once again, was to be there at the beginning, to set the parameters of the discussion and so determine the direction change would take. Her 'uncompromising' arguments were far more congruent than the separatist view with the long 'Women's Rights' tradition that was already part of the general radical creed, and so more appealing to the unattached male intellectual prepared to devote himself to fighting for a cause. Her practice provided a blueprint for the Ladies' Educational Associations to follow. The 'uncompromising' group showed what could be done, whereas the separatists did little more than utter protests and make sentimental appeals like Ruskin's to the Angel in the House myth.

## Medical education

At the same time as Emily Davies had been battling to gain access for women to university courses, other women had been working to achieve their entry into at least one of the liberal professions: medicine. This step had already been taken in the United States, and the English response had not been wholly disapproving (HW 1853: 576; *Saturday Review* 1857: 64). The Langham Place circle had from the first listed medicine among the new occupations which might be opened to women. The first practical moves were made by Emily Davies' friend Elizabeth Garrett between 1860 and 1865. While Emily Davies argued the case for women physicians in the *English Woman's Journal* in 1861 and at a Social Science Congress in 1862 (Davies 1910: 19–27, 34–40), Elizabeth Garrett studied privately for the examinations of the Society of Apothecaries, and was licensed in 1866. Her success, however, provoked such outrage in the medical profession that the path she had followed was officially closed in 1868, and could not serve as a model for other women (Manton 1965: 82–163; Stephen 1927: 55–67, 78–81).

Another way had to be found, and this task was taken up by a former student and tutor at Queen's College, Sophia Jex-Blake (1840–1912). In 1869 she undertook not only the monumental task, similar to that performed by Emily Davies at Cambridge, of collecting a group of students and arranging for lectures, demonstrations and examinations for them, but also to study these courses herself at the same time.

The story of the battle for women's medical education has been told a number of times (Bell 1953; Roberts 1993; Todd 1918): how Edinburgh University accepted Sophia Jex-Blake's group and then refused to allow the women to finish their courses, how some of them obtained degrees in Switzerland, the opening of first the Dublin and then the London medical examinations to women, the founding of the London School of Medicine for Women and the Hospital for Women which could provide teaching and ward experience when other institutions refused to accept women students, and the propaganda battle which resulted in support for women's medical education becoming part of the progressive creed.

The result of the campaign can be seen in the census figures for women doctors given in Table 4.4, 25 in 1881 rising to 477 by 1911. The percentage increases each decade were dramatic: 1881–91, 304 per cent; 1891–1901, 110 per cent; 1901–11, 125 per cent. A precedent had been set, and in one at least of the liberal professions the belief that it was an exclusively male sphere had been transformed from doxa to orthodoxy, while progressives held to the heterodox view developed by the Women's Movement that it was an appropriate occupation for a woman.

## The high schools

Though Emily Davies' own energies went chiefly into the campaign for higher education, and co-opting the young women 'going mad for want of something to do' for her purpose, a group of women she had converted to her 'uncompromising' beliefs turned to a different and even larger client group: the parents looking for a cheap but respectable education to occupy their daughters' teenage years. They were able to use her two achievements of the early 1860s, the Taunton Report and the local examinations, to give legitimacy to a new school system that offered a curriculum similar to that in boys' schools and advocated preparing girls for an occupation before marriage.

The Taunton Commission on Education, usually seen as the turning point for the reform of girls' secondary education (Burstall 1938: 38–9; Kamm 1971: 30–1), recommended the establishment in major towns of large – by this they meant about a hundred pupils – day schools for girls offering an academic education (PP 1867–8 vol 28: 559–60). The commissioners hoped that the work of the Endowment Commission would achieve this, but it was obviously going to be a slow process. The press interest which the report created, however, paved the way for these women to intervene and hasten the course of events, and in doing so to determine the form the later schools would take, and to link them firmly with the aims and ideals of the Women's Movement.

The initial move was made by Maria Grey (1816–1906), the daughter of an admiral, and widow of a connection of the powerful Whig family, who had long been interested in girls' education and who had, with her sister, Emily Davies' supporter Emily Shirreff, published a book on the subject, *Thoughts on Self-Culture*, in 1850. In June 1871 she read a paper to the Society of Arts arguing the case for endowed girls' schools and proposing the foundation of an 'Educational League' to carry out this work. As a result, the Council of the Society of Arts issued a circular inviting people to join such an association. At the Social Science Congress in October Maria Grey again read a paper on the subject, and a provisional committee was formed. The committee established the National Union for the Education of all Classes above the Elementary which, because of its social science backing and Maria Grey's aristocratic connections, had a titled president, an imposing list of aristocratic vice-presidents, and the Princess Louise as patron (Kamm 1971: 37–45).

The real work was, however, done by Maria Grey and three other women: Emily Davies' two Girton supporters, Emily Shirreff and Lady Stanley, and Mary Gurney (1836–1917), who had read a paper at the same Social Science Congress as Maria Grey on the schools established by Frances Buss, recommending that they should be taken as a model for 'middle class' girls' education (TNAPSS 1871: 367-8; Kamm 1971: 36)

The main achievement of the National Union was the founding of the Girls' Public Day Schools Company (GPDS) to open a series of proprietary schools, that is, schools where the initial capital was raised from investors who supported the cause and were prepared to accept a very low return on their money. This mode of establishing schools had proved successful in the case of a number of boys' schools and the girls' school Cheltenham Ladies' College. For internal organisation, however, it was not the Cheltenham school which provided the model, but Frances Buss's North London Collegiate School (Grey 1884: 50). A great deal had happened to this school since it was set up as a private venture by Frances Buss in 1850 on the model of Queen's College. It had flourished and grown, but further than this it had come to embrace the 'uncompromising' ideals of the Women's Movement. Frances Buss had found in Emily Davies someone whose ideas were sympathetic and she was prepared to allow her school to be used for trying them out. Unlike Dorothea Beale at Cheltenham, she had grasped eagerly at the prospect of external examinations and had entered twenty-five girls in the first Cambridge Locals examination. At this date, too, links were in the process of being formed between her school and Girton (Burstall 1933: 55).

The North London Collegiate School seemed to be offering in practice what the GPDS hoped to provide. Its fees were low enough to make it accessible to girls from quite modest homes, yet its examination results proved that a sound academic education could be offered at this cost, and its curriculum was adapted to the requirements of the public examinations.

However it was not just the curriculum policy that the new high schools took over from the North London Collegiate School. The GPDS also chose to follow this school in ignoring the status line between upper middle class and lower middle class. At the North London Collegiate School, though girls came from both professional men's and tradesmen's families, no notice was taken of family background. As one ex-pupil put it: 'No-one asked you who you were or where you came from' (Price and Glenday 1975: 13), while Frances Buss insisted that 'the same high tone of feeling' was expected of all the pupils, 'the same attention to instruction' (Bryant 1979: 117). Mary Gurney had publicly praised this policy, and though the Taunton Commission had advised against it, this blurring of status lines was accepted as a guiding principle by the GPDS, together with a specific commitment to non-denominational religious teaching which went further even than Frances Buss had done (PP 1867–8 vol 28: 560; TNAPSS 1871: 368). Lady Stanley wrote that it was decided from the beginning that in their schools 'all distinctions of class or sect should be absolutely ignored. It was largely predicted that this latter condition would bring ruin for the undertaking' (Stanley 1879: 317).

There was apparently a good deal of concern among upper-middle-class parents about the possible results of this mixing of classes, but it does not seem to have prevented a significant number from sending their daughters to the new schools (Delamont 1978b: 175–6; Yonge 1888a: 7, 10, 38). The benefits offered by the high schools, the combination of excellence and cheapness, seem to have overcome the status fears of many parents, for the schools flourished, presenting in Lady Stanley's words, 'the strange spectacle of perfect success in the first bold attempt ever made to found a wide system of education without grant or endowment' (Stanley 1879: 316). By the end of the century thirty-eight schools had at different times been opened, though there had been some closures and mergers (Kamm 1971: 207–14).

Other local bodies were soon opening proprietary girls' schools without

GPDS backing. By 1873 similar schools had been opened at Southampton and Guernsey, and others were being planned in Plymouth, Liverpool, and Manchester, while endowments were slowly becoming available. When in 1870 Frances Buss decided to make her school public, some of the funds of the Brewers' Company and the Clothmakers' Company were made over to it, and Manchester High School also received endowments. As a result of the Endowed Schools Commission's activities, other schools were founded or re-established on the high school model, some of them sharing the endowments of established boys' schools, as did the girls' school attached to Christ's Hospital, St Paul's School for Girls, and the Bradford and Leeds Girls' Grammar Schools. By 1897 there were eighty-six endowed schools for girls, some following the high school pattern, and some offering a 'middle school' – ending at fifteen or sixteen – education only (Bryant 1979: 101; Burstall 1907: 6; Burstall 1938: 41; Kamm 1965: 218–9).

There were other supporters of the general concept of improved education for girls who nevertheless could not accept the non-denominational nature of, or the lack of class distinction in the high schools. In 1883 the Church of England set out to establish its own system of high schools on the GPDS model through the Church Schools Company, the main difference being that the religious instruction was specifically Church of England. By the end of the century twenty-eight schools were under its control (Bell 1958). Those who objected to the mixing of classes, and could afford to pay for their exclusiveness, were catered for in the new girls' 'public' schools like St Leonard's, Roedean, and Wycombe Abbey, mostly boarding schools, some of which did not simply rely on high fees to avoid a mixing of ranks but carefully screened all the pupils admitted (Beale 1865: 278; Delamont 1978b: 176–7; Kamm 1965: 219–20; Percival 1939: 229–32).

Yet, in spite of these differences, the movement grew more rather than less homogeneous as the century progressed. The headmistresses of these new schools, unlike the headmasters of boys' secondary schools, established a single professional body under Frances Buss's leadership in 1874. Their recurring contact with one another, and their discussions of problems which all the schools faced, tended to create a consensus of opinion among them and a general convergence of practice within the schools (Price and Glenday 1975: 22–34). Even though historians, reading the speeches and writings of individual headmistresses, find it possible to divide them into conservatives and feminists, the uncompromising and the separatists, the movement saw itself as a unified one (Delamont 1978a: 154; Pederson 1981: 463–4).

It needs to be recognized that even the separatists were not strictly 'conservative', or at least that an even more conservative position, that girls' education should continue to be private, was possible. They too were involved in bringing about a 'revolution' in girls' education. It is only in hindsight, and in comparison with the more radical position taken by those adhering to Women's Movement ideas, that they appear conservative. The difference between the separatists and the uncompromising seems largely to have been determined by whether their support for women's education was based on the religious heterodoxy, developed by the evangelicals and tractarians, or on the theories of the Women's Movement. Joyce Pederson sees the separatists as drawing their inspiration not from the 'liberal feminist tradition of reform' but from belief in a 'corporate social order composed of diverse ranks differing in status and function but united in the pursuit of a common spiritual ideal' (Pederson 1981: 463–4). They held, that is, to the aristocratic ideal, whereas the uncompromising based their views on the entrepreneurial ideal which underlay the Women's Movement. Yet they proved able to work together in the Headmistresses' Association.

This was in part, no doubt, because the high school movement was built on the foundations established by the unequivocally separatist ladies' colleges.[3] A really uncompromising stand would have been to insist, as 'progressive' educators did in the 1920s, on co-education. Yet had this been done in 1870, support for the movement would have been minimal, whereas the aim of Maria Grey's National Union was to offer those parents who were prepared to pay for the education of their daughters something that the union regarded as superior to what was offered by governesses and private schools. Consequently, as I have demonstrated elsewhere (Jordan 1991), though the policy of the high schools was to build the curriculum around the requirements of the local examinations and so in practical terms bring it into conformity with that in boys' schools, their apologists made frequent use of what was described in Chapter 5 as the 'bluestocking syllogism', the argument that the purpose of academic education was to create 'good wives and mothers'. Since these arguments were the mainstay of their separatist critics, direct ideological confrontation between the two groups seldom took place, and their differences were treated as disagreements about organization and strategy rather than principles. By never explicitly stating their practical aims, the 'uncompromising' were able to maintain the support of parents, patrons and even teaching staff far more committed to the domestic ideology than they.

The gradual triumph of the uncompromising programme can be traced in the writings of committed separatists. The novelist Charlotte M. Yonge, for example, had, as her early novels show, adopted the bluestocking, separatist view in the 1840s and 1850s. Yet she seems to have accepted most of the 'uncompromising' initiatives, at least after a certain lapse of time. In the 1870s she recommended the local examinations, both as an incentive for girls studying at home and as a qualification for governesses, and supported the view that educated women from less than wealthy backgrounds ought to become self-supporting. The high school movement seems to have met with her qualified approval almost from its inception, and though she rejected Emily Davies' initial request for support for Girton, she later came to accept a period at a university as an appropriate conclusion to the education of a clever girl (Battiscombe 1943: 146; Yonge 1873, vol. 2: 232–3; 1877: 4–8, 33; 1888a: 7, 10, 38; 1890: 243). F. D. Maurice's views showed a similar modification. Though in 1860 he spoke against the idea of university education and professions for women, he later gave support to a number of Emily Davies' ventures (Kaye 1972: 87).

## Education for employment

If the headmistresses of the new public girls' schools were reticent about the 'uncompromising' nature of the curriculum, they were increasingly committed to urging on their students the Women's Movement argument that women should be trained for an occupation. In essence, the ideals presented to the students had their roots in the religious heterodoxy: philanthropy and self-actualization. Dorothea Beale saw her school as aiming at 'the perfection of the individual and the good of the community'; the aim of St Leonard's was 'to give each girl in the school the best chance of self-development, not for selfish ends, but for the good of the community'; Sara Burstall saw the high schools as providing 'a liberal education in school, and preparation for service to the community when school is over' (Burstall 1907: 11; Pederson 1975: 158; Percival 1939: 216).

However the schools also saw themselves as preparing girls for a paid occupation, and pressed this on their students as the third aim of their education. The Taunton Commission had used Women's Movement arguments on the subject, suggesting that late marriage and the greater number of women than men made it necessary for many middle-class girls to earn their own living, and that therefore their education should serve this purpose (PP 1867–8 vol. 28: 546). Even before this, however, such an aim had been adopted at the North London Collegiate School. One of Frances Buss's pupils recalled:

> She was very strongly impressed by the absolute necessity for young girls to be trained to some employment by which they might, if necessary, earn a livelihood. For women to be dependent on brothers and relations, she considered an evil to be avoided at all costs, and she tried to keep before us the fact that training for any work must develop a woman's intellect and powers, and therefore made her – married or single – a better and nobler being.
>
> (Burstall 1907: 8, quoted)

For the first twenty years of the life of her school Frances Buss could presumably have done nothing more than train girls to be governesses, relying at first on the reputation of her school to gain places for them, and then, after 1863, on the qualifications attested by the Cambridge Locals. In 1870, however, perhaps because of her contacts with the Langham Place circle, she began to widen the field. When her school became a public trust and moved to new quarters, the old school and its furniture were passed to a new foundation, the Camden School. In this school, designed for girls leaving at sixteen and with very low fees, the curriculum consisted largely of the skills needed for work as a clerk: English, arithmetic, bookkeeping (Burstall 1933: 38; Gurney 1872: 16–22). This school may have been modelled on the one run by the Employment Society, and even if it was not, Frances Buss seems to have adopted the new definitions of women's work being put forward by that society. Thus, when her schools began to serve as a model for the GPDS schools, the new definition of women's work was integrated into the curriculum. Self-dependence, in the Langham Place use of the term, became one of their ideals. In 1907 Sara Burstall wrote:

> Thus, into the schools officered by teachers who knew how hard it was for gentlewomen to earn a living, there entered also the ideal of giving to girls of the middle class the thoroughness and accuracy and real intellectual training which would fit them to work like their professional brothers for something like a living wage.
>
> (Burstall 1907: 8)

This was accepted by the GPDS leaders as one of their aims (Gurney 1872: 20; Stanley 1879: 320), and Sara Burstall, a product of Frances Buss's schools and Girton, and for many years headmistress of Manchester High School, linked it with the service ideal, stating that the aims of the high schools were to 'prepare their girls for work in the world, paid or unpaid, and urge on them the duty of service to the community' (Burstall 1907: 11).

Sara Burstall could talk so confidently of training for a paid occupation because by this time it had become fairly well established in practice that middle-class women, even upper-middle-class women, could practise a profession and earn an income for themselves without being forced into the position of 'status incongruence', at once a lady and a wage-earner, that had plagued the governess at mid-century (Peterson 1972; Poovey 1988: 163).

By 1900 the early discussions at Langham Place had borne fruit. Working ladies saw themselves as just as entitled as working gentlemen to a salary for the work they did, whether they needed it or not. It had been argued by F. D. Maurice as early as 1855 and by Barbara Leigh Smith in 1857 that acceptance of a salary was no more derogatory to a lady's status than to a gentleman's (Maurice 1855: 18; Smith 1857: 47–9), but while the Women's Movement still saw ladies' work as entry into 'public life' the point was not much stressed. For in public life many men, including Members of Parliament, still worked unpaid. When, however, it was seriously proposed that women enter the liberal professions the situation changed. As Elizabeth Garrett realized, it ran counter to the whole professional code to do professional work for nothing. She told a Social Science Congress in 1866:

It would be far better that it should be accepted as a point of honour among women, as it is among professional men, to take without question the salary or fee which belongs to any post or work, even when the recipient is not without some private income.

(Garrett 1866: 477)

A contributor to *Macmillan's Magazine* argued in 1869:

There seems to be a deep-rooted feeling that a woman who is not under the direst necessity is disgraced by earning money by her own exertions. Society considers it a venial offence for a young lady to waste her father's money on her extravagant vanity, but a very black crime that she should do profitable work with her brains. We are gradually abandoning the savage idea that work dishonours a man: may we hope that we shall become sufficiently civilized to feel idleness discreditable even to a woman?

(Holland 1869: 329)

That ladies should accept a salary became the accepted doctrine within the Women's Movement, and then spread beyond it. By 1893 even writers in the High Church girls' magazine *The Monthly Packet* accepted this view:

The best way of ascertaining that one's work is both intrinsically good and adapted to the wants of the age is to carry it into the labour market . . . I should advise even those who do not absolutely need the pecuniary remuneration to compete with paid workers, in order that their work may supply a real want; may be intrinsically good; may be done with more sustained effort, and consequently with less expenditure of effort.

(Wallas 1893: 114–15)

The view that ladies should enter the paid workforce was accepted almost from the beginning at the new women's colleges at Cambridge and Oxford, and it was because of this influence that female teaching was brought into line with the male professional tradition. As Joyce Pederson has pointed out, most of the women who attended these colleges were unequivocally ladies. Of those enrolled before 1895 and whose fathers' occupations were known, 11 per cent were daughters of 'noblemen', 'gentlemen' and 'farmers', 64 per cent of professional men, while most of the fathers of the 25 per cent from business backgrounds were upper middle-class: bankers, merchants, manufacturers. Very few of these women would have needed to earn their own livings, and yet more than half of them chose to become teachers, many of them reaching this decision as a result of the prevailing atmosphere within the colleges (Pederson 1975: 153–5).

Teaching, in consequence, was transformed beyond recognition by the efforts of the movement, and the situation of those at the top of the profession approached that of their male counterparts. The conditions under which women teachers worked in the new endowed and proprietary schools were very different from those of private governesses and under-teachers at select seminaries. Their hours and holidays were good (Bird 1911: 159, 161; Hogarth 1897: 929), and being employed by public bodies rather than private individuals they were free from the petty indignities and snobberies governesses encountered. The atmosphere in the high schools was different from that in private schools. The headmistresses who set the tone were committed to low living and high thinking and the schools strongly repressed the displays of wealth and the status worship which had characterized the ordinary private school (Pederson 1975: 154; Yonge 1857: 92–3). The salaries remained low; for form teachers around the £100 mark, though there were possibilities of rising. Headmistresses usually earned about £400, though in exceptional cases they could receive as much as £3,000. This was the result not so much of meanness in the employing bodies as of lack of the endowments which made it possible to offer the men teachers in boys' schools so much more (Fawcett 1878: 860; Pederson 1975: 150).

Nevertheless, the high school teacher had a self-esteem as a professional that the governess had lacked, and this was being mirrored by the 1880s, so observers implied, in the general community. By 1897 the president of the Association of Headmistresses claimed that 'the time had come when teachers should take their place as a learned profession' (Barnett 1884: 109; Pederson 1975: 149).

These teachers of the new type inspired not just respect in their pupils, but the schoolgirl 'pashes' which caused much concern in the schools, but which also led girls to adopt wholeheartedly the values of their idols (Burstall 1907: 160–1; Collet 1902a: 9; Percival 1939: 224). Thus, the commitment to a paid occupation which developed in the university colleges spread down through the high schools. The universities, it was accepted, were only open to the cleverest, but even the others, it was assumed, should do something. Other forms of teaching were open to the less academically inclined girls, primarily physical education and domestic science (Bird 1911, 121–2, 163–4; Burstall 1907: 200), but it was no longer assumed that the only appropriate work for ladies was teaching. Other occupations were coming to be considered suitable. Here the blurring of the status lines within the high schools seems to have played a crucial role. Well before the end of the century lower-middle-class parents had come to expect the schools to prepare their girls for employment as clerks either in private business or the civil service (Burstall 1907: 202), while the early restriction of work in insurance and the savings banks to 'ladies' blurred the lines between upper- and lower-middle-class occupations still further. The coming of the typewriter and the increasing employment of women as shorthand typists led the schools in the early twentieth century to begin offering clerical training as an alternative to the straight academic course for girls aged sixteen to eighteen (ibid.: 202).

It was not just in the high schools that upper-middle-class girls were steered into the same range of occupations as lower-middle-class ones. Even girls from the public boarding schools where the pupils were almost exclusively upper middle class, entered the same wide range of occupations. By 1927 ex-pupils of St Leonard's School had become missionaries, barristers, editors, journalists, secretaries, photographers, dispensers, nurses, warders, doctors, schoolmistresses, lecturers, authors, musicians, dressmakers, milliners, and public speakers, and had gone into farming, gardening, dairy work, weaving, embroidery, and stained glass work (Percival 1939: 227–8). It would seem that almost all the occupations (hairdressing and typesetting would seem to be the exceptions) which the Society for Promoting the Employment of Women had set out to redefine as 'women's work' had by the 1920s come to be regarded as 'ladies' work' as well.

## Women and the professions

This was certainly not the outcome that Emily Davies had hoped for when she began her campaign. Instead of fulfilling her vision of upper-middle-class women entering the same professional occupations as their brothers, the bulk of them, though now accepting that they would enter the paid workforce before marriage, were working in 'semi-mechanical occupations' for what were still, given their family background, pin money wages. Even university graduates were predominantly going into teaching, particularly after local authority grants became available, and indeed, as Carol Dyhouse has shown, the newer universities relied heavily on such women to keep up the numbers in the arts and science faculties (Dyhouse 1995: 18, 30–1). A few women took advantage of the opening of all university faculties to women to undertake other professional courses. Several studied accountancy and law in the 1890s, and Ray Strachey studied electrical engineering in the next decade. Women graduates were also found among the handful of women inspectors appointed by the government, and a few more were employed gathering statistics for the Board of Trade (Bulley and Whitley 1894: 21–2; Martindale 1938: 41, 47, 63, 183; Strachey 1928: 4).

Nevertheless, in the 1911 census women scarcely figured in any of the independent professional categories besides medicine. There were seven architects, nineteen accountants, and though there were apparently 200 registered pharmacists in the chemist/druggist category, and about twelve qualified dentists among the 250 in the 'dentists (including assistants)' category (Bird 1911: 195, 196), and though a few more than the two veterinary surgeons of the 1901 census may have been included in the composite 'veterinary surgeon and subordinate medical service' category, there were no lawyers, engineers, or surveyors listed.

I would suggest that the explanation lies, once again, with the change in the causes that appealed to feminist activists. The growing interest of Women's Movement members in the suffrage seems to have altered the direction of the most fervent of the movement's supporters, just as involvement with the trade union movement had absorbed those concerned with women's work at the other end of the scale. The campaign to get women into the medical profession was not followed by determined attacks on the other professional bodies (Reader 1966: 181). Instead, the energies of leading Women's Movement members began, during the 1870s, to be directed towards getting the vote. Their belief in its powers was extreme. Frances Power Cobbe, in a powerful and horrifying article on brutality in the working-class family, 'Wife Torture', claimed that 'were women to obtain the franchise tomorrow, it is morally certain that a Bill for the Protection of Wives would pass through the legislature before the Session was over' (Cobbe 1878: 80). Those interested in opening the professions, witnessing the struggle in medicine, seem to have felt that while the chartered bodies might hold out forever against individual women claimants for admission, an enfranchised female population would be able to put pressure on parliament, the authority which gave power to the chartered societies.

Yet the vote did not in fact bring an automatic expansion of professional work in its train. Although the 1919 Sex Disqualification Removal Act not only gave some women the vote, but opened the legal profession and the Chartered Society of Accountants to them, and set the scene for a struggle to have women admitted on the same terms as men to the administrative and executive classes of the civil service (Martindale 1938: 87–102; Strachey 1928: 375–7), this was not followed by any significant rise in the number of women entering the male-dominated professions. In the 1920s more and more women studied at the universities, and the 'career woman' became an accepted part of the social scene, but these careers were the same as those open at the end of the 1870s: literature, journalism and the arts, the civil service, medicine, and teaching. There were no widely canvassed campaigns to get women into other professions, and few women seem to have made individual choices. As was the case with lower-middle-class occupations, once the Women's Movement stopped targeting new occupations, no new occupations opened.

Nevertheless, the initiatives taken in the 1860s and early 1870s by both the Society for Promoting the Employment of Women and the Education Movement continued to have long-term effects which altered the country's occupational structure, and came close to destroying the economic dependence of, and hence patriarchal control over, grown up daughters. The efforts of the Employment Society to change employers' 'knowledge' had borne fruit, and work was available to young middle-class women in a number of areas previously restricted to men or older women.

Meanwhile, the ideas of the gospel of work and self-dependence, first applied to women in 1857, had become strongly entrenched in the women's university colleges and the high schools established through the efforts of the Women's Movement, and passed on the modification of 'knowledge' of women's work .which the movement had initiated. Furthermore, these trends then acquired a momentum of their own. The numbers of women in the occupations opened by the Employment Society multiplied, and so did the numbers of high schools and of women attending universities. Once the ideological barriers had been broken, more and more people saw that their self-interest lay in the areas pointed out by the Women's Movement.

What was not achieved was Emily Davies' hope of making upper-middle -class women's occupational opportunities identical with men's, of destroying the concept of separate spheres for men and women in the workforce. Though the Women's Movement had succeeded in redefining both women's and ladies' work, it had not abandoned them as concepts. Even after the vote was gained, most of the professions and trades were still closed to women and defended by their male membership most jealously. All the movement's successes in expanding women's occupations had occurred in the period 1860 to 1880, and thereafter, though the spread of the belief that women should work swelled the numbers in the new occupations, the range of occupations remained stationary. It was not to be seriously altered until the rise of second-wave feminism a hundred years later.

Yet the initial task which had confronted the Women's Movement should not be underrated, nor should the magnitude of its achievement. Women were still a long way from economic equality with men, but work which allowed them to support themselves in some dignity was at least available. In 1863 Jessie Boucherett wrote, in terms which would have seemed to many contemporaries ludicrously divorced from any relation to reality:

> If women were quite positively certain to marry before their father's death, the present system would not be so bad, but as they are not, it is wicked and cruel and based on a fallacy. Some day the contrary principle will be universally admitted. In course of time newspapers will take up the subject, leaders will be written, and lectures given on the duty of parents to their daughters; clergymen will preach about it, and tracts will be distributed, and then it will be recognized that a father who cannot leave his daughter a fortune, ought to teach her a trade, that she may be able to earn an honest livelihood; and the man who fails to do this will be thought less well of by his neighbours. Then the position of women will begin to improve, and this superfluity of helpless miserable creatures will gradually diminish till it ceases to exist.
>
> (Boucherett 1863: 47–8)

Before she died in 1905 her prediction was on the way to becoming a reality.

# NOTES

## 1 MIDDLE-CLASS WOMEN'S WORK

1 British historians, most notably Leonore Davidoff and Catherine Hall, began to use the term 'domestic ideology' to describe this collection of beliefs in the 1970s (Delamont 1978: 164). 'The cult of true womanhood' was the more usual term in the works of historians from the United States, for example Helsinger *et al.*, 1983.

## 2 THE CONSTRAINTS OF GENTILITY

1 Tilly and Scott use the terms 'family wage economy' and 'family consumer economy' to describe these latter forms of family organization, but these terms have not passed into general currency in the same way as the term 'family economy'.
2 For example, the 1851 census enumerators' books list as the occupations of the heads of households in Fitzroy Square in London two physicians, two surgeons, two barristers, a solicitor, an accountant, a colonel in the East India Company, an auctioneer, an organ builder, a proprietor of houses, a fundholder and a gentleman. Bedford Square housed families headed by four physicians, a civil engineer; a barrister, a solicitor and parliamentary agent, an inspector of letter carriers, GPO, a tin plate merchant, a wholesale jeweller and watch manufacturer, a malt distiller, a landed proprietor, a fundholder and an unmarried woman of no occupation.
3 The definition of the professional man gradually broadened as the century progressed. By 1902 A. C. Benson could write:

> It may roughly be said that the professions which stand highest in the social scale are the army, the navy, the bar, land agency, and the civil service. We may perhaps include with these artists, architects, and literary men. In the second rank come the solicitor, the engineer, the doctor, the schoolmaster; the Church, which formerly belonged to the upper grade, now stands somewhat apart, and may be called a vocation rather than a profession.
>
> (Benson 1902: 2)

4 One writer in the 1860s, discussing families 'in the rank of gentlefolk', wrote of

'the Paterfamilias, be he lawyer, doctor, divine, or man of letters', while another wrote that ladies were to be found 'in endless rows of terraces and crescents and squares – wherever the poor but genteel merchant and the second rate professional men reside, men with £300 to £400 per annum' (Cobbe 1862 : 228; Parkes 1865: 82).

5 Anne Summers has suggested that this was *the* significant distinction between the ladies and the nurses who nursed in the Crimean War. The ladies were prepared if necessary to do any of the heavy and dirty jobs required. 'The one constant distinction,' she notes, 'remains the paid or unpaid status of the worker' (Summers 1983: 51–3).

6 In both 1851 and 1871 15.5 per cent of households had general servants, but this hardly accounts for all the families which the male head's occupation would seem to place in the lower middle class, or the number suggested by Baxter's figures, as revised by Harold Perkin (1969: 420) of families with incomes between £60 and £300 a year. Thus it would seem that servant-keeping was not a defining characteristic of the status group, but a mark of prosperity for a particular family like a larger house or a piano, a step up from the weekly charwoman and the neighbour's boy who cleaned the boots and knives on a Saturday.

## 3 THE CONSTRAINTS OF FEMININITY

1 Sylvana Tomaselli (1985: 109–15) has shown that many Enlightenment philosophers like Diderot and Montesquieu saw the progress of civilization as necessarily leading to increased liberty for women, though whether this implied ultimate equal citizenship with men is not clear from her account.

2 Carol Pateman (1988, chap. 4) has made an ambitious and exciting attempt in proposing her theory of a 'sexual contract' underlying the social contract. When men agreed to overthrow the fathers they also agreed that they should take from them control over women. Part of the contract between the brothers is thus a sexual contract, an agreement that they will respect one another's rights to dominate the women in their own family.

3 If Carol Pateman is right, it may have been because women would be depriving their fathers or husbands of their patriarchal rights under the sexual contract if they entered into contracts with men who were not their relations.

4 This topic does not seem to have been much investigated by historians. Nevertheless even a glance at a thesaurus shows that the terms describing sexual licence are heavily gendered, that far more apply to women than to men, and that the ones applied to women are more abusive and condemnatory. While men are typically rakes, roués, lechers, profligates and libertines, women are whores, strumpets, trollops, trulls, hussies, drabs, bitches, jades and sluts.

5 There were, however, one or two dissidents who felt that there was no reason why married women should not work if they could keep their babies under their own eyes or while their children were at school (Martineau 1859: 299; TNAPSS 1868: 604).

6 Sylvana Tomaselli (1985: 120–2) suggests that the basis was laid in some of the writings of pro-women eighteenth century philosophers like Diderot and Antoine-Leonard Thomas in France and John Millar and William Alexander in

Britain who saw respect for women as a sign of increasing civilization. Other French origins have been identified by Jane Rendall (1985: 17–20) in the works of a number of female writers, notably Mme de Montbart, Mme Roland and Mme de Genlis, who used Rousseau's suggestion that training for citizenship was the province of the family to argue for better female education.

7 It was, however, to surface again in the 1870s with the advent of Social Darwinism (Fee 1974; Conway 1972; Duffin 1978).

8 The gradual insistence on recognized credentials for the practice of a profession had the effect of moving these occupations from a family economy to a male-breadwinner context. Pharmacy, a late entrant to the process, was a case in point. The Pharmacy Act of 1868 made it mandatory for all future chemists and druggists to have passed the Minor Examination of the Pharmaceutical Society before being placed on its register. The act, however, contained a 'grandfather' clause allowing all those who were already in business as chemists and druggists to go immediately on the list. The result was that the names of 215 women (about 2 per cent of the total number) appeared on the Register. Fifty of these women were still listed in 1900 (Holloway 1991: 261–2; Jordan 1998: 387–9). In other professions, where a retail department was not involved, though women might still continue to help during a man's lifetime, once registration through a professional association had been established by legislation, there was no provision for their carrying on after his death.

## 4 WHAT WAS WOMEN'S WORK?

1 These girls were quite distinct from the workers in the ready-made clothing industry which was conducted largely on outwork principles, employing the seamstresses and shirt-makers of the census categories, the women whose plight Thomas Hood recorded in his poem 'The Song of a Shirt'.

After the introduction of the sewing machine in the 1850s these workers tended to be brought together to work in factories, but they were still regarded as a group quite separate from those who had served an apprenticeship in one of the bespoke houses. The existence of outdoor hands in these houses, however, blurred the distinction somewhat, and a number of women seem to have existed on the borderline between seamstress and dressmaker, while the increase in the production of high quality ready-made garments made it harder to distinguish between the workshop and the 'private house' (PP 1864 vol. 22: 11, 121).

2 The large drop in the domestic service figures between 1891 and 1901 may reflect simply a change in classification; the General Report of the 1901 census says that many women engaged on domestic duties within their own families had previously been added to the domestic service totals (Bellamy 1978: 169).

## 5 BLUESTOCKINGS AND PHILANTHROPISTS

1 I am grateful to Sheldon Goldfarb for suggesting this example in response to a query to the Victoria e-mail discussion list.

2 There is now a large literature on 'liminality' in both anthropology and sociology, but Digby's term has the advantage of using the same metaphor while dealing specifically with the establishment of gender boundaries in nineteenth

century Britain. Digby in fact focuses primarily on the activities of members of the women's movement in the last few decades of the century, tending to regard the activities discussed here as already established as feminine, and accepted by 'conservatives'. This chapter suggests, however, that strong-minded women undertook a similar invasion of borderlands in the first part of the century.

3 The actual number who gave this as their occupation to the census takers remained small, only 109 women (compared with 1,504 men) being included in the category 'author, editor, journalist' in the 1851 census, many apparently choosing to emphasize their domestic role. Anne Mozley, for example, though she had been engaged in paid literary pursuits as a journalist and editor for over forty years, gave her occupation as 'annuitant' to the 1881 census takers. George Eliot also appeared simply as the wife of G. H. Lewes. Charlotte M. Yonge, on the other hand, gave her occupation as 'novel writer'.

4 Her advocacy was so successful that by the end of the century, a survey of female Oxford and Cambridge graduates found that almost all had at some time undertaken Sunday school teaching (Sidgwick 1890: 55).

5 The *Englishwoman's Review*, after describing how, when in 1863 a home for 300 soldiers' and sailors' daughters in Wandsworth was found to be mismanaged, a ladies' sub-committee was appointed to make recommendations, and how, when these were rejected, most of the ladies resigned, made the following comment:

> This is an excellent illustration of the way in which institutions for women are managed. First, a committee, composed exclusively of gentlemen, is appointed to govern it. They neglect or mismanage the institution; and this mis-management is quoted as a reason for doing nothing more for women in that direction.
>
> (EWR 1868: 70–1)

6 My thanks to the members of the Victoria e-mail list, in particular Amy Stephenson, Arpita Ghosal and Kris Garrigan, who reminded me of these depictions.

## 6 DETERMINING GIRLS' EDUCATION

1 There must, of course, have been some public schools founded during this period that did not survive until the 1940s. It seems unlikely, however, that adding these to the figures would alter the general picture of the 1840s to 1860s as the major period of expansion for boys' schools and 1870 to 1890 for girls' schools.

2 It also needs to be noted that much of the criticism of schools was directed at the physical conditions, poor food, cramped quarters, lack of exercise, rather than the curriculum. Charlotte Bronte, for example, has no complaints about the education Jane Eyre received at Lowood, only about the other conditions.

3 It was also possible to defend it as a solution to the problem of overstocking, and to argue, as the *Athenaeum* did in 1846, that art and music schools would 'rescue many from suspense and misery by teaching what is so appropriate to females' (*Athenaeum* 1846: 227).

4 In 1850 the *Athenaeum* referred to the opening of 'the Ladies' College,

Woodlands, Clapham Rise:—an institution founded on the same principles as Queen's College in London' (834), and in 1858 the editor of the *Englishwoman's Review* wrote of 'the numerous other colleges that have sprung up in and around London' (357). Three of the pre-1870 schools listed by Banks were founded before 1848, while besides the four mentioned here, he lists Loughborough High School (1850), St Dunstan's Abbey, Plymouth (1850), Badminton School (1858) and Howell's School (1859) (Banks 1954: 229).

## 7 TRANSFORMING NURSING

1 The anonymous author of 'Hospital Nurses as they are and as they Ought to Be', published in *Fraser's Magazine* in 1848, equated them with Sairey Gamp (*Fraser's* 1848: 539–40). On the other hand, an 1849 pamphlet by Edward Sieveking (1849) called *The Training Institutions for Nurses and the Workhouses: An Attempt to Solve One of the Social Problems of the Present Day*, which proposed a scheme for transforming the pauper women who had gained experience in the workhouse infirmaries into paid nurses who could earn their livings nursing both rich and poor, made no mention of a need to improve the nursing within the workhouses

2 A 1934 history of the organisation says that the first house was situated 'in the midst of a poor population to whom the sisters freely administered in sickness, when not otherwise engaged' (QNIA/W.9), and according to the *English Woman's Journal* (1860: 281) the 1860 *Annual Report* showed 'that the average number of nurses supplied gratuitously to the poor, is about twenty-five to thirty quarterly'while the 1861 Report was quoted as stating that one or two nurses were 'granted by the Committee to devote the whole of their time to visiting the sick poor, under the direction of the Clergy of the Parish to which they are appointed' (Howson 1862: 130). These annual reports have, however, vanished, and there was little attention paid by the committee to this charitable work in the pre-1860 records I examined (QNIA/W.2/3).

3 The 1851 census gives her age as 48, and records her as living with a 70-year-old father and 36-year-old brother in Bedford Square. Her father's occupation is given as 'magistrate, solicitor and land-owner'. The establishment consisted of these three and eight servants. Other correspondence suggests that there was also a country estate.

4 It would be fascinating to know of what this training consisted, but there seems little chance of finding out unless an account turns up in some memoirs. Certificates given to the probationers by the sisters at the hospital have survived in the St John's House archives, but they are completely unspecific. The second Lady Superintendent, Mrs Morrice, at one point outlined a plan for running a convalescent home within the House where probationers could get experience of home nursing under the guidance of the Sisters, but this did not happen and there is no evidence that the Sisters gave any instruction at all, beyond exercising 'woman's mission' of setting an example of a refined and religious way of life (Summers 1988: 3, 22).

5 In fact the succeeding history of St John's House was far from smooth. There were altercations between the Lady Superintendent and the Master, between the House and the hospital, and a number of splits within the sisterhood itself.

These have been fully and well described in Judith Moore's *A Zeal for Responsibility: The Struggle for Professional Nursing in Victorian England, 1868–1883* (1988).

6 A major theme in the historiography of nursing has been the creation of a matron independent of doctors and chaplains (Abel-Smith 1960: 24–8; Summers 1990; Moore 1988: 2–39). Yet though matrons and Lady Superintendents may have battled with male administrators and committees, they allowed no questioning of their own right to exact 'Christian obedience' from the women under them.

## 8 REDEFINING 'WOMEN'S SPHERE'

1 The campaign was a long one – lasting until 1882 – and the leadership soon passed out of the hands of Barbara Leigh Smith and Bessie Rayner Parkes (Holcombe 1977).

2 The notion that these women should turn to the ideal of self-dependence was already in the air (*Athenaeum* 1851: 631; *Fraser's* 1844: 583; *Fraser's* 1845: 703; Grey and Shirreff 1850: 19; Patmore 1851: 535; Yonge 1854: 30). It was the Women's Movement, however, which suggested that this should be the ideal for all women, not just society's casualties.

3 A number of ideas that were finally named by second-wave feminism a hundred years later were raised in this discussion. In 1865 F. W. Newman described 'male chauvinism': 'Men who are not personally conceited, often display conceit, at once offensive and injurious, in the claims which they make for their church, their country, their race, or (we will add) for their sex' (Newman 1865: 353). In 1866 Emily Davies tried to come to grips with the distinction since made between 'sex' and 'gender':

> The question under debate is not whether, as a matter of fact, there is such a thing as distinctive manhood or womanhood; for that no one denies. The debate is rather the degree to which certain qualities, commonly regarded as masculine and feminine characteristics, are such intrinsically or only conventionally; and further, as to the degree of prominence which it is desirable to give to the specific differences in determining social arrangements.
>
> (Davies 1866: 165)

## 9 REDEFINING 'WOMEN'S WORK'

1 These women seem to have been a constant worry and drain on the energies of workers for the Women's Movement. At first Bessie Rayner Parkes was sympathetic to these claims:

> An honest observer must feel that there is something noble – something beyond a mere effort after 'gentility', in the struggle to preserve the habits, the dress, and the countless moral and material associations of the rank to which they were born.
>
> (Parkes 1860: 814)

As the years passed, however, sympathy for their aspirations seems to have withered before their sloppiness, incompetence, and general impracticality. Louisa Hubbard complained of 'their grand ignorance of needlework and the inability to write an ordinary capable, well-expressed letter' and their refusal to set themselves to learn anything new:

> With admirable composure they assure you that it is the one thing they have no taste for, and on the suggestion that the difficulty might be overcome in the attempt, they mildly assure you that they feel it to be quite out of the question.
>
> (Hubbard 1875: 7)

2 This article was unsigned, and Harriet Martineau maintained the fiction that the author was a man. She adopted a similar persona for some of her contributions to *Once a Week*.

3 Other researchers who have used the Post Office records housed at Mount Pleasant (most notably Samuel Cohn (1985), Meta Zimmeck (1984) and Keith Grint (1988)) have not noted this connection, perhaps unaware that at this date the phrase 'persons who take a prominent part in obtaining [suitable] employment for educated women' could only signify the Society for Promoting the Employment of Women.

4 I have described in detail elsewhere the circumstances under which the Prudential Insurance came to employ female clerks (Jordan 1996). The fate of the women in Birmingham has yet to be explored by historians.

## 10 REDEFINING 'LADIES' WORK'

1 By and large the Women's Movement left the modification of lady-like manners to the 'fast' girls of the upper class and to the bohemians. In the 1840s, before the movement began, the landed gentry had its Lady Gay Spankers (satirised in Dion Boucicault's play *London Assurance*) who joined the men in the hunting field. In the 1860s the 'girl of the period' was taking over some of the freedoms of Society men (Crow 1971: 195–7). 'Dress reform' was left to the bohemians – the aesthetic ladies of the 1880s and 1890s who abandoned their corsets and wore collarless day dresses, and the 'crop-head' art students of the pre-First World War period. The education movement only followed these changes after Society had approved them, though it led the way in team sports and the adoption of the 'gym slip' as the appropriate sports dress (Atkinson 1978: 118; Delamont 1978: 146, 150).

2 In 1873 the daughter of an Oxford professor did so well that she became eligible for an exhibition offered by Worcester College. It was suggested to the father that he make a test case of the matter. He declined, not wanting to subject his daughter to the publicity, though stating that 'it appears to me to be the highest injustice, and therefore the most suicidal folly, to refuse women the means by which they may prove the possession of that capacity by which they can be so serviceable to society' (EWR 1874: 43–4).

3 Even the uncompromising did not follow the boys' schools blindly. Accounts of subjects studied show that far more attention was paid to needlework, art, and

music than could have been the case in boys' schools (Atkinson 1978: 110; Burstall 1933: 50; Price and Glenday 1975: 32), and the schools were still hampered by the need for their girls to be 'ladylike' and 'inconspicuous' – the 'double conformity' noted by Sara Delamont – so their policies on dress and exercise were closer to those of the select seminaries than to the boys' schools (Delamont 1978a: 140; Price and Glenday 1975: 42).

# BIBLIOGRAPHY

Abel-Smith, Brian. 1960. *A History of the Nursing Profession.* London: Heinemann.
—— 1964. *The Hospitals 1800-1948.* London: Heinemann.
Adams. 1849. 'Woman's mission.' *Westminster Review* 52: 352–78.
Adams, Carole Elizabeth. 1988. *Women Clerks in Wilhelmine Germany: Issues of Class and Gender.* Cambridge: Cambridge University Press.
Adburgham, Alison. 1964. *Shops and Shopping 1800-1914.* London: Allen and Unwin.
Aimé-Martin, Louis. 1834. *The Education of Mothers of Families; or, the Civilisation of the Human Race by Women.* Trans. Edwin Lee. 1842 edn. London: Whittaker and Co.
Alexander, Sally. 1984. 'Women, class and sexual differences in the 1830s and 1840s: some reflections on the writing of feminist history.' *History Workshop Journal* (17): 123–49.
Allchin, A. M. 1958. *The Silent Rebellion: Anglican Religious Communities 1845-1900.* London: SCM Press.
Anderson, Gregory. 1976. *Victorian Clerks.* Manchester: Manchester University Press.
—— 1988. 'The white-blouse revolution,' in *The White-Blouse Revolution*, ed. G. Anderson. Manchester: Manchester University Press.
Anderson, Michael. 1984. 'The social position of spinsters in mid-Victorian Britain.' *Journal of Family History* 9: 377–93.
Armstrong, W. A. 1972. 'The use of information about occupation,' in *Nineteenth Century Society: Essays in the Use of Quantitative Methods for the Study of Social Data*, ed. E. A. Wrigley. Cambridge: Cambridge University Press.
Atkinson, Alan. 1978. 'Fitness, feminism and schooling,' in *The Nineteenth Century Woman: Her Cultural and Physical World*, ed. S. Delamont and L. Duffin. London: Croom Helm.
Atkinson, J. B. 1861. 'Social Science.' *Blackwood's Edinburgh Magazine* 90: 463–78.
Austen, Jane. 1813. *Pride and Prejudice.* 1951 edn. London: Macdonald's Illustrated Classics.
—— 1816. *Emma.* 1950 edn. London: Collins Classics.
—— 1963. *Catherine*, in *Minor Works: The Works of Jane Austen*, ed. R. W. Chapman. London: Oxford University Press.

Aytoun, W. E. 1862. 'The Rights of Woman.' *Blackwood's Edinburgh Magazine* 92: 183–201.

Baly, Monica E. 1980. *Nursing and Social Change.* 2nd edn. London: William Heinemann.

—— 1987. 'The Nightingale nurses: the myth and the reality,' in *Nursing History: The State of the Art*, ed. C. Maggs. London: Croom Helm.

—— 1988. *Florence Nightingale and the Nursing Legacy.* 2nd edn. London: Croom Helm.

Banks, J. A. 1954. *Prosperity and Parenthood.* London: Routledge and Kegan Paul.

—— 1978. 'The social structure of nineteenth century England as seen through the census,' in *The Census and Social Structure: An Interpretative Guide to Nineteenth Century Censuses for England and Wales*, ed. R. Lawton. London: Frank Cass.

Banks, J. A. and Olive Banks. 1965. *Feminism and Family Planning.* Liverpool: Liverpool University Press.

Barnett, Henrietta O. 1884. 'Women as philanthropists,' in *The Woman Question in Europe*, ed. T. Stanton. London: Sampson Low.

Baron, Ava. 1991. 'Gender and labor history: learning from the past, looking to the future,' in *Work Engendered: Toward a New History of American Labor*, ed. A. Baron. Ithaca: Cornell University Press.

Barrett, Michele. 1992a. *The Politics of Truth: From Marx to Foucault.* Cambridge: Polity Press.

—— 1992b. 'Words and things: materialism and method in contemporary feminist analysis,' in *Destabilizing Theory*, ed. M. Barrett and A. Phillips. Cambridge UK: Polity Press.

Battiscombe, Georgina. 1943. *Charlotte Mary Yonge: The Story of an Uneventful Life.* London: Constable.

Beale, Dorothea. 1865. 'The Ladies' College at Cheltenham.' *Transactions of the National Association for the Promotion of Social Science*: 274–87.

Beale, Dorothea, Lucy H. M. Soulsby, and Jane Frances Dove. 1898. *Work and Play in Girls' Schools by Three Headmistresses.* London: Longman's Green.

Bell, E. Moberly. 1953. *Storming the Citadel: The Rise of the Woman Doctor.* London: Constable.

—— 1958. *A History of the Church Schools Company: 1883-1958.* London: S.P.C.K.

Bellamy, Joyce M. 1978. 'Occupation statistics in the nineteenth century censuses,' in *The Census and Social Structure: An Interpretative Guide to Nineteenth Century Censuses for England and Wales*, ed. R. Lawton. London: Frank Cass.

Benenson, Harold. 1984. 'Victorian sexual ideology and Marx's theory of working class.' *International Labour and Working Class History* 28: 1–23.

Benson, Arthur Christopher. 1902. *The Schoolmaster.* 1914 edn. London: John Murray.

Bergen, Barry H. 1982. 'Only a schoolmaster: gender, class, and the effort to professionalize elementary teaching in England, 1870-1910.' *History of Education Quarterly* 22: 1–21.

Bird, M. Mostyn. 1911. *Woman at Work: A Study of the Different Ways of Earning A Living Open to Women.* London: Chapman and Hall.

Blackburn, Helen. 1902. *Women's Suffrage*. London: Williams and Norgate.

Bodichon, Barbara. 1970. *Letters From Various Writers to Barbara Bodichon, 1869–1885*, vol. reel 13: box 2, *The Papers of Emily Davies and Barbara Bodichon: From Girton College, Cambridge*: Harvester Microform.

Booth, Charles. 1902. *Poverty*. 1970 edn. New York: A.M.S. Press.

Boucherett, Jessie. 1861. 'Local societies.' *English Woman's Journal* 8 (46): 217–29.

—— 1863. *Hints on Self-Help: A Book for Young Women*. London: Partridge.

—— 1864a. 'On the cause of the distress prevalent among single women.' *English Woman's Journal* 12 (72: 400–9).

—— 1864b. 'Adelaide Anne Procter.' *English Woman's Journal* 13 (73): 17–21.

—— 1869. 'How to provide for superfluous women,' in *Woman's Work and Woman's Culture*, ed. J. E. Butler. London: Macmillan.

—— 1884. 'The industrial movement,' in *The Woman Question in Europe*, ed. T. Stanton. London: Sampson Low.

Bourdieu, Pierre. 1977. *An Outline of a Theory of Practice*. Trans. Richard Nice. Cambridge: Cambridge University Press.

—— 1990a. *In Other Words: Towards a Reflexive Sociology*. Trans. Matthew Adamson. Cambridge: Polity Press.

—— 1990b. *The Logic of Practice*. Trans. Richard Nice. Cambridge: Polity Press.

Bremner, Christina. 1888. 'Woman in the labour market.' *National Review* 11: 458–70.

Bronte, Charlotte. 1849. *Shirley*. 1974 edn. Harmondsworth: Penguin.

Brown, Frank P. 1912. *South Kensington and its Art Training*. London: Longmans.

Bryant, M. 1979. *The Unexpected Revolution: A Study of the History of the Education of Women and Girls in the Nineteenth Century*. London: University of London Institute of Education.

Buchanan, Margaret, and Anne Neve. 1926. 'The late Mrs Clarke-Keer.' *Pharmaceutical Journal and Pharmacist*: 374–5.

Bulley, A. Amy and Margaret Whitley. 1894. *Women's Work*. London: Methuen.

Burstall, Sara A. 1907. *English High Schools for Girls*. London: Longmans Green.

—— 1933. *Retrospect and Prospect: Sixty Years of Women's Education*. London: Longmans.

—— 1938. *Frances Mary Buss, an Educational Pioneer*. London: S.P.C.K.

Burton, Hester. 1949. *Barbara Bodichon, 1827-1891*. London: Murray.

Buss, Frances M. 1871. 'Boarding schools for girls.' *Englishwoman's Review* 2 (5): 10–12.

Butler, A. S. G. 1954. *Portrait of Josephine Butler*. London: Faber.

Butler, Josephine E. 1868. *The Education and Employment of Women*. London: Macmillan.

Caine, Barbara. 1992. *Victorian Feminists*. Oxford: Oxford University Press.

Cartwright, F. F., V. H. Hall, D. I. Williams, L. T. Cotton, and I. D. Gainsford. 1991. *The Story of King's College Hospital and its Medical School*, ed. D. J. Britten. London: Farrand Press.

Casteras, Susan P. 1987. *Images of Victorian Womanhood in English Art*. Rutherford NJ:

Fairleigh Dickinson University Press.

Chapone, Hester. 1773. *Letters on the Improvement of the Mind.* 1825 edn. London: Hailes.

Clark, Alice. 1919. *Working Life of Women in the Seventeenth Century.* 1992 edn. London: Routledge.

Clark, G. Kitson. 1962. *The Making of Victorian England.* London: Metheun.

Clarke, A. K. 1953. *A History of Cheltenham Ladies College 1853–1953.* London: Faber.

Clough, Blanche Athena. 1903. *A Memoir of Anne Jemima Clough.* London: Edward Arnold.

Cobbe, Frances Power. 1862a. 'Celibacy v. marriage.' *Fraser's Magazine* 65: 228–35.

—— 1862b. 'What shall we do with our old maids?' *Fraser's Magazine* 66: 594–610.

—— 1863. *Essays on the Pursuits of Women.* London: Emily Faithfull.

—— 1869. 'The final cause of woman,' in *Woman's Work and Woman's Culture*, ed. J. E. Butler. London: Macmillan.

—— 1878. 'Wife torture in England.' *Contemporary Review* 32: 55–87.

—— 1894. *Life of Frances Power Cobbe. By Herself.* 2 vols. London: Bentley.

Cockburn, Cynthia. 1983. *Brothers: Male Dominance and Technological Change.* London: Pluto Press.

Cohn, Samuel. 1985. *The Process of Occupational Sex-Typing: The Feminization of Clerical Labor in Great Britain.* Philadelphia: Temple University Press.

Coleridge, Christabel. 1903. *Charlotte Mary Yonge: Her Life and Letters.* London: Macmillan.

Collet, Clara. 1902a. *Educated Working Women. Essays on the Economic Position of Women Workers in the Middle Class.* London: King.

—— 1902b. 'West End tailoring (women),' in *Poverty: I,* ed. Charles Booth. 1970 edn. New York: A. M. S. Press.

Comte, Auguste. 1865. *A General View of Positivism.* Trans. J. H. Bridges. 1957 edn. New York: Speller.

Connell, R. W. and T. H. Irving. 1992. *Class Structure in Australian History.* Melbourne: Longman Cheshire.

Conway, Jill. 1972. 'Stereotypes of femininity in a theory of sexual evolution,' in *Suffer and be Still: Women in the Victorian Age*, ed. M. Vicinus. Bloomington: Indiana University Press.

Conway, Moncure D. 1868. 'The suppressed sex.' *Westminster Review* 90: 437–62.

Cornwallis, Caroline Frances. 1857. 'The capabilities and disabilities of women.' *Westminster Review* 67: 42–72.

Crafts, N. F. R. 1989. 'The industrial revolution: economic growth in Britain, 1700–1860,' in *New Directions in Economic and Social History*, ed. A. Digby and C. Feinstein. London: Macmillan.

Craik, Dinah Mulock. 1858. *A Woman's Thoughts about Women.* London: Hurst and Blackett.

—— 1887. 'Concerning men: by a woman.' *Cornhill* 9: 368–77.

Crompton, Rosemary and Gareth Jones. 1984. *White Collar Proletariat: Deskilling and Gender in the Clerical Labour Process.* London: Macmillan.

Crosswaithe, John. 1863. 'Needlewomen.' *Good Words* 4: 684–8.

Crow, Duncan. 1971. *The Victorian Woman.* London: George Allen and Unwin.

Davidoff, Leonore. 1974. 'Mastered for life: servant and wife in Victorian and Edwardian England.' *Social History* 7: 406–28.

—— 1979. 'The separation of home and work? Landladies and lodgers in nineteenth and twentieth century England,' in *Fit Work for Women*, ed. S. Burman. London: Croom Helm.

—— 1990 '"Adam spoke first and named the Orders of the World": masculine and feminine domains in history and sociology,' in *Politics of Everyday Life: Continuity and Change in Work and the Family*, ed. H. Corr and L. Jamieson. London: Macmillan.

Davidoff, Leonore and Catherine Hall. 1987. *Family Fortunes: Men and Women of the English Middle Class, 1750–1850.* Chicago: University of Chicago Press.

Davies, Emily. 1863. 'The influence of university degrees on the education of women.' *Victoria Magazine* 1: 260–71.

—— 1966. *The Higher Education of Women.* London: Strahan.

—— 1910. *Thoughts on Some Questions Relating to Women, 1860–1908.* Cambridge: Bowes and Bowes.

—— 1970. *Family Chronicle*, reel 1: box I, *The Papers of Emily Davies and Barbara Bodichon: From Girton College, Cambridge*: Harvester Microform.

Davies, James. 1866. 'Female education.' *Quarterly Review* 119: 499–515.

Davies, Margery. 1974. 'Woman's place is at the typewriter: the feminization of the clerical labor force.' *Radical America* 8: 1–28.

Davies, J. Ll. 1855. 'District visiting,' in *Lectures to Ladies on Practical Subjects,* ed. F. D. Maurice. London: Macmillan.

Delamont, Sara. 1978a. 'The contradictions in ladies' education,' in *The Nineteenth Century Woman: Her Cultural and Physical World,* ed. S. Delamont and L. Duffin. London: Croom Helm.

—— 1978b. 'The domestic ideology and women's education,' in *The Nineteenth Century Woman: Her Cultural and Physical World,* ed. S. Delamont and L. Duffin. London: Croom Helm.

Dex, Shirley. 1985. *The Sexual Division of Work: Conceptual Revolutions in the Social Sciences.* Brighton: Harvester.

Diamond, Marion. 1996. 'Maria Rye: the primrose path,' in *Wollstonecroft's Daughters: Womanhood in England and France 1780–1920,* ed. Clarissa Campbell Orr. Manchester: Manchester University Press.

Digby, Anne. 1992. 'Victorian values and women in public and private,' in *Victorian Values: A Joint Symposium of the Royal Society of Edinburgh and the British Academy,* ed. T. C. Smout. Oxford: Oxford University Press.

Drake, Barbara. 1984. *Women in Trade Unions.* 1920 edn. London: Virago.

Du Maurier, George. 1894. *Trilby: A Novel.* 1917 edn. London: Constable.

Duffin, Lorna. 1978. 'Prisoners of progress: women and evolution,' in *The Nineteenth Century Woman: Her Cultural and Physical World,* ed. S. Delamont and L. Duffin. London: Croom Helm.

Dyhouse, Carol. 1981. *Girls Growing Up in Late Victorian and Edwardian England.* London: Routledge and Kegan Paul.

—— 1995. *No Distinction of Sex? Women in British Universities, 1870–1939.* London: UCL Press .

Eastlake, Elizabeth. 1848. 'Vanity Fair and *Jane Eyre*.' *Quarterly Review* 84: 153–85.

Edgeworth, Maria. 1801. *Moral Tales.* 1857 edn. London: Simpkin Marshall.

Eliot, George. 1860. *The Mill on the Floss.* 1953 edn. London: Collins.

—— 1861. *Silas Marner.* 1953 edn. London: Collins.

Elshtain, Jean Bethke. 1981. *Public Man, Private Woman.* New Jersey: Princeton University Press.

Empson, William. 1833. 'Illustrations of political economy: Mrs Marcet – Miss Martineau.' *Edinburgh Review* 57: 1–39.

Exeter, Henry, Lord Bishop of. 1852. *A Letter to Miss Sellon, Superior of Sisters of Mercy, at Plymouth.* London: John Murray.

Faithfull, Emily. 1860. 'The Victoria Press.' *Transactions of the National Association for the Promotion of Social Science*: 819–22.

—— 1871. 'Women's work, with special reference to industrial employment.' *Journal of the Society of Arts*: 378–83.

—— 1884. *Three Visits to America.* Edinburgh: Douglas.

Fawcett, Millicent Garrett. 1867. 'The education of women in the middle and upper classes.' *Macmillan's Magazine* 17: 511–17.

—— 1878. 'The old and the new ideals of women's education.' *Good Words* 19: 853–60.

Fee, Elizabeth. 1974. 'The sexual politics of Victorian social anthropology,' in *Clio's Consciousness Raised*, ed. I. M. Hartman and L. W. Banner. New York: Harper.

Fiddes, Edward. 1941. 'Introductory chapter. The admission of women to Owens College,' in Mabel Tylecote, *The Education of Women at Manchester University.* Manchester: Manchester University Press.

Foucault, Michel. 1980. 'Truth and power,' in *Power/Knowledge: Selected Interviews and other Writings, 1972–1977*, ed. C. Gordon. Brighton: Harvester.

Fraser, Nancy and Linda Nicholson. 1988. 'Social criticism without philosophy: an encounter between feminism and postmodernism,' in *Universal Abandon? The Politics of Postmodernism*, ed. A. Ross. Minneapolis: University of Minneapolis Press.

Garrett, Elizabeth. 1866. 'Hospital nursing.' *Transactions of the National Association for the Promotion of Social Science*: 472–77.

Gay, Peter. 1984. *The Bourgeois Experience: Victoria to Freud. I: Education of the Senses.* London: Oxford University Press.

Gibbons, Stella. 1932. *Cold Comfort Farm.* 1938 edn. Harmondsworth: Penguin.

Gleadle, Kathryn. 1995. *The Early Feminists. Radical Unitarians and the Emergence of the Women's Rights Movement.* London: Macmillan.

Greenwell, Dora. 1862. 'Our single women.' *North British Review* 36: 62–87.

Greer, Germaine. 1979. *The Obstacle Race: The Fortunes of Women Painters and Their Work.* London: Secker and Warburg.

Greg, W. R. 1844. 'Juvenile and female labour.' *Edinburgh Review* 79: 130–56.

——— 1868. 'Why are women redundant?' in *Literary and Social Judgements*. London: Bungay.

Gregory, Dr. 1774. *A Father's Legacy to His Daughters*. 1825 edn. London: Hailes.

Grey, Maria. 1884. 'The Women's Educational Movement,' in *The Woman Question in Europe*, ed. T. Stanton. London: Sampson Low.

Grey, Maria and Emily Shirreff. 1850. *Thoughts on Self Culture Addressed to Women*. London: Simpkin Marshall.

Grint, Keith. 1988. 'Women and equality: the acquisition of equal pay in the Post Office 1870–1961.' *Sociology* 22 (1): 87–108.

Grylls, Rosalie Glynn. 1948. *Queen's College, 1848–1948*. London: Routledge and Sons.

Gurney, Mary. 1872. *Are We to Have Education for Our Middle Class Girls?* London: William Ridgway.

Haddon, Charlotte. 1871. 'Nursing as a profession for ladies.' *Saint Paul's* 8: 458–61.

Hakim, Catherine. 1979. *Occupational Segregation: A Comparative Study of the Degree and Pattern of the Differentiation between Men and Women's Work in Britain, the United States and Other Countries. Vol. 9, Department of Employment Research Papers*. London: Department of Employment.

Halévy, Elie. 1951. *A History of the English People in the Nineteenth Century, vol. 4: The Victorian Years 1841–95*. Trans. E. I. Watkin. London: Benn.

——— 1934. *A History of the English People in the Nineteenth Century. Epilogue. Vol. II*, Trans. E. I. Watkin. London: Benn.

Harmon, Rebecca Lamar. 1968. *Susanna Mother of the Wesleys*. London: Hodder and Stoughton.

Harrison, J. F. C. 1961. *Learning and Living 1790–1960: A Study in the History of the English Adult Education Movement*. London: Routledge and Kegan Paul.

Haward, Warrington. 1879. 'Ladies and hospital nursing.' *Contemporary Review* 34: 490–503.

Helsinger, Elizabeth K., Robin Lauterbach Sheets and William Veeder. 1983. *The Woman Question: Society and Literature in Britain and America 1837–1883. Vol. II, Social Issues*. New York: Garland.

Hill, Bridget. 1989. *Women, Work and Sexual Politics in Eighteenth-Century England*. Oxford: Basil Blackwell.

Hill, Michael. 1973. *The Religious Order: A Study of Virtuoso Religion and its Legitimation in the Nineteenth Century Church of England*. London: Heinemann.

Hinton, James. 1870. 'On nursing as a profession.' *Cornhill Magazine* 22: 451–6.

Hobsbawm, E. J. 1963. *Labouring Men: Studies in the History of Labour*. London: Weidenfeld and Nicolson.

Hogarth, Janet E. 1897. 'The monstrous regiment of women.' *Fortnightly Review* 62: 926–36.

Holcombe, Lee. 1973. *Victorian Ladies at Work: Middle Class Working Women in England and Wales, 1850–1914*. Newton Abbot: David and Charles.

——— 1977. 'Victorian wives and property: Reform of the married women's property law, 1857-1882,' in *A Widening Sphere: Changing Roles of Victorian Women*, ed. M. Vicinus. Bloomington: Indiana University Press.

Holland, Penelope. 1869. 'Two girls of the period. The upper side: our offence, our defence and our petition: by a Belgravian young lady.' *Macmillan's Magazine* 19: 323–31.

Holloway, S. W. F. 1959. 'All Saints' Sisterhood at University College Hospital, 1862–1899.' *Medical History* 3: 146–56.

—— 1991. *Royal Pharmaceutical Society of Great Britain 1841–1991*. London: The Pharmaceutical Press.

Houghton, Walter E. 1957. *The Victorian Frame of Mind, 1830-1870*. New Haven: Yale University Press.

Houston, Arthur. 1862. *The Emancipation of Women from Existing Industrial Disabilities Considered in its Economic Aspect*. London: Longman, Green, Longman and Roberts.

Howson, J. S. 1860. 'Deaconesses.' *Quarterly Review* 108: 342–87.

—— 1862. *Deaconesses; or the Official Help of Women in Parochial Work and in Charitable Institutions*. London: Longman, Green, Longman, and Roberts.

Hubbard, Louisa M. 1875. *The Year Book of Women's Work*. London: Labour News.

Humphries, Jane. 1990. 'Enclosures, common rights, and women: the proletarianization of families in the late eighteenth and early nineteenth centuries.' *Journal of Economic History* 50 (1): 19–42.

Jameson, Anna. 1843. 'Condition of the women and the female children.' *Athenaeum*: 257–9.

—— 1846. *Memoirs and Essays Illustrative of Art, Literature and Social Morals*. London: Bentley.

—— 1855. *Sisters of Charity: Catholic and Protestant, Abroad and at Home*. London: Longman, Brown, Green, and Longmans.

—— 1856. *The Communion of Labour*. London: Bentley.

Jefferys, James B. 1954. *Retail Trading in Britain, 1850–1950*. Cambridge: Cambridge University Press.

Jeffreys, Sheila. 1985. *The Spinster and her Enemies: Feminism and Sexuality 1880–1930*. London: Pandora,.

Jeune, M., ed. 1893. *Ladies at Work: Papers on Paid Employments for Ladies by Experts in the Several Branches*. London: Innes.

Johnston, Judith. 1997. *Anna Jameson: Victorian, Feminist, Woman of Letters*. Aldershot: Scolar Press.

Jordan, Ellen. 1988. 'Female unemployment in England and Wales 1851–1911: an examination of the census figures for 15–19 year olds.' *Social History* 13 (2): 175–90.

—— 1989. 'The exclusion of women from industry in nineteenth century Britain.' *Comparative Studies in Society and History* 31 (2): 273–96.

—— 1991. 'Making good wives and mothers'? The transformation of middle class girls' education in nineteenth century Britain.' *History of Education Quarterly* 31 (4 ): 439–62.

—— 1994. 'Defining the "woman question" 1855–1858.' *Proceedings*. Brisbane: Victorian Studies Association.

—— 1996. 'The lady clerks at the Prudential: the beginning of vertical segregation by sex in clerical work in Great Britain.' *Gender and History* 8 (1): 65–81.

—— 1998. '"The great principle of English fair-play": the admission of women to the Pharmaceutical Society of Great Britain.' *Women's History Review* 7 (3): 381–409.

Joyce, Patrick. 1993. 'The imaginary discontents of social history: a note of response to Mayfield and Thorne, and Lawrence and Taylor.' *Social History* 18 (1): 81–5.

Kamm, Josephine. 1958. *How Different From Us: A Biography of Miss Buss and Miss Beale.* London: Methuen.

—— 1965. *Hope Deferred: Girls' Education in English History.* London: Methuen.

—— 1971. *Indicative Past: A Hundred Years of the Girls' Public Day School Trust.* London: Allen and Unwin.

Kaye, Elaine. 1972. *A History of Queen's College.* London: Chatto and Windus.

Kaye, J. W. 1855. 'The "non-existence" of women.' *North British Review* 23: 536–62.

—— 1856. 'Outrages on women.' *North British Review* 25: 233–56.

—— 1857. 'The employment of women.' *North British Review* 26: 291–338.

Kessler-Harris, Alice. 1976. 'Women, work, and the social order,' in *Liberating Women's History: Theoretical and Critical Essays*, ed. B. A. Carrol. Urbana: University of Illinois Press.

—— 1993. 'Treating the male as "other"; Redefining the parameters of labor history.' *Labor History* 34 (2–3): 190–204.

Kingsley, Charles. 1855. 'The country parish,' in *Lectures to Ladies on Practical Subjects*, ed. F. D. Maurice. London: Macmillan.

Laqueur, Thomas W. 1990. *Making Sex: Body and Gender from the Greeks to Freud.* Cambridge Mass.: Harvard University Press.

Levine, Philippa. 1987. *Victorian Feminism 1850–1900.* London: Hutchinson.

Lewis, Jane E. 1988. 'Women clerical workers in the late nineteenth and early twentieth century,' in *The White-Blouse Revolution*, ed. G. Anderson. Manchester: Manchester University Press.

Lewis, Sarah. 1839. *Woman's Mission.* London: Parker.

—— 1848. 'On the social position of governesses.' *Fraser's Magazine* 37: 411–14.

Liddon, Henry Parry. 1893. *Life of Edward Bouverie Pusey.* 4 vols. London: Longmans.

Lister, T. H. 1841. 'Rights and condition of women.' *Edinburgh Review* 73: 189–209.

Lockwood, David. 1989. *The Blackcoated Worker: A Study in Class Consciousness.* Second edn. Oxford: Clarendon Press.

Lowe, Graham S. 1987. *Women in the Administrative Revolution: The Feminization of Clerical Work.* London: Polity Press.

M.M.H. 1858. 'Florence Nightingale and the English soldier.' *English Woman's Journal* 1 (2): 73–9.

McWilliams-Tullberg, Rita. 1977. 'Women and degreees at Cambridge University, 1862–1897,' in *A Widening Sphere: Changing Roles of Victorian Women*, ed. M. Vicinus. Bloomington: Indiana University Press.

Maggs, Christopher. 1983. *The Origins of General Nursing.* London: Croom Helm.

Manners, Janetta. 1881. 'The employment of women in the public service.' *Quarterly Review* 151: 181–200.

Mannheim, Karl. 1936. *Ideology and Utopia: An Introduction to the Sociology of*

*Knowledge.* London: Kegan Paul.

Manton, Jo. 1965. *Elizabeth Garrett Anderson.* London: Methuen.

Marshall, Dorothy. 1973. *Industrial England 1776–1851.* London: Routledge and Kegan Paul.

Martindale, Hilda. 1938. *Women Servants of the State 1870–1938: A History of Women in the Civil Service.* London: Allen and Unwin.

Martineau, Harriet. 1859. 'Female industry.' *Edinburgh Review* 109: 293–336.

—— 1865. 'Nurses wanted.' *Cornhill Magazine* 11: 409–25.

Marx, Karl. 1867. *Capital: A Critique of Political Economy.* Trans. B. Fowkes. 1977 edn. Vol. 1. New York: Vintage.

Maurice, Frederick. 1884. *The Life of Frederick Denison Maurice. Chiefly told in his own letters. Edited by his Son, Frederick Maurice.* 2 vols. London: Macmillan.

Maurice, Frederick Denison. 1848. *Queen's College London: Its Objects and Method.* London: Rivington.

—— 1855. *Plan of a Female College.* Cambridge: Macmillan.

—— 1860. 'Female School of Art: Mrs Jameson.' *Macmillan's Magazine* 2: 227–35.

Mayor, Joseph B. 1869. 'The cry of the women.' *Contemporary Review* 11: 196–215.

McBride, Theresa M. 1976. *The Domestic Revolution: The Modernisation of Household Service in England and France 1820–1920.* London: Croom Helm.

McCord, Norman. 1991. *British History 1815–1906.* Oxford: Oxford University Press.

McGregor, O. R. 1955. 'The social position of women in England, 1850-1914: a bibliography.' *British Journal of Sociology* 6: 48–60.

McGuinn, Nicholas. 1978. 'George Eliot and Mary Wollstonecraft,' in *The Nineteenth Century Woman: Her Cultural and Physical World,* ed. S. Delamont and L. Duffin. London: Croom Helm.

McKendrick, Neil. 1974. 'Home demand and economic growth: a new view of the role of women and children in the Industrial Revolution,' in *Historical Perspectives: Studies in English Thought and Society in Honour of J. H. Plumb,* ed. N. McKendrick. London: Europa.

Meynell, Viola. 1929. *Alice Meynell: A Memoir.* New York: Charles Scribner's Sons.

Middleton, Chris. 1985. 'Patriarchal exploitation and the rise of English capitalism,' in *Gender, Class and Work* ed. E. Gamarnikow. Aldershot: Gower.

Mill, John Stuart. 1869. *The Subjection of Women.* 1929 edn. London: Everyman.

Millet, Kate. 1972. 'The debate over women: Ruskin vs Mill.' in *Suffer and be Still: Women in the Victorian Age,* ed. M. Vicinus. Bloomington: Indiana University Press.

Milne, John Duguid. 1857. *Industrial and Social Position of Women in the Middle and Lower Ranks.* London: Chapman and Hall.

Mingay, C .E. 1963. *Landed Society in the Eighteenth Century.* London: Routledge and Kegan Paul.

Mitchell, Sally. 1977. 'The forgotten woman of the period: penny weekly family magazines of the 1840s and 1850s,' in *A Widening Sphere: Changing Roles of Victorian Women,* ed. M. Vicinus. Bloomington: Indiana University Press.

—— 1995. *The New Girl: Girls' Culture in England 1880–1915.* New York:

Columbia University Press.

Moore, Judith. 1988. *A Zeal for Responsibility: The Struggle for Professional Nursing in Victorian England, 1868–1883.* Athens and London: University of Georgia Press.

More, Hannah. 1799. *Strictures on the Modern System of Female Education.* 1811 edn. Vol. 2. London: Cadell and Davies.

—— 1809. *Coelebs in Search of a Wife.* Vol. 2. London: Cadell and Davies.

Mozley, Anne. 1846. *Tales of Female Heroism.* London: James and Burns.

—— 1888. 'Introduction,' in *J. B. Mozley, DD, Essays Historical and Theological,* ed. Anne Mozley. London: Rivingtons.

Mumm, Susan. 1996. '"Not worse than other girls": the convent-based rehabilitation of fallen women in Victorian Britain.' *Journal of Social History* 29 (1): 527–46.

Nestor, Pauline. 1982. 'A new departure in publishing: the *English Woman's Journal* and the *Victoria Magazine.*' *Victorian Periodicals Review* 15: 93–106.

Newman, F. W. 1865. 'Capacities of women.' *Westminster Review* 84: 352–80.

Nicholson, Linda. 1986. *Gender and History: The Limits of Social Theory in the Age of the Family.* New York: Columbia University Press.

Nightingale, Florence. 1868. 'Una and the lion.' *Good Words* 9: 360–6.

Nussbaum, Felicity A. 1984. *The Brink of All We Hate: English Satires on Women, 1660–1750.* Lexington: University of Kentucky Press.

Nutting, M. Adelaide and Lavinia L. Dock. 1907. *A History of Nursing.* 2 vols. New York: Putnam.

Oliphant, Margaret. 1858. 'The condition of women.' *Blackwood's Edinburgh Magazine* 83: 139–54.

—— 1860. 'Social science.' *Blackwood's Edinburgh Magazine* 88: 698–715.

—— 1869. 'Mill's "The Subjection of Women".' *Edinburgh Review* 130: 572–602.

Parkes, Bessie Rayner. 1858. 'The profession of the teacher.' *English Woman's Journal* 1 (1): 1–13.

—— 1859a. 'The market for educated female labour: a paper read at the meeting of the Association for the Promotion of Social Science, Bradford, 1859.' *English Woman's Journal* 4 (21): 145–52.

—— 1859b. 'What can educated women do?' *English Woman's Journal* 4 (22): 217–26.

—— 1860. 'A year's experience in woman's work.' *Transactions of the National Association for the Promotion of Social Science*: 811–19.

—— 1862. 'The balance of public opinion in regard to women's work.' *English Woman's Journal* 9 (53): 340–4.

—— 1865. *Essays on Women's Work.* London: Strahan.

—— 1861. 'The Condition of Working Women in England and France.' *Transactions of the National Association for the Promotion of Social Science*: 632–40.

Pateman, Carole. 1988. *The Sexual Contract.* Oxford: Polity Press.

Paterson, Emma A. 1875. 'The position of women engaged in handicrafts and other industrial pursuits.' *Englishwoman's Review* 6: 1–12.

Patmore, Coventry. 1851. 'The social position of woman.' *North British Review* 14: 515–40.

Payne, P. L. 1974. *British Entrepreneurship in the Nineteenth Century*. London: Macmillan.

Pederson, Joyce Senders. 1975. 'Schoolmistresses and headmistresses: elites and education in nineteenth-century England.' *Journal of British Studies* 15: 135–62.

—— 1981. 'Some Victorian headmistresses: a conservative tradition of social reform.' *Victorian Studies* 24: 463–88.

Pennington, Lady. 1761. *A Mother's Advice to her Absent Daughters*. 1825 edn. London: Hailes.

Percival, Alicia C. 1939. *The English Miss Today and Yesterday*. London: Harrap.

Perkin, Harold. 1969. *The Origins of Modern English Society 1780–1880*. London: Routledge and Kegan Paul.

—— 1989. *The Rise of Professional Society: England since 1880*. London: Routledge.

Perry, Ruth. 1985. 'Radical doubt and the liberation of women.' *Eighteenth Century Studies* 18: 472–93.

Peterson, M. Jeanne. 1972. 'The Victorian governess: Status incongruence in family and society,' in *Suffer and be Still: Women in the Victorian Age*, ed. M. Vicinus. Bloomington: Indiana University Press.

Phillips, L. F. M. 1861. *My Life and What Shall I Do With it? A Question for Young Gentlewomen: by an Old Maid*. London: Longman, Green, Longman and Roberts.

Pinchbeck, Ivy. 1930. *Women Workers and the Industrial Revolution 1750–1850*. 1969 edn. London: Cass.

Pollard, Sidney. 1965. *The Genesis of Modern Management: A Study of the Industrial Revolution in Great Britain*. London: Arnold.

Poovey, Mary. 1988. *Uneven Developments: The Ideological Work of Gender in Mid-Victorian England*. London: Virago.

Pratt, Edwin A. 1898. *A Woman's Work for Women: Being the Aims, Efforts, and Aspirations of "L. M. H".' (Miss Louisa M. Hubbard)*. London: Newnes.

Price, Mary and Nonita Glenday. 1975. *Reluctant Revolutionaries: A Century of Head Mistresses 1874–1974*. London: Pitman.

Prochaska, Frank. 1980. *Women and Philanthropy in Nineteenth Century England*. Oxford: Clarendon.

—— 1988. *The Voluntary Impulse: Philanthropy in Modern Britain*. London: Faber.

Purvis, June. 1991. *A History of Women's Education in England*. Milton Keynes: Open University Press.

Reader, W.J. 1966. *Professional Men: The Rise of the Professional Classes in Nineteenth Century England*. London: Weidenfeld and Nicolson.

Rendall, Jane. 1985. *The Origins of Modern Feminism: Women in Britain, France and the United States, 1789–1860*. London: Macmillan.

—— 1987. '"A moral engine?" Feminism, liberalism and the English Woman's Journal,' in *Equal or Different: Women's Politics 1800–1914*, ed. J. Rendall. Oxford: Basil Blackwell.

—— 1989. 'Friendship and politics: Barbara Leigh Smith Bodichon (1827–91) and Bessie Rayner Parkes (1829–1925),' in *Sexuality and Subordination: Interdisciplinary Studies of Gender in the Nineteenth Century*, ed. S. Mendus and J. Rendall. London: Routledge.

Rich, R. W. 1933. *The Training of Teachers in England and Wales during the Nineteenth Century.* Cambridge: Cambridge University Press.

Ritchie, Anne Thackeray. 1861. 'Toilers and spinsters.' *Cornhill Magazine* 3: 318–31.

Roberts, Shirley. 1993. *Sophia Jex-Blake: A Woman Pioneer in Nineteenth-Century Medical Reform.* London: Routledge.

Roebuck, Janet. 1973. *The Making of Modern English Society from 1850.* London: Routledge and Kegan Paul.

Rogers, Katherine M. 1982. *Feminism in Eighteenth-Century England.* Urbana: University of Illinois Press.

Routledge, Florence and Emilia F. S. Dilke. 1891. 'Trades unionism among women.' *Fortnightly Review* 49: 741–50.

Rowbotham, Sheila. 1975. *Hidden from History.* Harmondsworth: Penguin.

Ruskin, John. 1865. *Sesame and Lilies.* 1920 edn. London: Dent.

Rye, Maria. 1859. 'The rise and progress of telegraphs.' *English Woman's Journal* 4 (22): 256–63.

Sadie, Stanley, ed. 1980. *New Grove Dictionary of Music.* London: Macmillan.

Schutz, Alfred. 1967. *The Phenomenology of the Social World.* Trans. George Walsh Frederick Lehnert. Chicago: Northwestern University Press.

Scott, Joan W. 1988. 'Deconstructing equality-versus-difference: or, the uses of poststructuralist theory for feminism.' *Feminist Studies* 14 (1): 33–50.

Scudamore, F. 1871. *Report by Mr Scudamore on the Re-organization of the Telegraph System of the United Kingdom.* London: HMSO

Seccombe, Wally. 1993. *Weathering the Storm.* London: Verso.

Seymer, Lucy. 1957. *A General History of Nursing.* 2nd edn. London: Faber.

—— 1960. *Florence Nightingale's Nurses: The Nightingale Training School 1860–1960.* London: Pitman.

Shellard, E. J. 1996. *Some Outstanding Women Pharmacists of the Late 19th Century.* London: Museum of Royal Pharmaceutical Society of Great Britain.

Shirreff, Emily. 1858. *Intellectual Education and its Influence on the Character and Happiness of Women.* London.

—— 1873. 'Girton College.' *Fortnightly Review* 14: 87–93.

Sidgwick, Mrs Henry. 1890. *Health Statistics of Women Students of Cambridge and Oxford and of Their Sisters.* Cambridge: Cambridge University Press.

Sieveking, Edward. 1849. *The Training Institutions for Nurses and the Workhouses: An Attempt to Solve One of the Social Problems of the Present Day.* London: Williams and Norgate.

Smith, Barbara Leigh. 1857. *Women and Work.* London: Bosworth and Harrison.

Smith, F. B. 1982. *Florence Nightingale: Reputation and Power.* London: Croom Helm.

Smith-Rosenberg, Carroll. 1979. 'The female world of love and ritual: relations between women in nineteenth century America,' in *A Heritage of Her Own: Toward a New Social History of American Women*, ed. N. F. Cott and H. Pleck. New York: Touchstone (Simon and Schuster).

Sonstroem, David. 1977. 'Millet versus Ruskin: a defense of Ruskin's "Of Queen's Gardens".' *Victorian Studies* 20: 283–97.

Spencer, M. G., ed. 1909. *The Fingerpost: A Guide to the Professions and Occupations of Educated Women.* 3rd edn. London: Central Bureau for the Employment of Women.

Stanley, Henrietta. 1879. 'Personal recollections of women's education.' *Nineteenth Century* 6: 308–21.

Steinberg, Marc W. 1996. 'Culturally speaking: finding a commons between post-structuralism and the Thompsonian perspective.' *Social History* 21 (2): 193–214.

Stenton, Doris Mary. 1977. *The English Woman in History.* New York: Schoken.

Stephen, Barbara. 1927. *Emily Davies and Girton College.* London: Constable.

Stone, James S. 1994. *Emily Faithfull: Victorian Champion of Women's Rights.* Toronto: P. D. Meaney.

Stone, Lawrence. 1977. *The Family, Sex and Marriage in England 1500–1800.* London: Weidenfeld and Nicolson.

Strachan, Glenda. 1995. '"It is natural for every woman to be, to some extent, a nurse": nursing in the latter half of the nineteenth century in Australia.' *Journal of Interdisciplinary Gender Studies* 1 (1): 23–32.

Strachey, Ray. 1928. *The Cause: A Short History of the Women's Movement in Great Britain.* 1978 edn. London: Virago.

Strom, Sharon Hartman. 1992. *Beyond the Typewriter: Gender, Class, and the Origins of Modern American Office Work, 1900–1930.* Chicago: University of Illinois Press.

Summers, Anne. 1979. 'A home from home – women's philanthropic work in the nineteenth century,' in *Fit Work for Women,* ed. S. Burman. London: Croom Helm.

—— 1983. 'Pride and prejudice: ladies and nurses in the Crimean War.' *History Workshop Journal* (16): 33–56.

—— 1988. *Angels and Citizens: British Women As Military Nurses 1854–1914.* London: Routledge and Kegan Paul.

—— 1990. 'Ministering angels: Victorian ladies and nursing,' in *Victorian Values: Personalities and Perspectives in Nineteenth-Century Society,* ed. G. Marsden. London: Longman.

Taylor, Barbara. 1983. *Eve and the New Jerusalem.* London: Virago.

Thackeray, William Makepeace. 1847. *Vanity Fair, A Novel without a Hero.* 1908 edn. London: Everyman.

Theobald, Marjorie. 1996. *Knowing Women: Origins of Women's Education in Nineteenth-Century Australia.* Cambridge: Cambridge University Press.

—— 1988. 'The accomplished woman and the priority of intellect: a new look at women's education in Britain and Australia 1800–1850.' *History of Education* 17: 22–6.

Thomas, Clara. 1967. *Love and Work Enough: The Life of Anna Jameson.* Toronto: Toronto University Press.

Thompson, Flora. 1954. *Lark Rise to Candleford.* 1954 edn. London: Oxford University Press.

Tilly, Louise A. and Joan W. Scott. 1979. *Women, Work and Family.* New York: Holt.

Todd, Janet, ed. 1991. *Dictionary of Brostish Women Writers.* London: Routledge.

Todd, Margaret. 1918. *The Life of Sophia Jex-Blake.* London: Macmillan.

Tomaselli, Sylvia. 1985. 'The enlightenment debate on women.' *History Workshop* (20).

Tosh, John. 1996. 'Authority and nurture in middle-class fatherhood: The case of early and mid-Victorian Britain.' *Gender and History* 8 (1): 48–64.

—— 1997. 'The making of masculinities: the middle class in late nineteenth century Britain,' in *The Men's Share: Masculinities, Male Support and Women's Suffrage in Britain, 1890–1920*, ed. A. V. John and C. Eustace. London: Routledge.

Trench, Maria. 1884. 'English sisterhoods.' *Nineteenth Century* 16: 339–52.

Trimmer, Mrs Sarah. 1787. *The Oeconomy of Charity; Or An Address to Ladies Concerning Sunday Schools; the Establishment of Schools of Industry Under Female Inspection; and the Distribution of Voluntary Benefactions.* London: Bensley.

Trollope, Anthony. 1865. *Miss Mackenzie.* 1988 edn. Oxford: Oxford University Press.

—— 1877. 'The young women at the London Telegraph Office.' *Good Words* 18: 377–84.

Tropp, Asher. 1957. *The School Teachers: The Growth of the Teaching Profession in England and Wales from 1800 to the Present Day.* London: Heinemann.

Tuke, Margaret J. 1939. *A History of Bedford College for Women 1849–1937.* London: Oxford University Press.

Turner, Barry. 1974. *Equality for Some: The Story of Girls' Education.* London: Ward Lock.

Twining, Louisa. 1887. 'Fifty years of women's work.' *National Review* 9: 659–67.

Usherwood, Paul and Jenny Spencer-Smith. 1987. *Lady Butler Battle Artist 1846–1933.* Gloucester: Alan Sutton.

Vicinus, Martha. 1994. 'Models for public life: biographies of "noble women" for girls,' in *The Girl's Own: Cultural Histories of the Anglo-American Girl, 1830–1915*, ed. C. Nelson and L. Vallone. Athens, Georgia: University of Georgia Press.

Walkerdine, Valerie. 1990. *Schoolgirl Fictions.* London: Verso.

Wallas, M.T. 1893. 'Teaching,' in *Ladies at Work: Papers on Paid Employments for Ladies by Experts in the Several Branches*, ed. M. Jeune. London: Innes.

Warren, Mrs. 1865a. *How I Managed My Children from Infancy to Marriage.* London: Houlston and Wright.

—— 1865b. *How I Managed my House on Two Hundred Pounds a Year.* London: Houlston and Wright.

Weber, Max. 1948. *From Max Weber: Essays in Sociology.* Trans. H. H. Wirth and C. Wright Mills. London: Routledge and Kegan Paul.

—— 1968. *Economy and Society,* ed. G. Roth and C. Wittich. 3 vols. New York: Bedminster.

Wedgwood, Julia. 1869. 'Female suffrage, considered chiefly with regard to its indirect results,' in *Woman's Work and Woman's Culture*, ed. J. E. Butler. London: Macmillan.

Weedon, Chris. 1987. *Feminist Practice and Poststructuralist Theory.* Oxford: Basil Blackwell.

Weibel, Kathleen, Kathleen M. Heim, and Dianne J. Ellsworth. 1979. *The Role of*

*Women in Librarianship 1876–1976: The Entry Advancement and Struggle for Equalization in One Profession.* London: Oryx Press.

Wells, H. G. 1934. *Experiment in Autobiography.* 1969 edn. London: Cape.

WG. 1877. 'A few hints to young candidates for the nursing profession.' *Woman's Gazette* 2 (8).

Whyte-Melville, George. 1863. 'Strong-minded women.' *Fraser's Magazine* 68: 667–78.

Widdowson, Frances. 1980. *Going up into the Next Class: Women and Elementary Teacher Training, 1840–1914.* London: Women's Research and Resources Centre.

Williams, Thomas Jay. 1965. *Priscilla Lydia Sellon.* London: S.P.C.K.

Wilson, H. Mary and R. Wilson. 1893. 'Hospital nursing,' in *Ladies at Work: Papers on Paid Employments for Ladies by Experts in the Several Branches*, ed. M. Jeune. London: Innes.

Wollstonecraft, Mary. 1792. *A Vindication of the Rights of Woman.* 1929 edn. London: Everyman.

Woodham-Smith, Cecil. 1950. *Florence Nightingale, 1820–1910.* London: Constable.

Wrigley, E. A. 1989. 'Population growth: England, 1680–1820,' in *New Directions in Economic and Social History*, ed. A. Digby and C. Feinstein. London: Macmillan.

Yonge, Charlotte M. 1844. *Abbeychurch, or, Self Control and Self Conceit.* 1976 edn. New York: Garland.

—— 1854. *Heartease, or, The Brother's Wife.* 1897 edn. London: Macmillan.

—— 1856. *The Daisy Chain.* 1906 edn. London: Macmillan.

—— 1857. *Dynevor Terrace, or The Clue of Life.* 1890 edn. London: Macmillan.

—— 1873. *Pillars of the House, or, Under Wode, Under Rode.* 1901 edn. Vol. 2. London: Macmillan.

—— 1877. *Womankind.* 1881 edn. London: Mozley and Smith.

—— 1879. *Magnum Bonum.* 1889 edn. London: Macmillan.

—— 1885. *The Two Sides of the Shield.* 1889 edn. London: Macmillan.

—— 1888a. *Beechcroft at Rockstone.* 1889 edn. London: Macmillan.

—— 1888b. *Hannah More.* London: W. H. Allen.

—— 1890. *More Bywords.* 1891 edn. London: Macmillan.

Young, G. M. 1953. *Victorian England: Portrait of an Age.* London: Oxford University Press.

Zimmeck, Meta. 1984. 'Strategies and stratagems for the employment of women in the civil service.' *Historical Journal* 27: 901–24.

## UNSIGNED PERIODICAL ARTICLES

*All the Year Round*
1858. 'My girls.' *All the Year Round* 2.

*Alexandra Magazine*
1864. 'Law-copying as an employment for women.' *Alexandra Magazine and Woman's Social and Industrial Advocate* (5): 305–8.

*Chemist and Druggist*
1892. 'Lady-pharmacists.' *Chemist and Druggist* 41: 143–6.

*Contemporary*
'The powers of women and how to use them.' *Contemporary Review* 14: 521–39

*Fraser's*
1833. The female character.' *Fraser's Magazine* 7: 591–601.
1836. 'Female education and modern matchmaking.' *Fraser's Magazine* 13: 308–16.
1844. 'Hints on the modern governess system.' *Fraser's Magazine* 30: 571–83.
1845. 'An inquiry into the state of girls' fashionable schools.' *Fraser's Magazine* 31: 703–12.
1846. 'Milliners' apprentices.' *Fraser's Magazine* 33: 308–16.
1848. 'Hospital nurses as they are and as they ought to be.' *Fraser's Magazine* 37: 539–42.
1860. 'Female labour.' *Fraser's Magazine* 61: 359–71.

*Good Words*
1866. 'Mary Merryweather: by the author of "Quaker Philanthropy".' *Good Words* 7: 748–52.

*Household Words*
1852. 'The new school for wives.' *Household Words* 5: 84–9.
1853. 'The iron seamstress.' *Household Words* 8: 575–6.
1855a. 'Hospitals.' *Household Words* 12: 457–61.
1855b. 'School-girls.' *Household Words* 12: 39–41.
1856. 'Health and education.' *Household Words* 14: 313–7.

*Pharmaceutical Journal and Transactinos*
1895. 'Qualifications of public dispensers.' *Pharmaceutical Journal and Transactinos* 25: 1178–9.

*St James's*
1862. "Governesses.' *St. James's Magazine* 4: 501–7.

*Saturday Review*
1855. 'The Nightingale fund.' *Saturday Review* 24 Nov.: 61–2.
1857a. 'Industrial occupations of women.' *Saturday Review* 18 June: 63–4.
1857b. 'Bloomeriana.' *Saturday Review* 12 Sept.: 238–9.
1858. 'The claims of governesses.' *Saturday Review* 30 Jan.: 110–11.

## PARLIAMENTARY PAPERS

1841 Census of Great Britain: Parliamentary.Papers 1844 vol. 27.

1851 Census of Great Britain: Parliamentary Papers 1852–3 vol. 88.

1861 Census of Great Britain: Parliamentary Papers 1863 vol. 53.

1871 Census of Great Britain: Parliamentary Papers 1873 vol. 71.

1881 Census of Great Britain: Parliamentary Papers 1883 vol. 80.

1891 Census of Great Britain: Parliamentary Papers 1893–4 vol. 106.

1901 Census of Great Britain: Parliamentary Papers 1903 vol. 84.

1911 Census of Great Britain: Parliamentary Papers 1913 vol. 78.

Second Report of the Commissioners on the Employment of Children: Parliamentary Papers 1843 vol. 13.

Report of Schools Inquiry Commission: Parliamentary Papers 1867–8 vol. 28 Part I.

First Report of the Civil Service Inquiry Commission: Parliamentary Papers 1875 vol. 23.

The Employment of Women: Parliamentary Papers 1893—4 vol. 37 Part I.

## ARCHIVE MATERIAL

*London Guildhall Library:*
Records of Society of Apothecaries

  MS 10,987: Court of Examiners – Nominal Register of Apothecaries' Assistants 1857–1900.

*London Metropolitan Archives:*
Records of St John's House

| HI/ST/SJ/A2/1 | Minute Book of Council 1848–1864 |
| HI/ST/SJ/AIO/l–9 | Rules and Regulations |
| HI/ST/SJ/A18/1 | Master's Reports to Council |
| HI/ST/SJ/AI9/1–2 | Lady Superintendent's Letters and Reports |
| HI/ST/SJ/CI/l–3 | St John's House: Admissions Register |

*Post Office Archives:*
  POST 30/275 D[E 361311875] File nos. I–XII: Savings Bank: First Employment of Female Clerks

*Wellcome Institute:*
Records of the Institution of Nursing Sisters
  SA/QNI/W.2/l–4 Committee Minute Books 1841–1867
  SA/QNI/W.9 A Short History of the Institution of Nursing Sisters [1934]

# INDEX

Becker, G. S. 192
Bedford College 118–19, 201, 205,
206
binary oppositions 15, 42, 45, 52, 99
Birmingham 188, 189
Bird, M. Mostyn 63, 81, 83, 84, 185,
197
*Blackwoods' Edinburgh Magazine* 42,
160
bluestockings 87, 92–5, 149, 165,
166, 206; 'bluestocking syllogism'
95–7, 108–9, 111, 214, 215
Bodichon, Barbara *see* Smith, Barbara
Leigh
bohemians 228
boredom 47–8, 88, 98, 147, 156, 199
bookkeepers, female 81, 180
'borderlands' 89, 92, 98, 99, 104, 105,
109, 114, 115, 126, 135, 143
Boscawen, Frances 92
Boucherett, Jessie 65, 159, 172–4,
180, 181, 196, 197
Boucicault, Dion 228
Bourdieu, Pierre 17–19, 89, 105
Bradford Girls' Grammar School 213
Brighton 176, 189
British and Foreign School Society 71
*British Critic* 129
Bronte, Charlotte 47, 225
Brougham, Lord 157, 158
Browning, Elizabeth Barrett 98
Bryant, Margaret 107, 201, 203
Bryce Commission 204
Bryn Mawr 209
Bulley, Amy and Margaret Whitley 81,
83, 197
Burney, Fanny 91
Burns, James 98
Burstall, Sara 215, 216
businesses, increase in scale 11–12,
184, 186–8
'busy idleness' 47, 87, 201
Buss, Mary Frances 119, 202, 205,
211–12, 215
butchers, wives of 57, 58
Butler, Lady *see* Thompson, Elizabeth
Butler, Josephine 206
Byron, Harriet Brownlow 141

Cambridge University 201, 202, 205,
206, 210; local examinations 215;
women's colleges 217, 206–7, 209,
225
Camden School, The 216
Canning, Lady 117, 135
capitalism 15–16, 27, 60
capitalist production 27
'career woman' 220
careers, choice of by men 30, 148; open
to talents 148, 167; for women 198,
200–1, 220
Carlyle, Thomas 152
catechism 105
celibacy 129, 130
census: reports 5, 9, 10–11, 16, 38–9,
57, 58, 66, 67, 69, 71, 75, 76–81,
113–14, 180–1, 210, 219;
enumerators' books 29, 37, 65, 131,
133, 178, 183–4, 222, 225, 226
Central Training School 113
Chadwick, Edwin 135
changes in women's employment
summarized 5, 43, 84, 106, 169,
218–19, 221
Chapone, Hester 93–4, 109
charities, voluntary subscription 35,
56, 90, 98, 102; women in 102–3,
127, 158, 225; women on
committees of 102–3, 115; employ
female clerks 180; *see also* philanthropy
Charity Commission 204
charwomen 126
Cheltenham Ladies' College 119–20,
211
Chisholm, Caroline 102
chivalry, age of 49
*Christian Remembrancer* 104
Christian Socialism 116, 171
Christianity 167; public school 55;
evangelical 90–4, 152, 154
Christ's Hospital School for Girls 204,
213
Chudleigh, Mary 149
Church Schools Company 213
citizenship 44, 45
civil servants 29, 30, 34, 120, 148,

Houston, Arthur 162
household economies 24; family 24, 28, 29, 36–7, 43, 46, 57, 61, 64, 222, 224; male-breadwinner 24, 29, 224; multi-wage 28
housework 35
housing 29; middle-class 29–30
Howitt, Mary 158
Hubbard, Louisa 57, 162, 197, 228
husband-hunting 108, 112, 161, 166

idleness 54, 165, 217; see also 'something to do'
'improvement of the mind' 94–7
'improvers' in dressmaking 65, 66
independence 20, 39, 44; male 45, 151; female 63, 64, 83, 84, 121, 151
individualism 7, 44, 148, 150
industrial capitalism 27
industrialism 6, 15, 17, 19, 24–7, 56
inferiority to men, women's 41, 43, 48, 55, 224
influence, women's 49, 50, 51, 96–7, 102, 153, 164
Inglis, Lady 128, 135
inn-keepers 37
inspectors, government: of schools 72; female 219
Institution for the Care of Sick Gentlewomen in Distressed Circumstances 135–6
Institution of Nursing Sisters 103, 127–8, 131, 226
insurance companies 186; as employers 13, 19, 30, 172; officers of 30, 32
insurance of life 58
Intellectual Education 97, 98
intellectuals 6, 17, 90; female 90–5, 195; male 158, 207–9; socially unattached 18–19, 149, 158, 168, 170, 195–6
International and Electric Telegraph Company 180
International Congress of Women 185

Jameson, Anna 51, 56, 151–5, 156, 158, 199

Jex-Blake, Sophia 35–6, 117, 210
*John Halifax, Gentleman* 159
Johnson, Samuel 92
Johnston, Judith 51, 98, 152
Jones, Agnes 140
Jones, Mary 134, 139
journalists, female 19, 81, 150, 151, 155, 159, 160, 219
justice, women's need to understand 109

Kaiserswerth 127, 130, 135
Kaye, J. W. 155–6
Kay-Shuttleworth, James 72
Kay-Shuttleworth, Mrs 117
Kessler-Harris, Alice 15
King, Gertrude 180
King's College, London 116
Kingsley, Charles 102, 117
'knowledge' 17, 19, 44, 61, 71, 74, 81, 84, 88, 99, 114, 125, 126, 136, 143, 159, 170, 179, 192, 193, 208, 220

labour: aristocracy 36, 40; -intensive occupations 74, 125, 142; turnover 13, 70, 73, 142, 184 (synthetic 13, 125, 187–8)
labourers 38, 73; see also agricultural
ladies 32, 33, 38, 39, 56, 84, 129, 132, 136, 139, 140, 143, 172, 180, 182, 193, 198; must not earn 35–6, 140, 216–7, 223
*Ladies at Work* 84
ladies' colleges 115–20, 144, 201, 206, 214; 'college system' defined 120
Ladies' Educational Associations 206–7, 208–9
'ladies' work' 35–6, 60, 147, 218–20, 221
Lady Emily Sheepshanks 87
Lady Gay Spanker 228
Lady Superintendents 130–4, 140
Laing, David 115, 116, 119
Lancashire 192
landed gentry see gentry
Langham Place 157–9, 164–5, 168, 170, 172–3, 198, 199, 210, 215–6

study, independent for women 89–91,
135, 136; essential to religion 94
*Subjection of Women, The* 167
suffragettes 87
suffrage, women's 149, 156, 168, 220
Summers, Anne 98, 102, 134, 136,
223
Sunday Schools 35, 99–100, 225
superannuation 128
superiority, male 41, 43, 48, 55, 224
'surplus women' *see* 'redundant women'
symbolic capital 18, 89, 91, 105, 136,
198
synthetic turnover *see* labour turnover

*Tales of Female Heroism* 53
'taste for discrimination' 192, 193
Taylor, Harriet 151
Taylorism 188, 194
Taunton Commission 108, 203–4, 211,
212
teachers, female 37, 59, 60, 76, 87, 88,
133, 137, 144, 147; accreditation of
72, 115–16, 170–1, 201; conditions
73, 121–2, 144, 218; elementary
school 60, 72–4, 170; high school
107, 121, 218; in new public girls'
schools 5, 11, 107, 121, 218;
influence of 218; of art and music
113–14; private school 66–7;
training of 66–7, 72–3, 116–17,
203; wages 218
teacher training colleges 72–3
telegraph operators, female 76, 81,
172, 180–1, 189, 198
telephonists 81
Thackeray, William Makepeace 87
Theobald, Marjorie 110, 111, 112
Thompson: Elizabeth (later Lady
Butler) 114; E. P. 15, 16, 127;
Flora 57, 83
*Thoughts on the Education of Daughters*
108
*Thoughts on the Self–Culture Addressed to
Women* 108, 211
Tilly, Louise and Joan Scott 24, 222
Tilly, Sir John 181–3
*Times, The* 136, 139, 203

Todd, Dr Robert Bentley 139
Tomaselli, Sylvana 223
trade unions 40, 171, 175–6, 179,
194–5; for women 196, 220
tradesmen 26, 29, 120; daughters of
137; *see also* craftsmen
training for work advocated 14, 17, 31,
83, 115–16, 120, 122, 127–8,
131–2, 136, 140, 156, 159, 168,
172, 173–4, 198, 205, 215–19, 221
Training Institution for Nurses, for
Hospitals, Families and the Poor *see*
St John's House
Transactions of the National
Association for the Promotion of
Social Science 157
Trimmer, Sarah 45–6, 92, 99–101
Trinity College, Dublin 209, 210;
Trollope, Anthony 103
'truth' 17, 40, 44, 54, 134
typewriter 179, 188, 193, 218
typists 193, 194, 218–19

uncompromising approach to women's
education 200–1, 205, 207, 209,
210, 212, 213, 214, 218
unemployment, female 9–11, 45, 75
unintended consequences 121, 219
Unitarianism 118, 151, 168
universities 20, 109
university education for women 7, 201,
204–9, 214, 221
University College, London 118
unpromotable category 13, 71, 73, 74,
125
'unsexing' activities 45, 63, 84, 88
upper class 33, 84, 96, 99, 135
upper middle class 29, 33–6, 40, 42,
56–7, 60, 70, 93, 141, 150, 222–3;
defined by female leisure 30–1,
34–5; defines society's manners and
morals 32–4; female occupations
29, 60, 70, 141; housing 29–30,
32; male education 33–4; male
occupations 32–3; size 34; women's
role to be refining influence 51–2;
*see also* middle class
United States of America 23, 70, 151,